The
BEST

Your Itemized Guide

LIFE

to the *Good Life*

LIST

Find the Perfect Gift,

Impress the CEO,

Beat a Cold Before It Beats You,

Say "I Love You"
Without Saying Anything,

Kiss Anxiety Goodbye,

Host an Unforgettable Party,

Prepare for Any Emergency,

and Much More

DEE DEE CLERMONT

AVON, N

Published by
Adams Media, a division of F+W Media, Inc.
57 Littlefield Street, Avon, MA 02322. U.S.A.
www.adamsmedia.com

ISBN 10: 1-4405-3007-6
ISBN 13: 978-1-4405-3007-4
eISBN 10: 1-4405-3304-0
eISBN 13: 978-1-4405-3304-4

Printed in the United States of America.

10   9   8   7   6   5   4   3   2   1

Library of Congress Cataloging-in-Publication Data
is available from the publisher.

This book is available at quantity discounts for bulk purchases.
For information, please call 1-800-289-0963.

For Hilary
who teaches by example how to live the best life.

Introduction

Life can be difficult to navigate. It's tough enough to live out your life well without asking yourself to attempt to live your *best* life as your *best* self. Yet it always seems that achieving mastery over any task still leaves room for improvement. There will always be better ways to close a hard-to-write e-mail at work, (seemingly) fewer minutes to spend pampering yourself, and endless things your mother would do differently if she were you.

But the real conundrum lies in the question, "Where do I begin?" For most of us, living our best lives seems an overwhelming grab for the impossible. While it's a nice idea—kind of like moving to the Caribbean and starting up a B&B— the reality of all that paperwork, legwork, and startup capital leaves most of us breathless and exhausted before we've even bought the sunscreen.

Enter *The Best Life List*, a book that lets you scale down your seemingly unachievable goals and achieve greatness. Living as your best self may take a lifetime to perfect. That's why this book breaks it down into bite-sized pieces, with lists in no particular order so you can be inspired or surprised with something every time you crack it open. Using ten enlightening ideas, ten easy steps, and ten simple tips, you will discover that you can have it all—from a longer, healthier life to a great and satisfying storybook romance with the man of your dreams whether or not you've already met!

Whether you've tried and failed to make improvements in your life, or never even thought to try, these 298 lists promise to do the heavy lifting with a one-foot-in-front-of-the-other approach to helping you wake up to a healthier, more confident, and better-fulfilled you.

Good luck—and good living!

Kick Your Garbage to the Curb

1 **Recycle:** Make sure you look for recycling symbols and separate the items that display them from your traditional garbage. You will be amazed by how much less waste you create.

2 **Pay Attention to Packaging:** When shopping, avoid products with a lot of disposable packaging. Avoid buying individual servings unless it's really necessary.

3 **Give Up Takeout:** A lot of unnecessary waste comes from restaurant takeout packaging. Eat in or eat out.

4 **Drink Out of Glasses Whenever Possible:** Buy drinks that come in larger sizes and ask your family to use glasses at home. Drinking out of cans and individual bottles is a major waste creator.

5 **Buy a Travel Mug:** No more disposable coffee cups for you. Also invest in an aluminum or glass bottle for carrying water.

6 **Buy Milk in Recyclable Glass Bottles:** The bottles will be washed and reused.

7 **Use Rags and Cloth Napkins:** Give up paper towels and paper napkins. They are expensive and wasteful.

8 **Use Only One Bag:** In some countries, the government-issue garbage bins look alarmingly similar to a bathroom garbage bin by American standards—but it keeps the production of trash down. Challenge your family to fill only one garbage bag per week.

9 **Recycle or Refill for Beauty:** A lot of brands offer rewards if you recycle your makeup cases or bring them in for refills instead of buying new. Find out if your favorite brands do this. If not, write a letter asking them to start.

10 **Make Your Own Products:** Use refillable bottles and make easy, eco-friendly products with which to clean your house!

Create a Blissful Spiritual Practice

1 **Use Crystals and Stones:** Thought by some to attract everything from love to success; investigate and invest in your own collection.

2 **Try Candle Burning:** Candles are used in some practices to bring health and monetary rewards, luck, and peace. Buy one, ask it for the thing you desire, and then burn it. One rule—do not blow it out. It must go out on its own.

3 **Build a Shrine:** If there is someone you miss or something you desire, place a picture in an uncluttered space and surround it with herbs and candles to help bring it to you.

4 **Have a "What Is" Box:** Cut phrases and pictures out of magazines of things you want to attract to your life and place them in a box. Every morning, go through it.

5 **Pray:** Take time to ask the universe in whatever form you are comfortable with, for safety, protection, and happiness. Also offer thanks.

6 **Employ the Elements:** Use earth, water, air, and fire to bring balance to your life. Place a lit match on a mound of dirt, then "pour" an empty glass over top to signify air. Finally, pour water on it to douse the flame.

7 **Start a Tarot Practice:** Read about the Tarot and begin each morning with a one-card reading.

8 **Cleanse:** Throw away one thing you no longer need each day in a short, but meaningful, ritual.

9 **Give Thanks Before Eating:** Offer thanks to all of those that brought your meal to you, from the ancestors of the animal to the butcher, the farmer, and the chef. Eat slowly and savor each bite.

10 **Reflect with Gratitude:** Twice a day, upon waking and before sleeping, take a moment to reflect on the things in life you are grateful for, and the things you hope will come.

Land the Perfect Job

1. **Network:** Employ websites, friends, and family. Look up people on social networking sites. Keep in touch and reach out when you are ready to look for a job.

2. **Get an Internship:** Even if it's unpaid, while you are on-site, take it more seriously than a paid position. Become invaluable and it could lead to a job.

3. **Shadow Someone:** Pay attention and be deferential, but also attempt to create a personal relationship so that he or she remembers you.

4. **Be Memorable:** Without being pushy or annoying, be someone memorable. Present yourself as capable, confident, and interesting to be around.

5. **Socialize:** In today's world, the line between professionalism and social contact has started to blur. Put yourself out there by attending industry events and making a point of talking to lots of people. You just never know!

6. **Offer to Work Free:** It is experience, and if you do it publicly, people will begin coming to you for your expertise. For starters, help out at your church or a retirement community.

7. **Offer a Workshop:** Contact HR at a company you like and let them know that you are available to teach a seminar on a topic the company's employees would like. (Of course, for this to work you'll need to have a seminar to teach.)

8. **Cold Call:** Be professional and tenacious but know when to back off. Leave one message and call back two more times with a week's buffer in between.

9. **Lean on Nepotism:** If you or your parents know people in the business, use the connection. Everybody else uses theirs.

10. **Build Your "Brand":** Create a website that reflects who you are. Include images that convey your skill set. Consider who you hope will see it and what you want them to take away.

Extend Your Life by Ten *Good* Years

(1) Become a "Yes!" Woman: Many believe the power of positive thought prolongs your life span by as much as ten years. So change your mindset and live longer.

(2) Lose Weight, But Not Too Much: Living at a healthy body weight is known to extend both the quality and length of your life.

(3) Sleep Less: Spending less time sleeping means more time living. Not to mention that statistically, people who sleep more than eight hours a night don't live as long as people who sleep between seven and eight hours a night.

(4) Don't Worry, Be Happy: People who choose a Zen approach to life are often far less stressed out than the rest of us. Find a way to stop worrying now.

(5) Don't Be a Hermit: Studies have shown that people who live with other people, even roommates, live longer lives.

(6) Get a Pet: Animal-lovers are more likely to survive accidents and heart attacks.

(7) Get Busy in Bed: People who have sex four or more times a week live longer than those who don't. So get on it!

(8) Get Rich: The more money you have, the more resources you can access to live a healthier life.

(9) Fall in Love: People in loving relationships live longer. So try to find as many reasons as you can to fall in love with your mate again and again.

(10) Laugh: It *is* the best medicine. So get giggling.

Enjoy Outdoor Space
(Even if You Don't Have Any at Home)

① **Grow a Garden:** Even if it is just a window garden, it is a way to get your hands dirty and grow something green.

② **Housesit:** See if you can water plants or tend to the pets of a person with outdoor space. Get comfortable on *their* patio.

③ **Host a Front-Stoop Dinner:** Get out the grill and cook out on your front stoop. It isn't the most private dining experience, but it's outdoors and it's fun.

④ **Utilize the Park:** Spend as much time as you can in the park soaking up the sun and frolicking in the grass.

⑤ **Open the Windows:** Turn off the air and use a fan instead. Then read your paper with your coffee and a gentle morning breeze.

⑥ **Use Your Roof:** Sneak up to the rooftop and lay out under the stars. If you can't get up there, see if you can borrow some else's roof.

⑦ **Host an Indoor-Outdoor Barbecue:** Crank up the nature sounds on your noise machine and grill burgers on the stovetop. Use candles and flashlights in lieu of regular lights and a fan in lieu of air conditioning.

⑧ **Roll Out Some Sod:** Lay out a large tarp and carpet your living room with synthetic turf. Roll around in your little yard until you've had enough, then roll it up again.

⑨ **Create Your Own Greenhouse:** Using plant lights if you lack direct sunlight, let plants flourish all over your house so that it feels vibrant, alive, and outside-like.

⑩ **Rent a Plot:** Community gardens are getting more and more popular in urban areas. Find one near you and start a garden for yourself and your family to ease some of the summer stir-crazies.

Vacation the Way Your Grandparents Did

(1) Visit the Red Lion Inn (Stockbridge, Massachusetts): Since the eighteenth century, this classic New England Inn has welcomed guests to sit on its large front porch.

(2) Roll the Dice at Golden Gate Casino (Las Vegas): Built in 1906, this, the oldest of the great Las Vegas casinos, is still going strong. And you can still get shrimp cocktail for $1.99.

(3) See the Statue of Liberty (Ellis Island, New York): Many of our grandparents saw it from a boat and knew they were home. Visit to remind yourself what they left to make your life what it is.

(4) Live Simply at the Wort Hotel (Jackson, Wyoming): Built by a homesteader, this historic hotel has been in operation since 1941.

(5) Get Glamorous at Grauman's Chinese Theatre (Hollywood): Opening in 1922, this Hollywood landmark immortalizes in cement the hands and feet of some of its very first stars.

(6) Unleash Your Imagination at the Kennedy Space Center (Orlando, Florida): When your parents were young, their parents took them to learn about the space program. Now you can go and teach your children about the stars.

(7) Let Loose at Disneyland (Anaheim, California): Disney's first park, Disneyland, opened in 1955 and continues to thrill and delight children of all ages.

(8) Trek Out to Coney Island (Brooklyn, New York): Nathan's Hotdogs and a newly updated boardwalk have halted Coney Island's fall from grace. It's time to ride one of America's very first wooden roller coasters!

(9) Drink Up at Mon Ami Winery (Catawba, Ohio): Built in 1873 and operating in its present incarnation since the 1930s, this historic Ohio winery produces 40,000–50,000 gallons of wine each year.

(10) Tackle the Frontier (Great Falls, Montana): In the middle of Lewis and Clark country, this uncrowded destination boasts the same historical trolley ride your grandparents took.

Sneak Veggies into Your Diet (with Satisfying Results!)

1. **Befriend a Blender:** Hand-held, countertop, or otherwise, if you don't have some kind of a blender, get one. Then move on to #2.

2. **Embrace Sauces:** When sneaking veggies into a diet, sauce is king. Make spaghetti sauce from scratch and go heavy on the fresh tomatoes, fresh spinach, mushrooms, and zucchini.

3. **Love Soups:** Similarly, soups are a wonderful way to incorporate vegetables into your diet.

4. **Sip a Stealth Smoothie:** Sweeten vegetable-based smoothies by adding some ripe fruit, a little honey, or even some ice cream!

5. **Nosh on Kale Chips:** You don't need a dehydrator. Just stick them in your oven at the lowest temperature until crispy. Sprinkle with salt and . . . yum!

6. **Make It a Slaw:** Red cabbage is higher in nutrients than white cabbage, so use red in your favorite coleslaw recipe. You can also julienne any other veggies you like and mix them in with vinegar and a dash of mayo.

7. **Make It Fun:** So your child (young or old) won't touch a vegetable with a ten-foot pole? Try making a smiley face in his or her sandwich using vegetables.

8. **Try Almond or Peanut Butter Celery:** How about this for a snack? Cut up celery and spread peanut or almond butter inside. Dot with a few sweet raisins and munch away.

9. **Hold the Meat:** The next time you order a hamburger, get it without the meat. It tastes remarkably similar as long as you hang on to the condiments, and add extra vegetables. If you have to have your meat, ask for extra veggies (if you can, get creative and pile on sprouts and lots of lettuce).

10. **Add Fat:** Add cheese or butter to vegetables or even cook them with bacon. Bacon makes *anything* good, even Brussels sprouts and spinach!

The Only Rules You Need to Love By

1 **Self-Love Is Key:** It's actually true—you must love yourself first and best.

2 **Love (Mostly) Feels Good:** Being in love should not cause everyday pain.

3 **Love Is Uplifting:** Love does not humiliate or degrade.

4 **Love Seeks Your Best Self:** Love should make you strive to reach the outermost limits of your most wonderful qualities, at least some—if not all—of the time.

5 **Love Sets You Free:** It does not tie you up and choke you. It makes you alive and able to fly.

6 **Love Doesn't Leave You Hanging:** Real love does not lose your number, get too busy to call, or forget agreements.

7 **Love Respects:** It knows your boundaries and works to protect them *with* you.

8 **Desperation Is *Not* Love:** And it is rarely about its object. Look inward to find what you are actually seeking.

9 **History Matters:** The best indicators of a lover's future behaviors can be seen by looking at his or her past.

10 **Fear of Rejection Does Not Protect You from Rejection:** Use your lessons in love as a touchstone rather than a ball and chain.

Feel Sexier Today Than You Did Five Years Ago

1. **Learn to Purr:** Lower your voice, add a gritty whisper to your words, and make everything you say sound like it's coming from a sex kitten.

2. **Learn a Sexy Hobby:** Take up the cello or set up a few jazz-singing lessons. Or maybe take a class on sculpting the human body.

3. **Try New Tricks in the Bedroom:** Never tried it? It's time you did.

4. **Take a Pole Dancing Class:** Learn to move . . . like that. It won't take long before you feel . . . like that.

5. **Match Your Bra and Panties:** Go out and buy a totally hot, matching set. Then when you go out, wear them and see how much sexier you feel. Better yet, forget the panties.

6. **Start Wearing Thong Underwear:** If you've never worn a pair, having that little secret every day will wake up your sexy. And when you share it with your partner, he'll agree.

7. **Invest in Thigh-Highs and Stilettos:** When he comes home, be wearing them with one of his suit jackets, and nothing else.

8. **Master the Flirt:** Practice how you move your eyes or work a subtle grin into a conversation. Best of all, make sure you get really good at tracing gentle circles on his forearm and tossing your hair back when you laugh at his jokes.

9. **Slow Down:** The sexiest women move with the greatest deliberateness and care. Do everything the same but slower and with more passion.

10. **Walk Like You Mean It:** Watch sexy women walk and add that bounce to your own step. Make sure you give him something to watch while you're walking away.

Add This to Your Kick-Ass Resume

1 **Summary of Skills:** They are more likely to read why you are qualified in a short but clearly stated summary.

2 **Professional Goals:** Inform your potential employer of how this position will help you achieve your goals. The company needs to know it is a part of your path.

3 **Hyperlinks:** Make sure that any of the work you want a potential employer to see, websites that would inform your skill set, or e-mail addresses of people they need to contact are properly formatted for easy access.

4 **A Head Shot:** Include a small one as an attachment, rather than a large 8" x 11" glossy, to give them a sense about you that will (hopefully) land you ahead of the pack. Keep it professional, warm, and not cheesy. If you're unsure, skip it.

5 **References:** Don't have them "available upon request." They might not bother and it could lose you the job.

6 **Milestones:** It's important to be very clear about where you are coming from and why they can trust you.

7 **Your Stats:** If you can quantify any of your successes or accomplishments, by all means, do so! Numbers talk. Use them.

8 **Your Whole Education:** If you took supplemental classes or spent time in an important program you did not complete, include them on your resume. Knowing you studied at all is almost as important as where you got your degree.

9 **Special Interests:** Yes, it matters that you know how to surf. Don't dedicate a great deal of space to this, but it's nice to see well-rounded and compelling candidates. Who knows? Maybe your future employer was once a Big Kahuna himself!

10 **Made and Saved:** Tell a future employer in numbers how much you made or saved your last employer.

Sling a Sarong with Style

1 **As a Halter Dress:** Hold the sarong lengthwise at the center and wrap just enough fabric around your neck, pinning at the nape. Wrap the rest of the fabric around your waist and tie it together at your navel.

2 **As a Beach Cover:** Hold the sarong lengthwise. Wrap it from front to back and then back again and tie it so that it hangs, strapless, like a towel.

3 **As a Bikini Top:** Fold the sarong lengthwise until the fabric only covers your bust. Pull it to the back and tie it. Let the excess fabric cascade down your spine.

4 **As a Skirt with a Side Slit:** Diagonally fold the fabric and bring it around your hips from back to front. Tie the sarong at the side.

5 **As a Mini Skirt:** Fold the fabric in half horizontally, then wrap it front to back and tie it on your hip.

6 **As a Halter Top:** Fold the sarong in half and wrap it from back to front across your bust. Cross over and then bring the sides up behind your neck and tie it.

7 **As Short Pants:** Bring the sarong around your waist horizontally and then tie a knot below your belly with each of the two corners. Pull fabric up from between your legs and stuff in or pin it over the knot.

8 **As a Shawl:** Fold it and drape it over your shoulders for light coverage on a breezy evening.

9 **As a Hair Scarf:** Fold the sarong in half diagonally, then place it on your head. Tie the two corners under your hair at the nape of your neck.

10 **As a Belt:** Fold the sarong diagonally, then tie it around your waist. Continue to fold the fabric until you get it to the desired length.

Clean Up in Five!

1 **Use Color-Coded Laundry Baskets:** Put a laundry basket in each person's room to be brought down on laundry day. After the "dry" cycle, sort laundry and leave for the owners to take back to their rooms.

2 **Put Your Supplies in a Carrier:** Having them all with you means you can clean the mirror, dust the shelf, and wipe down the table without stopping.

3 **Make Piles:** For efficiency, if you come across something that goes in the bedroom, put it in a bedroom pile, etc.

4 **Do a Little Every Day:** Wipe down the bathroom sink after you brush your teeth, give the kitchen a good wipe-down after you wash the dishes, make your bed as soon as you get out of it.

5 **Clean the Shower:** . . . while you shower. Spray down the walls before you get in (don't use a toxic cleaner for this), then wipe them clean before you wipe yourself clean.

6 **Sort on a Good TV Night:** Go through bills and organize items to file into piles. Put them away during the commercial break.

7 **Have a System in Place:** It might take you a weekend to set up a good foundation—a filing cabinet for papers, a linen closet for towels and sheets—but after that, putting everything away is easy.

8 **Make It a Party:** Put on music that you enjoy and make a date with yourself to clean at the same time each week. Pour yourself a drink and get to work.

9 **Set a Goal for Bigger Jobs:** Plan a yard sale to motivate yourself to clean out the closet or the basement.

10 **Offer Rewards:** Treat yourself. If the house looks good, go out to dinner.

Veggie Meals That Even a Carnivore Will Crave

1   **Mac and Cheese:** Cook macaroni al dente, then stir in cream and a mix of cheeses. Top with butter and bread crumbs, and bake at 350°F for one hour. (It's still good without the hotdogs.)

2   **Cheese Quesadilla:** Buy soft taco shells, place them in a lightly greased pan, and sprinkle with shredded cheese. Place a second shell on top. Flip it and then add more cheese and any vegetables you like. (Cover with a lid to melt the cheese.)

3   **Baked Stuffed Mushrooms:** Lightly sauté a mixture of celery, carrot, onion, and the mushroom stems; in a bowl mix them with butter, bread crumbs, Parmesan cheese, and an egg. Fill each mushroom and bake at 350°F for 30 minutes.

4   **Stuffed Acorn Squash:** Cut an acorn squash in half, clean out the seeds, and sprinkle the remaining squash with cinnamon, honey, and salt and pepper. Bake at 425°F for 30 minutes. Stuff with a mixture of yellow split peas, lightly sautéed onion and garlic, wild rice, and an egg to bind. Bake for another hour at 350°F and top with more Parmesan.

5   **Potato Pancakes:** Grate potatoes, carrots, and onions. Squeeze out excess fluid. Bind with one egg and lightly fry in a shallow pan, browning both sides.

6   **Lasagna:** Use cooked noodles topped with cheese, tomato sauce, and veggies, then more noodles and more cheese, tomato sauce, and veggies.

7   **Chili:** Use your favorite recipe but swap out the meat for extra beans.

8   **Portabella Mushroom Burgers:** Add a piece of cheddar and some veggies on a brioche bun.

9   **Fried Tomatoes:** Slice tomatoes (multiple colors suggested). Dip them in egg, coat them in panko bread crumbs, fry, and smother with Parmesan cheese.

10   **Breakfast for Dinner:** Make a big omelet stuffed with your favorite veggies. Serve with a piping side of wheat toast and roasted potatoes.

Master Any Airport

1 **Join a Frequent Flyer Program:** Ever notice how some people just get to walk right up and pass through any line first at the airport? Those people probably either work there or are part of a frequent flyer program. It is worth your time to look into joining no matter how often you fly.

2 **Use a Carry-On:** Checking baggage is so 2005. Now airlines let you bring a good-sized carry-on to the gate and check it there. It forces you to pack economically and saves you time.

3 **Dress the Part:** Wear something sophisticated but nice. Look put together and like you are somebody and you will be treated accordingly.

4 **Check in at Home:** Almost every airline lets you print your boarding pass before you get to the airport.

5 **Don't Get There Too Early:** If you don't check your baggage and you take care of check-in at home, you need no more than forty-five minutes to get through the checkpoint and walk to your gate.

6 **Get Organized While Waiting:** While in line, get ready. Contain metal objects in one bag and get your ID out.

7 **Bring Your Own Snacks, Buy Beverages:** You can't get liquid through security, but you can bring food. Since airport prices are outrageous for mediocre food, bring your own.

8 **Remember, Kindness Pays Off:** People who work for airlines deal with a lot of cranky travelers. You will stand out if you are *not* one of them.

9 **Relax:** When you are in an airport you have no control. Take a deep breath, relax, and accept it. Then go people-watch.

10 **Be Proactive:** If your flight is delayed, or canceled, don't dawdle. Call the airline on your cell phone *and* seek out a ticket agent. Flights fill up quickly and it is first come, first served.

Bad Beauty Habits You Need to Break

1 **Cigarettes:** Nothing makes you uglier than cigarettes. They stain your teeth, smell terrible to anyone not smoking them, destroy your complexion, and cause premature wrinkles. If that wasn't enough, they also dull your hair.

2 **Sugary Cereal:** Most cereals are just basically white flour in a fancy package. Add all that sugar to it and you are basically eating candy for breakfast—good for a minute, until your teeth start rotting.

3 **Diet Soda:** Regular soda's evil twin because it arrives packaged as "healthier." Actually, when your body tastes something sweet your pancreas goes into overdrive and then you need more sugary food to soak it up. This equals not pretty.

4 **Processed Foods:** Since there are so few nutrients in them, eating them is not giving your body what it needs, leaving it hungry and wanting more.

5 **Coffee:** Some say that in moderation, coffee is good for you. But let's face it, it stains your teeth and does a number on your breath.

6 **Margarine:** Few kinds are actually a healthy alternative to butter since they are generally made with very-bad-for-you trans fats, which lead to hormone imbalances and bad skin.

7 **Salt:** It makes you bloated and over time it makes your skin less elastic.

8 **Soy Sauce:** Unless you want almost *half* of your sodium in one tablespoon of soy sauce, skip it. If it contains MSG, you'll also be bloated.

9 **Chewing Gum:** One sugary stick will actually cause your breath to *worsen* once you've spit it out. It causes the bacteria in your mouth to reproduce.

10 **Spicy Fried Foods:** Take hot wings, for instance—they make you sweaty and because they are high in fat, sugar, *and* sodium, they will keep you sweaty for a while.

Have a No-Tantrum Naptime

1 **Stick to a Schedule:** Make nap time the same every day; consistency is key. You will start to recognize when your toddler feels tired.

2 **Have Downtime Before:** Experts suggest that at least twenty minutes before naptime, you give your child a bottle or juice, play quiet music, read a book, and enjoy quiet games.

3 **Darken Her Room:** Block out sun with blinds or hang a heavy curtain. Turn off lights and make it a sleepy environment.

4 **Stick to the Same Place:** If possible, put your child down for a nap in his bed. If he goes to school, give him a blanket or stuffed animal from his bed to take for naptime.

5 **Avoid Car Naps:** Try not to let your child sleep outside of naptime, which means keep her awake in the car and in strollers.

6 **Make It Quiet Time for Everyone:** When the kids are napping, everyone should be quiet.

7 **Make It a Priority:** Don't sacrifice naptime too often. Make it something everyone expects.

8 **Have Active Mornings:** Keep your kids moving in the morning so that they are worn out enough to welcome sleep.

9 **Keep It Pleasant:** If your baby is shrieking and miserable for more than ten minutes, go in and try rocking him. If that doesn't help, offer toys to play with in his crib.

10 **Let Her Play:** You can't force a child to sleep. But you can give yourself an hour to relax or get things done. Let your baby play in bed. Once you have had some time to yourself, go get her.

Find the Man of Your Dreams Online

1. **Keep the Goals Achievable:** Setting a goal like, "I will chat with ten men this week," is far more manageable than an unwieldy and almost impossible, "I'm going to meet my husband today."

2. **Don't Take It Too Seriously:** Make your profile funny and self-deprecating. Have fun and don't get attached before you've even met!

3. **Look at It as a Shopping Spree—but Cheaper:** "Collect" these little square headshots like they are pretty pairs of shoes. Shop for perfect guys, acceptable guys, and fixer-uppers.

4. **Move It Into the Real World:** Throw a party using the dating site as a guest list.

5. **Seek *Them* Out:** Don't wait to get winked at; send messages to guys you think might be compatible, or at least fun on a date.

6. **Have a Plan:** If you decide to e-mail five times and then ask for a date, stick to it. If you can't nail him down, move on.

7. **Skip the Phone:** Adding a step between the computer and real life is just stalling. So pick a place to meet and go ahead and meet.

8. **Arrive with a Plan:** Definitely have someplace to go so that you arrive with a time limit. Whether you like him or not, enjoy your date and get out.

9. **Search Other Cities:** Open up your search if you aren't finding anyone local. Your soul mate might live an hour away. It's worth it to look there.

10. **Fix Your Picture:** Guys are visual creatures. If you aren't getting the right responses, try using a photo with an artful shadow obscuring some of your face so that you look hotter and younger. It's not a lie, it's intrigue.

Stop an Argument Before It Begins

1. **Know Your Triggers:** Are you tired? Pre-coffee? Stressed? Any of these might mean you are itching for a fight—so decide not to and then don't.

2. **Know His Triggers:** Same goes for your man. If you know he is more fragile than usual, give him a break.

3. **Defuse:** If things start to get heated, try to defuse it with a joke or change the subject and revisit when neither of you is feeling so sensitive.

4. **Walk Away:** Not every fight has to happen right away. The old adage, "Don't go to bed angry"? Horseshit. Sometimes going to bed angry is the best way to wake up peaceful.

5. **Be Deliberate:** Choose your words carefully when you have a peeve, a frustration, or a concern. Begin by knowing that you are in a loving and safe relationship and go forward from there without name-calling or humiliation.

6. **Implement a "Safe Word":** Choose an innocuous word like "apple" that you agree will turn around an escalating conversation.

7. **Feel Good:** Make sure you're eating right, getting enough sleep, and exercising to keep stressful confrontations to a minimum.

8. **Let It Go:** Some of us are raised believing we have to express every feeling we have, but do we? Some fights aren't worth having. Know when it's okay *not* to talk about it.

9. **Find Your Goal:** On the other hand, if you have something you have to say, be very clear about your desired outcome. Do you want an acknowledgment? An apology? Attention? Knowing what it is you want will help you lay out the path to getting it.

10. **Say What You Mean:** Don't get off track; just say what you mean and then leave it.

Dress Your Closet Well

1 **A Little Black Dress:** This must-have is good for everything from business meetings to Saturday-night dates.

2 **A Hat:** A good hat can take any outfit from blah to glamorous *and* serve a practical purpose if you're having a bad hair day.

3 **A Leather Belt:** A good leather belt will keep your pants up and look good.

4 **At Least One Wig:** Even if you'll only ever wear it on Halloween, sometimes a girl just has to step out of her own skin—or at least hair.

5 **A Pair of Amazing Shoes:** It's okay to splurge on that one perfect pair.

6 **A Jacket That Goes with Everything:** A trench coat or blazer you can wear to work or play and makes you feel put together is a must for your closet.

7 **A Worn-in Pair of Jeans:** It doesn't matter how many times you've had them patched, if they are your go-to pair on the weekends, they should stay in your closet until they turn to dust.

8 **A Suit:** Even if you work on a farm, someday, somewhere, someone is going to care whether or not you show up in a suit. When that day arrives, you'd better have one.

9 **Comfy Kicks:** Own a great pair of tennis shoes you can wear to the club or to the gym.

10 **Something Overpriced and Trendy That You Love:** Just make sure you don't go overboard. But then again, why not? You only live once.

Simple Styles, Fabulous Hair

1 **Side Part:** Part your hair on the opposite side using a comb for a dramatic change. Pin it at your ear to keep it out of your eyes.

2 **Braids:** If your hair is long, divide it into two halves, then braid each one. For extra flair, challenge yourself to braid a ribbon through it.

3 **Schoolgirl Pony:** This ponytail goes high on your head and bounces when you walk.

4 **Twists:** This style works best on short hair. Divide your hair into one-inch sections, twist each against your head, and secure with a pin.

5 **Wig Curls:** Medium to long hair works best for this funky style. Using a comb, divide your hair into squares. Twist the hair into small, tight buns all over your head and secure with a pin.

6 **Hippie Part:** Use a flat iron to straighten out the kinks and part your hair with a comb down the middle. Use a little bit of product to keep it Marcia Brady smooth.

7 **Finger Waves:** Run product through wet hair and then secure hair with large metal pins that draw it into waves. Sleep in them and wake up looking like you stepped off the silver screen.

8 **Beachy Wild:** Sleep with your hair damp and braided. When you wake up, take out the braids and shake out your hair. Massage your scalp to loosen it up.

9 **Flower Power:** Pin a flower just above your ear on the smaller section of your side-parted hair.

10 **Bold Bangs:** If you are blessed with a large enough forehead, go ahead and cut choppy bangs to wake up a tired look.

Books Best Read on the Beach (Cocktail in Hand)

1 The *Twilight* Series **(Stephenie Meyer):** Nothing like a little vampire romance, read in direct sunlight, to stay engrossed, entertained, and bite free.

2 *The Great Gatsby* **(F. Scott Fitzgerald):** This book summers on Long Island in the 1920s with Nick Carraway, his cousin, Daisy Buchanan, and, of course, the great and ingratiating Gatsby himself.

3 *The Joy Luck Club* **(Amy Tan):** A story about Chinese mothers and their American-born daughters, the story splits its time between pre-war China and a present-day game of mahjong.

4 *The Girl with the Dragon Tattoo* **(Stieg Larsson):** Follow the sexy Lisbeth Salander as she solves the Mikael Blomkvist case. Fight the Scandinavian cold by reading on the beach.

5 *Gone with the Wind* **(Margaret Mitchell):** Scarlett O'Hara and Rhett Butler—and Tara—have the *real* love story in this beguiling classic, even though if you asked Scarlett she'd say it was Ashley Wilkes.

6 *Bridget Jones's Diary* **(Helen Fielding):** Bridget is a girl with whom you'd love to grab a cocktail. Read it on the beach, no matter how you look in a bikini.

7 *This Is Where I Leave You* **(Jonathan Tropper):** This novel from 2009 takes you into the hilarious dysfunction of one family mourning their father.

8 *The Unbearable Lightness of Being* **(Milan Kundera):** If you'd like to read something smart and sexy, try this masterpiece.

9 *Under the Tuscan Sun* **(Frances Mayes):** This memoir-cum-cookbook makes a compelling case for starting a new life in an abandoned villa in Tuscany after a bad divorce.

10 *How Stella Got Her Groove Back* **(Terry McMillan):** A successful forty-something woman falls for a much younger heartthrob on a first-class vacation to Jamaica. Cheers!

Books Best Read Out Loud
(with Your Partner)

1 **For Fun:** Read the *Harry Potter* series by J. K. Rowling or another young adult treasure like *His Dark Materials* by Philip Pullman.

2 **For Romance:** *Perfume* by Patrick Suskind is a wonderfully exciting mystery with a dark romantic edge. Or try Jane Austen's *Pride and Prejudice* for something more classically romantic.

3 **For the Intellectual Challenge:** *Lincoln: The Biography of a Writer*, by Fred Kaplan, analyzes the writing of a great president.

4 **For a Laugh:** Read *America* by Jon Stewart or any of Chelsea Handler's autobiographies.

5 **To Test Your Moral Compasses:** *The Stoned Family Robinson* by J. D. Wyss and J. P. Linder or any of the other hilarious literary mashups on sale today. Any list of ethics questions will also fulfill this purpose quite well, like a purity test.

6 **For Hot Sweaty Lust:** *The Delta of Venus* by Anaïs Nin or any Harlequin Romance will get your blood pumping as you read to each other before bed . . . naked.

7 **For Sex Tips:** Try *The Good Girl's Guide to Bad Girl Sex* by Barbara Keesling or *The Kinsey Report*.

8 **To Better Understand Each Other:** *Men Are from Mars, Women Are from Venus*, by John Gray, or *You Just Don't Understand*, by Deborah Tannen, will definitely inform your next fight, positively.

9 **To Learn Something:** *Why Do Men Have Nipples*, by Mark Leyner and Billy Goldberg, or any other short answer compilation, will make you and your honey the team to beat at the next pub quiz.

10 **To Get Moving:** Try a travel guide or a Bill Bryson book of hilarious travel essays.

Throw a Page-6 Cocktail Party

1 **Let Cocktails Be the Star:** A cocktail party should feature, *what else?* The cock-tail. So do some research and find a few that look nice and taste good.

2 **Choose the Menu:** Small one-bite appetizers are a must. Choose delicacies like mini crab cakes, vegetarian sushi rolls, and chicken sate with dipping sauce.

3 **Get the Tools:** You will need attractive pitchers or glass dispensers that go together to dispense the cocktails, as well as serving trays for the hors d'oeuvres.

4 **Send a Formal Invite:** To set the tone even before your guests arrive, make sure your invitation has the right look along with a suggestion of attire; in this case, "cocktail." You can send online invitations as long as they are classy.

5 **Hire a Staff:** Hire a bartender and one or two waiters to walk around serving your beverages and appetizers. If your space feels too cramped for either of these things, make sure your stations for both food and drinks are simple and clean and remain as such.

6 **Make a Playlist:** Set your iPod with songs that will complement the mood. Jazz standards and some classical music interpretations will give the area a warm, calm feel.

7 **Invest in Your Attire:** You are the hostess. Make sure you look like the part.

8 **Set the Space:** Keep the lights at a warm glow and add safe, decorative candle-light to supplement. (Floating votives add a nice touch.)

9 **Prepare in Advance:** Have your cocktails already made and the garnish ready to go. Keep second rounds in Tupperware in your refrigerator and refill as your mixtures get low.

10 **Start with a Toast:** When your guests have arrived, find an opportunity to wel-come them with a toast.

Bust Out These
Tried-and-True Dance Moves

1. **The Grind:** With a suitable partner, match your hips together and gyrate together in a circle.

2. **The Put a Ring on It:** Slide your shoulders back and forth as you twist your hand front to back in front of your mouth. Keep your other hand on your hip.

3. **The Wave:** Arms out shoulder height, begin at the tips of the fingers on one hand and follow through in a waving motion to the fingertips on the other hand.

4. **The Charleston:** This popular 1920s dance has you with bent arms, fingers splayed out in front of you, alternating one hand in front of you chest at a time in rhythm. The opposite foot should accompany each hand with a forward kick.

5. **The Moonwalk:** Begin by rolling one foot from toe to heel, then the other. Smooth the move until you look like you're sliding.

6. **Hip Gyration:** You can thank Shakira for this one. Arms up in the air, it is all about doing a rapid side-to-side or complete circle with the hips.

7. **The Running Man:** Separate your feet one in front of the other. Hop together and reverse. Don't slide. Just hop.

8. **Walk Like an Egyptian:** Meet your palms above your head so that your face is framed by your arms. Move your head, keeping it upright toward one elbow and then the other.

9. **The Sock Slide Entrance:** What makes this move look good is that you appear from out of nowhere. Stand off to the side, then propel yourself smoothly as you slide into view. Stop yourself midway.

10. **The Gator:** Just like John Belushi, yell "Gator!" and fall to your back, spastically flailing your arms and legs.

Blow Your Accountant's Mind:
Work Your Way to a Million Dollars

1 **Start a Business:** If you have a great idea and you execute it well, down the road, your business could definitely make you a million.

2 **Earn Money:** The goal is to earn substantially more than you spend. You can earn through a job, investments, and side projects.

3 **Don't Go Into Debt:** Live below your means if down the road you hope to have a million dollars.

4 **Invest:** You can put money into a 401(k), and over time the amount of money you amass will be significant. There are other plans that a financial adviser might point you toward if you're interested.

5 **Save Money:** You can spend as long as you are saving more. Calculate your earnings and only buy what you need.

6 **Stay the Course:** People who change jobs, move regularly, and have a tendency to cash out stocks earn less over time than those who are patient.

7 **Buy Collectibles:** Find items you think will be valuable down the road and buy them while they are still relatively inexpensive.

8 **Inherit:** Show a little kindness to an aging relative. Spend time with her and help her with everyday needs. It might not guarantee you a place in the will, but it might, and more than that, it will make you spiritually richer.

9 **Buy Real Estate:** Find parts of town where property isn't too expensive. When you find something you like, research it to see if it looks like the property value will go up or down. If it looks promising, get in there.

10 **Save Ten Percent:** A lot of financiers suggest that every time money comes in, you move ten percent to a savings account. Do not invest it or spend it. Just save.

Become a Baby (and Man) Whisperer

1. Address Them: Use their name for emphasis to let them know that you are serious.

2. Keep It Short: You want to make sure what you say is to the point and is clear. So plan it in advance and then relay it quickly and plainly.

3. Hear It from Them: Ask them to repeat what you've explained back to you that so you are certain you were understood.

4. Stay Positive: Rather than telling them what you don't want them to do, explain a better option. For example, "When it comes to people we love, we hug them," instead of telling them not to hit.

5. Don't Holler: Walk to wherever they are and join in the activity for a few minutes. When you spot a good end point, you can ask them to stop and move on to a different activity.

6. Don't Leave It to Them: Especially if you don't mean it. If you know they can't properly choose their own outfit, give them a choice: this shirt, or that shirt?

7. Don't Make Them Explain Themselves: It's difficult for anyone to know clearly why they did something, wrong or right. Instead discuss it with them to try to get to the bottom of a naughty behavior.

8. Use Cause and Effect Reasoning: Let them know that something good will come after they do something they don't necessarily want to do. *After* they clean up they will get to watch their show.

9. Echo Correct: When they make the wrong choice of activity or behavior, show them or explain what the right choice would have been.

10. End It: If you are not open to discussion, don't discuss. Let them know in plain terms that the matter is settled.

Inspire, Engage, and Influence: How to Get People to Do What You Want Them to Do

1. **Empathize:** Putting yourself in someone else's shoes offers valuable perspective when attempting to sway them. Anticipate what they want you to say.

2. **Lead by Example:** Whatever you're selling, make sure you'd buy. If you walk the talk, others will follow.

3. **Establish Your Expertise:** Where you learned what you know is less important than what you know. If you know what you're talking about, no one will challenge you.

4. **Effectively Compare:** Show how happy others are with the results, and illustrate the ways in which lives were improved through example and testimonial.

5. **Emphasize Exclusivity:** Everyone wants to feel special, so drive home the ways in which the experience, product, or idea cannot be duplicated.

6. **Be Honest:** People can smell a lie a mile away. Use the truth, even if that means selectively choosing your points.

7. **Employ Body Language:** If attempting persuasion in person, keep your body open. Folded arms suggest a lack of truthfulness.

8. **Make Eye Contact:** When face-to-face, look the person in the eye. If persuading on paper, address the person by name when you can.

9. **Speak Clearly and with Purpose:** Positive, reinforcing language will help you avoid spending too much time focusing on the negatives.

10. **Don't Lecture:** Lectures are dull and often preachy. No one likes to be talked *at*. So make sure you allow for discussion. Listen thoughtfully to questions and answer them plainly. Allow your subject to move toward your position at her own pace.

Jet-Set with Royalty

1. **The Royal Box at Wimbledon (England):** Take in the world's most prestigious tennis championship in the box where monarchs sit.

2. **High Tea at the Savoy (London, England):** Set between lunch and dinner, high tea is believed to have started in the 1800s when the Duchess of Bedford grew hungry between meals,.

3. **Versailles (France):** This royal chateau, built for Louis XIV, has gilded ceilings and lush gardens.

4. **Château de Bagatelle (Paris):** Formerly the hunting grounds of French royalty, these public gardens are now home to an exquisite English rose garden.

5. **Castles of Bavaria (Germany):** A tour of these historic castles will include Neuschwanstein, one of several castles after which Disney modeled Sleeping Beauty's Castle at Disneyland.

6. **The Taj Mahal (India):** This mausoleum was built for Indian Empress Mumtaz Mahal—a monument to great love fit for royalty.

7. **The Shangri-La Hotel (Abu Dhabi, United Arab Emirates):** This luxury hotel has its own private beach. Guests each have a private balcony, use of any of the four pools, private service, and of course, a spa fit for a princess.

8. **Forbidden City (China):** China's last emperor lived in this fifteenth-century palace before it became a monument and a museum.

9. **Four Seasons Hotel (New York City):** With marble bathrooms and personal sitting areas, this Manhattan luxury hotel is renowned for offering the royal treatment.

10. **Cinderella's Castle (Orlando, FL):** Walt Disney knew how to make every little girl's fantasy world into a reality. At Disney World, anyone can be a princess.

How to Ask Him Out

1 **Read the Paper:** Know what's going on in town so that you are always prepared with—if not the *who to ask*—then the *where to ask*.

2 **Forget Coy:** Shyness can be sweet and charming, but it isn't going to get you a date. Be bold and forward for a change.

3 **Look Confident:** Practice walking into rooms with confidence. When you meet a guy you like, make eye contact and speak clearly in declarative sentences.

4 **Make Yourself Known:** While some people are happy to go on a blind date, it's always better to have heard good things about a date in advance. So encourage friends to spread the word about this amazing girl who's on the market . . .

5 **Get a Friend's Stamp of Approval:** Approach one of his friends and let her know you are interested in her friend. If you come off well, her thumbs-up will mean a lot to him.

6 **Make It a Group Outing:** Be the organizer of a group outing, but be very clear with your crush that he is the reason you are going through the trouble.

7 **Buy Tickets in Advance:** If you already have the tickets to an event you know he would enjoy, it will be harder for him to turn you down.

8 **Take a Deep Breath and Pick Up the Phone:** Just bite the bullet. The worst that can happen is that he will say no.

9 **Take His Answer in Stride:** Whether he says yes or no, save your celebratory dance party, or pity party, for later. A simple, "Great" or "Okay" will suffice.

10 **Ask Again:** Odds are, if you ask a lot of guys out, someone is bound to say yes. So keep asking.

Drop That Bad Habit Now!

1. **Read Books:** Read books that detail people breaking bad habits. Focus on tricks they used to get through the hard parts and try to incorporate them into your own "detox."

2. **Change Your Habits:** Forbid yourself from partaking of your habit at the usual times. Smoke *before* you eat instead of after. Only eat sweets when you feel good instead of when you are depressed.

3. **Own a Mantra:** Look yourself in the eye five times a day and say, "I will not (insert bad habit). I am stronger than (insert bad habit). I will overcome (insert bad habit)."

4. **Wake Up to Success Stories:** Type up ten paragraphs about people who have overcome their cravings. Read it first thing in the morning.

5. **Wait Five Minutes:** Before you eat that delicious cake, drink that mojito, or chomp on your nails, make yourself wait five minutes. It's possible that the urge will pass.

6. **Plan a Vacation:** Every time you catch yourself thinking about your bad habit, plan a vacation. Often just changing the thought will keep you from going through with the behavior.

7. **Set Achievable Goals:** Don't tell yourself you can never drink or eat a cupcake again. Just decide not to drink or eat that cupcake *now*. Keep your goals easy and doable.

8. **Make It a Game:** People are competitive, so get friends to quit with you and race them to a healthier life.

9. **Go Places Where You Can't Enjoy Your Vices:** If you can't smoke someplace, studies have shown that not smoking while there becomes easier. So make sure you go to those places and surround yourself with people that keep you from your bad habit.

10. **Put It Off:** At the first time in the day that you typically engage in the bad behavior, wait an hour. The next day, wait two hours. The following day, three hours, etc.

Open Your Mind, and the Heart Will Follow

1 **Stimulate Your Senses Differently:** Listen to different musical styles than you're used to. Try foods you've never tasted. Look at the world through new eyes.

2 **Argue the Opposite Point of View:** Have a worthy opponent take your side and see how you do arguing against it.

3 **Hear Without Judgment:** Someone else's *opinion* does not change what *is*. So let them speak and reflect without becoming insulted or feeling threatened.

4 **Assume the Best:** If you encounter people with a different idea or a different lifestyle, begin by deciding they are not coming from a place of evil but from a place that is right for them.

5 **Read about Other People and Places:** If you have some sense of the world beyond your own, it's easier to open your mind to different ideas.

6 **Travel:** Go someplace entirely unlike the place you live and see how the world looks to someone else.

7 **Be Culpable:** Take full responsibility for yourself, your choices, and the life you live. Don't worry so much about what everybody else is doing.

8 **Step Back:** When you get too close to a person or topic it's sometimes difficult to see the forest for the trees. Try to step back and get a better view.

9 **Say Yes:** Decide that you will agree to any new experience offered up and you will look for all the ways you *agree* with any argument made rather than disagree.

10 **Don't Expect Anything:** Before you enter the room, imagine it empty. No ideas, no people, no tables or chairs. When you walk in, see it all as if it is the first room you have ever seen. And learn more about it from that point forward.

Get the Promotion That Everybody Wants

1 **Keep Your Accomplishments Visible:** Without bragging or needing too much praise, be sure you make plain when you are kicking butt.

2 **Excel at What You Do:** Be the best and you will be the one to beat.

3 **Watch for Overloaded Execs:** Reach out to them and let them know why you'd be particularly good at something they coincidentally are in need of help with.

4 **Ask Superiors for Tasks:** Send periodic e-mails letting them know you'd be happy to take on more work.

5 **Help Define a New Position:** If you can see that your business would benefit from an additional position, lay it out and present it clearly and with confidence. Then let your boss know you hope to fill it.

6 **Make Yourself Known and Respected:** Let's be clear—don't be "renowned" for your desktop dance at the office party. Instead be known for your hard work and overall positive attitude.

7 **Hold a Private Meeting:** At some point ask your boss privately what she suggests you do to get ahead. People like to impart wisdom. Doing so will make her feel respected and important.

8 **Find a Mentor:** Choose someone in the company who is successful and well-liked, then get him to take you under his wing.

9 **Keep Learning:** Get better than those around you at important things, like information technology. Within your business, always keep up with new trends and point them out—not as a know-it-all, but to be helpful.

10 **Ask for It:** If you know that you are up for the promotion, don't be afraid to let the company know that you are very interested in getting it. A little excitement and ambition is a good thing.

Mix Up These Cocktails to Impress at Any Party

1 **Mojitos:** Prepare a pitcher with rum, crushed mint leaves, sugared lime juice, and soda water. Garnish with whole mint leaves.

2 **Cosmopolitans:** Prepare a pitcher with vodka, Cointreau, fresh lime juice, and cranberry juice. Garnish martini glasses with a salt rim and a twist of lime.

3 **Margaritas:** Combine tequila, triple sec, and lime juice over rocks. Garnish with a salted rim and a slice of lime.

4 **Watermelon Vodka:** Cut the top off a large watermelon horizontally. Take out the meat and refill the rind with vodka. Put some of the fruit back into the vodka. Cover and let it stand in the refrigerator overnight. Use a punch dipper to serve and garnish with extra watermelon.

5 **Mint Julep:** Fill a pitcher with lightly crushed mint leaves, bourbon, powdered sugar, and water. Garnish a tumbler with a sprig of mint.

6 **Mai Tais:** Combine equal parts light and dark rum, crème de almond, triple sec, sweet and sour mix, and pineapple juice. Garnish a punch glass with a toothpick skewered with a cherry and a piece of pineapple.

7 **Sangria:** Fill a punch bowl with red or white wine and the fruit of your choice. Add rum and ginger ale.

8 **Vodka Infusions:** Buy airtight glass bottles and fill them with orange slices, mint leaves or basil, and cucumber; add a bottle of vodka and let it infuse for a week or two. Strain, then serve to your guests with the mixers of their choice.

9 **Black or White Russian:** Put equal parts Kahlua and vodka in a pitcher. Pour two tablespoons of heavy cream into a tumbler for a white Russian and over ice for the black version.

10 **Iced Irish Coffee:** Prepare iced coffee. Add Irish cream liqueur to taste. Serve over rocks in a pint glass.

Learn to Skip a Rock on Water

1 **Choose the Body of Water:** An ideal surface for skipping rocks shouldn't have too many waves or be too shallow. Find a pond or lake with a somewhat deep, smooth surface.

2 **Choose Your Rock:** Find a flat, smooth stone. Some experts swear that rounder is better. For beginners, choose one that is smaller than your palm.

3 **Consider Weight:** You don't want to choose a stone that is cumbersome or difficult to throw. Similarly, you don't want one that is too slight to support itself against the water.

4 **Gather Extra Stones:** Make sure you have a pile ready to go. It will likely take a bit of practice before you get it right.

5 **Master the Hold:** Nestle the stone between your thumb and index or middle finger. (Whichever is more comfortable.)

6 **Toss:** Stand sideways in the water with your feet at hip-width. Using a flicking of the wrist, skim the stone over top of the water.

7 **Be Aware of Trajectory:** Did the stone sink? Try elevating the front of the stone slightly before the next toss. Was it too slow to bounce on the water? Lay the stone flatter and try again.

8 **Count the Skips:** Do several in a row and see each time if you can beat your best "score." When you're ready, compete against someone else.

9 **Try Rough Waters:** It is possible to skip stones over waves. Find a manageable but heavier stone that will be able to break through them.

10 **Experiment:** Once you have the hang of it, try out different stones and see which ones feel the easiest to you. Soon you will be able to skip any rock, anywhere. Even in a puddle!

Make That Headache Yesterday's News

1. **Relax:** Tension headaches are often caused by tense muscles in the neck and back. Try lying down with your eyes closed and picturing each muscle group releasing.

2. **Go for a Run:** Or do yoga or take a swim—anything to get your muscles primed and relaxed.

3. **Hydrate:** Drink plenty of water and eat foods high in electrolytes, like bananas and coconut, so that your body can retain it. It will cut down on headaches.

4. **Apply Lemon Juice:** Dab externally just below your nose and breathe the fresh fragrance. Soaking gingerroot in lemon juice to drink can also help stop headaches.

5. **Use Acupressure:** Apply gentle pressure to your temples. Also try squeezing the area between your thumb and index finger with the thumb and index finger of the other hand, then releasing.

6. **Get Acupuncture:** Another tried-and-true method for relieving headaches, especially if you get them a lot, is to go to an accredited acupuncturist for a few specifically placed needles.

7. **Stretch:** As soon as the headache comes, stretch out to release tension in your neck, shoulders, and back.

8. **Have Sex:** It sounds counterintuitive; isn't this how we *avoid* sex? But having sex releases all kinds of happy headache-fighting chemicals into our bodies.

9. **Reduce Stress:** Try to keep stress in your life at a minimum. If your job or family life has gotten out of hand, step back and see if there is some way to calm things down.

10. **Change Your Diet:** Eat foods that are high in omega-3 fatty acids and cut out food high in caffeine (sorry, chocolate) and sugar. Also, make sure you eat regularly and are getting enough protein.

Power Down and Enjoy Some Quiet Time

1. **Go for a Walk:** Rain, sun, or snowstorm, you can always go for a walk as long as you dress accordingly. In fact, the worse the weather, the better the adventure!

2. **Take a Bath:** Fill the tub with your favorite scents and break out some major mindless reading. Your favorite magazine or romance novel should keep you entertained.

3. **Masturbate:** Read some soft-core porn essays or simply let your mind take you into a great arousing fantasy.

4. **Dance:** No one's watching. Turn on something that gets you moving and go crazy doing your worst Elaine-Benes-from-*Seinfeld* impression.

5. **Paint:** Set up a little art studio somewhere in your home and paint your masterpiece. Use a good photograph you've taken as inspiration.

6. **Cook:** Take some time to make yourself something delicious. Simply use what you know or, if you must, find a recipe in one of those cookbooks you got for a college graduation present that's been collecting dust.

7. **Meditate:** While you're turning off power switches, why not also turn off the lights and music, then sit in silence and focus on your breath.

8. **Pray:** You might also let yourself focus on asking God or the Universe (or both) for what you most want. Not sure what that is? Use the quiet time to figure it out.

9. **Accept the Oscar for Your Life:** Present yourself with an award and then thank those who helped you "win" it. Feel free to give and accept as many awards as you can think of.

10. ***Write* a TV Show:** Since you aren't watching one, get out a pen and paper and outline a great idea for a show starring, who else, *you.*

Stretch Out Your Energy, Anytime, Anywhere

1 **Torso Twist:** Sit with your legs outstretched, then bend one knee and place the bottom of that foot over the knee of the opposite leg. Place the opposite arm against the elevated knee and gently twist your torso.

2 **Shoulder Stretch:** Put both arms above your head. Grab one elbow with one hand and gently pull while your elbow pulls back in the other direction.

3 **Shoulder Opener:** Place the back of one hand against the middle of your spine. Reach up in the air with the other hand, then bring it down behind your back and try to touch your hands together.

4 **Head and Neck Stretch:** Sitting down, slowly roll your head down toward your chest until it hangs free. You can gently place a hand on your head to stretch it a little more.

5 **Back Stretch:** Sit up straight in a chair. Place your hands on your hips. Then carefully move your elbows toward each other behind your back.

6 **Upper Leg Stretch:** Standing up, pull your knee in toward your chest. Stand against the wall if you need to for balance.

7 **Lower Leg Stretch:** Place the toes of one foot against the wall, and bend your knee toward the wall. Keep your other leg one step behind you. Allow a gentle stretch to extend down the front of your leg.

8 **Calf Stretch:** Place one foot flat on the floor and then carefully step forward with your other leg. Gently bend the knee of the front leg, leaving both of your feet flat on the floor.

9 **The Hang:** Bend forward, letting your head hang free. Be careful not to hyperextend the backs of your legs. Then slowly, one vertebra at a time, roll back up.

10 **Child's Pose:** Sit on your knees and then bend forward until your face touches the floor in front of your knees, extending your arms above your head.

Nail a Free Throw in Basketball

1 **Step Up:** Walk up to the line with purpose. Own it. This is your line.

2 **Line Up:** Your dominant leg should be out in front against the line and perfectly aligned with the basket. (If you are right-handed, use your right leg; left-handed, your left.)

3 **Stand:** Your feet should be shoulder-width apart as you are standing facing the basket, your nondominant leg in back.

4 **Balance:** This is an important point. Stand in the center of the free-throw line and center yourself so that you are in perfect balance.

5 **Make an L:** Use your elbow to make the shape of an L beneath the ball. Place your other hand just behind the ball.

6 **Focus:** Watch the back of the rim so that your eyes are generally focused on the net. Aim for the back of the rim.

7 **Bend Your Knees:** Give yourself an edge by bouncing your knees up and down a few times so that when you are ready to throw, you are prepared.

8 **Use Only One Hand:** You don't need help from your nondominant hand on this one. Just fire it up with your hand under the ball. Your other hand is simply a guide.

9 **Toss It:** Make sure your bounce up from your knees is perfectly timed to flicking your wrist and the subsequent release.

10 **Follow Through:** Keep your hand up after you let go of the ball to ensure that you have guided it in the right direction.

Foods That Will Surprise You

1 **Stinky Cheese:** These rich, complex cheeses are usually made with vinegar and/or mold. The smell should not deter you from the opportunity to eat them.

2 **Caviar:** Despite the fact that they can be cost prohibitive—and the fact that they are fish eggs—caviar has a salty tang and a delicate texture that literally "pops" on your tongue.

3 **Raw Oysters:** These silky shellfish with their creamy briny flavor is a proven aphrodisiac, if you can forget for a moment that they are also slimy and raw.

4 **Foie Gras:** There's a reason foodies talk about this stuff like it's better than sex. It might be goose liver, but the rich, sumptuous flavor will change your mind about its edibility.

5 **Cracklings:** While the idea of deep-fried animal skins might be repulsive to some, cracklings, including pork rinds, are very popular in southern states and worth a try.

6 **Tongue:** Almost salami-like in consistency, this lean meat has been a cultural delicacy for some time. If you don't think about it, you might like it.

7 **Beets:** This nutritional powerhouse gets a bad wrap. A sweet root vegetable, it's sometimes pickled and other times boiled fresh in soups, sauces, or on its own.

8 **Quinoa:** Granted, it's hard to pronounce (try "keen-wah"), and looks a little like bird seed; but, this highly nutritious, protein-rich grain is as versatile as pasta. And some say it's tastier.

9 **Squid Ink Pasta:** This black pasta looks dramatic and has doctors claiming it can help prevent cancer. And while it *is* black pasta made from squid ink, it's also delicious.

10 **Escargot:** When prepared properly, snails are truly one of the very best things ever to be dipped into melted butter.

How to Survive the Loss of a Loved One

1 **Give Yourself Time:** Don't expect to "get over it." Let yourself cycle through the pain.

2 **Join a Support Group:** Death is a very personal experience, except, the thing is, it happens to everyone. Joining a support group can give you a chance to grieve openly where you feel safe.

3 **Talk to the Dead:** Sometimes you must come to terms with the fact that there will always be things unsaid. So say what you have to.

4 **Be "Inappropriate":** People in the throes of mourning have cited feeling as if the world is going on around them and without them; they feel embarrassed and inappropriate at strange times. Let it go. When grieving, it's absolutely fine to be "inappropriate."

5 **Put One Foot in Front of the Other:** The goal here is to get through your grief and get on with your life. So be deliberate. Wake up, meet your responsibilities, and one day you will come back to life.

6 **Get Involved with Something She Loved:** Take over her charity work or learn to play her guitar. Do something that makes you feel like you are carrying on her legacy.

7 **Talk about the One Who Died:** Don't pretend like you never knew him. Share stories and celebrate his life.

8 **Don't Torture Yourself:** You don't have to miss her all the time. Some people say that they found a parent's death liberating. Remember: Grief feels different for everyone.

9 **Focus on the Future:** You will heal and your life will go on. Believe that and hold on to it. Your loved one would want you to.

10 **Don't Make Any Major Life Choices:** Wait a year before deciding to marry, move, quit your job, or join the circus. That's about how long it takes to reassess your life and begin moving forward.

Learn to Like Just about Anyone

1 **Focus on the Good Points:** Maybe she has nice nails, makes very good brownies, or has fun Christmas sweaters. Whatever it is, remind yourself whenever you begin to feel annoyed.

2 **Imagine Him as His Child Self:** It's easier to forgive flaws in children, so imagine him as a child to awaken your compassion.

3 **Consider Where People Have Been:** You don't know their history or what made them the way they are. Give them the benefit of the doubt.

4 **Ask Better Questions:** Find out if people have ever volunteered, had a sick loved one, or lost a great love. That will help you find their humanity, which will make it harder to dislike them.

5 **Think of It This Way:** You only have to meet her. She has to *be* her. Maybe that will make the pill a little easier to swallow.

6 **Spend One-on-One Time with Them:** If you are having a hard time with someone, ask him or her out alone to see if you can't get to the bottom of it.

7 **Recognize the Potential:** Imagine that a little effort on your part now might lead to a good friendship down the road.

8 **Tune Out Tone:** If a person is aggressive or even downright cold, try to focus on what he said and not how he said it. If you just hear the words without the inflection, you might find the information was even useful.

9 **Ask: "Am I Missing Something?":** Even the most abhorrent of people have something to love inside. Keep digging until you find it.

10 **Remember: It Takes Less Energy to Love Than to Hate:** You can like people for selfish reasons. Hating them is a waste of your energy.

Grow the Greenery Every Home Needs

1. **Aloe:** These light-green beauties are not just pretty to look at. Cut them and use the gel on burns! Fine in low light, and good for people who forget to water.

2. **Hoya Plant:** These grow quickly, so you'll feel good about your skills. Keep it on the dry side and in indirect light.

3. **Peace Lily:** The name alone is enough to make you want this plant in your home. They flourish in low light and they practically call out "water me!" with wilting leaves.

4. **Jade:** With beautiful, bulbous leaves, jade plants make wonderful decoration. They only require a little indirect sunlight and can go months without water.

5. **Donkey Tail:** Another succulent, like jade and aloe, these plants are interspersed with delicate pink flowers. Like other succulents, they do better with little water and indirect light.

6. **English Ivy:** English ivy vines are gorgeous and grow like a weed. They thrive in indirect light and almost can't be *overwatered*.

7. **Asparagus Fern:** The delicate emerald green leaves make this a very pretty plant. It has poisonous berries, so hang it where the cats and kids can't reach. Keep it moist and in low light.

8. **Spider Plant:** You can easily plant the hanging "babies" and make new plants. Anyone will tell you that as long as you sometimes water them, they're tough to kill.

9. **Ficus Tree:** This large plant can fill that empty corner you haven't decided about. You never have to move it and it rarely needs water, but it does like a little sun.

10. **Cactus:** As long as you don't use them as ashtrays, cacti are hardy, need very little water, and can live well in almost any home environment.

Clean the Mess Out of Your Fridge

1. **Alert the Masses:** Let people know your plan ahead of time. Your kids, room-mates, or partner may have been conducting a science project with that zucchini. Give them a say.

2. **Get Your Tools Together:** Make sure you have a trash bag, a recycling bag, a compost bin, cleaning supplies (including a sponge and dish soap), and a chilled cooler.

3. **Wait, then Unplug:** Let your groceries dwindle so you can clean when your fridge is at its most empty. When it's time to clean, begin by unplugging it to save energy and keep you from catching a chill.

4. **Save the Freezer:** Don't clean your freezer on the same day you clean your refrig-erator. Defrosting your freezer is a whole different ball game. But keep the door closed so that it retains its freeze.

5. **Dispose:** Put acceptable kitchen scraps you no longer want into your composting bin and throw away or recycle the packaging. Put things you are keeping into the cooler.

6. **Wash Your Fridge Like You Wash Your Dishes:** Scrub all the nooks and crannies with a nonabrasive sponge. Run the removable bins and emptied reusable con-tainers through the dishwasher.

7. **Make It Shine:** Don't be afraid to dust with an old T-shirt from top to bottom, and use an old toothbrush on corners, drawer tracks, and other hard-to-clean areas.

8. **Put the Food Away:** Plug in the refrigerator and let it cool down, then replace the food.

9. **Add Baking Soda:** Place an open box of baking soda in the door and one at the back wall to keep odors to a minimum.

10. **Know Your Grocery Needs:** Before you go shopping next, make a list of items that need replacing and items that are running out. Don't buy too much stuff. And if you do, donate the extras to a food pantry as soon as possible.

Classical Music That Really Is, Well, Classic

1. **Embrace the Calm:** Classical music has some wild, roaring parts to it; however, it will never be a headbanger's ball. Enjoy the floating sounds and peaceful notes.

2. **Feel the History:** Much classical music was of a particular time and place. Try to imagine the people who listened to it before you—what they wore, who they were.

3. **Consider How It Fits Together:** It's amazing to think that nearly every sound is a blend of several notes and several instruments.

4. **Play It While You Work:** Mozart in particular is said to inspire and motivate, so play it while you are trying to get things done.

5. **Tell Yourself a Story:** Make one up that follows each part of each movement. If you can, read about the story that inspired the composer.

6. **Follow It:** Check out the sheet music from the library and follow the notes as you listen. It will help you see the nuances and subtleties of the piece.

7. **Listen to Modern Classical:** You might be surprised to know that the *Star Wars* theme, by John Williams, is a classical piece. Go out and buy the album so that you can hear it in its entirety.

8. **Try Popular Classical:** If there is something or a part of something you are familiar with, start there. Listen to Beethoven's Fifth Symphony or find an opera you know a little bit about. Many orchestras offer a summer "pops" program that can include rock music reimagined as classical.

9. **Hear It Live:** There is no better way to enjoy classical music than live. Go to the symphony or to a smaller venue or music school in your area.

10. **Play It:** Learn to play something on the piano or guitar and really get a feel for the music and what making it entails.

Easy-to-Mix Mocktails for Any Occasion

① **Shirley Temple:** Add grenadine to Sprite and garnish with maraschino cherries.

② **Sherbet Punch:** In a large punch bowl combine ginger ale and colored sherbet.

③ **Witch's Brew:** For this spooky Halloween treat, combine purple Kool-Aid, ginger ale, peeled grapes, and dry ice in a clear punch bowl.

④ **Virgin Daiquiri:** Mix two parts Sprite to one part sweet and sour mix, and add a handful of frozen raspberries, a dollop of frozen Cool Whip, and ice to a blender. Pour into a tall glass and add whipped cream to garnish.

⑤ **Virgin Bloody Mary:** Use a Bloody Mary mix or prepare your own with tomato juice, horseradish, Worcestershire sauce, Tabasco, celery salt, and cumin. Add club soda and a celery stalk.

⑥ **Tommy Collins:** Combine club soda, rum extract, lime juice, sugar, and ice in a blender and mix to a froth. Use a lime wedge to garnish a tumbler.

⑦ **Sparkling Julep:** Mix sparkling grape juice and mint-infused soda water (set overnight) and garnish a glass with mint.

⑧ **Texas Sunrise:** Add grenadine to a glass of orange juice over ice. Garnish with an orange wedge and a maraschino cherry.

⑨ **Sparkling Fruit:** Freeze fresh raspberries, blueberries, or strawberries and use them as ice with seltzer water or clear soda poured over them. It looks great and tastes refreshing.

⑩ **Amaretto Smoothie:** Combine nonalcoholic amaretto liqueur, milk, and vanilla ice cream in the blender. Blend until smooth. Pour into a milkshake glass and garnish with a dash of powdered chocolate.

Rock a Live Show (Even if You Haven't Been to One in a While)

1 **Get a Recommendation:** Before you choose a show, ask friends who are musically inclined if they have any suggestions for venues or performers.

2 **Choose Music You Know:** Look in community papers and on websites to see what bands or performers are coming to your area.

3 **Don't Overspend:** If it is the first time you are seeing a performer live, don't spend a lot on tickets until you find out if the show will be right for you. Go online and look at venue reviews and read fan blogs to get a sense of what to expect.

4 **Be Polite:** Don't talk or walk around during the performance. Wait until a song ends.

5 **Get Comfortable:** If the show is crowded, try to find a corner where you can lean against a wall. If you can find one, get a seat.

6 **Hold Your Space:** Music venues are pushy places. If people get too close, turn so that your elbow forces them away. Keep a wide stance—legs apart, hands on hips.

7 **Use Ear Plugs:** Most live music is unnecessarily loud. You will have a much more pleasant experience if you protect your ears.

8 **Know Some of the Songs:** If possible, get your hands on a CD or listen to the music online before you get to the show. Knowing a few songs in advance will make your experience that much richer.

9 **Dress in Layers:** No matter what the weather is like outside, be prepared for the venue to be hot. Have something on you can strip down to if you are overwhelmed.

10 **Leave:** If the music is bad or the crowd is unruly, go ahead and get out of there. Live music should be fun.

Alternatives to Deodorant (That Really Work!)

1. **Baking Soda:** Applying just a little with a towel or a powder puff will mask body odor—some would argue, better than deodorant—and is much less expensive.

2. **Lemon:** Lemon juice is said to kill odor-causing bacteria. Since studies indicate that smell comes from bacteria and not from sweat, it's really all you need.

3. **Zinc Oxide Mixtures:** Fill a spray bottle with a zinc oxide powder mixed with an essential oil with a smell you like. You can mix water with the powder and infuse herbs in the mixture over a few days in place of the oils if you'd prefer.

4. **Cornstarch:** Mixed with baking soda, cornstarch is a key ingredient in homemade deodorants.

5. **Rubbing Alcohol:** Spraying this on your armpits from a spray bottle has the added benefit of healing any minor cuts from shaving. But it does sting a little.

6. **Essential Oils:** An ancient remedy used for masking B.O., a few drops of an essential oil in your rubbing alcohol will add a lovely scent to an effective deodorant alternative.

7. **Rock Crystal Salt:** This mineral cuts body odor without harsh chemicals.

8. **"Stones":** Often made from a variety of minerals, these natural deodorant stones are sold in organic stores nationwide.

9. **Baby Wipes:** Instead of one dose of chemical deodorant in the morning, for a quick freshener, wipe your pits with baby wipes or soap whenever you go to the bathroom.

10. **Shower:** A shower a day is actually enough for most people to keep their body odor under control.

Must-Have Magazine Subscriptions

(1) **For the Maven—*In Style*:** This is your ultimate monthly guide to the hottest celebrity fashion and beauty ideas.

(2) **For the Gossip—*People*:** Find out what all your favorite celebrities are doing, who they are seeing, and what they are wearing. It's a guilty pleasure, but it's fun.

(3) **For the Cool Girl—*Elle*:** Articles in *Elle* make you think and act. Find out the best new books to read and where to go to see and be seen.

(4) **For the Health Nut—*Shape*:** Learn the smartest ways to get in shape and stay in shape, with up-to-date ideas for exercising and eating right.

(5) **For the Smarty Pants—*The New Yorker*:** This literary digest excerpts the greatest writers, new and old, of our day and keeps you in-the-know about goings on around the world.

(6) **For the Curious—*Time Magazine*:** Limit your global news intake to a manageable weekly dose. *Time Magazine* has been delivering the goods since 1923 with memorable covers that have marked some of the greatest moments in our nation's history.

(7) **For the Sophisticate—*Vogue*:** If you want to be the first of your friends to know anything about fashion and living the high life (whether or not you can afford to), this is the magazine for you. Or just *appear* sophisticated by purchasing the September issue.

(8) **For the Family Woman—*Good Housekeeping*:** Moms, meet your magazine! Founded in 1885, it was also your great-grandmother's magazine and perhaps even your great-great grandmother's . . .

(9) **For the Chef—*Cook's Illustrated*:** Learn what's new in foodie heaven and how to bring it down to Earth. For people who are serious about food and interested in technique.

(10) **For the Rest of You—*O Magazine*:** If Lady O says you should know about it, you should know about it.

Tie the Knot (Without Breaking the Bank)

1 **Call It Anything but a Wedding:** All vendors tack on what may as well be called a "wedding tax," so make sure you tell them you are planning a family reunion, or when buying your cake, a christening.

2 **Have a Picnic:** Host your big day at a local park. Enlist a cousin to grill dinner on the barbeque and set up horseshoes or bocce.

3 **Find a Cheaper Venue:** You can rent a room in a church or community center for less than a formal event hall.

4 **Go Buffet:** Order family style from a restaurant you like and buy sterno heaters from a dollar store.

5 **Go Super Casual:** Set up in your backyard or the backyard of a close friend and ask everyone to bring a dish instead of presents.

6 **Hire Your Own Staff:** Hire a cousin's college friends to serve, run the bar, and replenish the buffet. Have at least one person overseeing them whom you pay or ask to perform this task in lieu of a wedding gift.

7 **Delegate!:** Put a friend in charge of the bar, another in charge of dinner, someone else in charge of music, and still another in charge of decorations. Be the point person but don't go bridezilla, or you could lose friends.

8 **Buy Your Flowers the Day Before:** The morning before, go to a local farm or farmers' market and buy your flowers. It's much cheaper.

9 **Shop Online:** Buy vases, favors, and even dresses online. A site like OnceWed .com offers designer gowns at a fraction of the prices.

10 **Keep It Small:** It will feel special knowing that you have a close relationship with everyone at your wedding.

Triage an Outfit That's on Its Last Legs

1 Make Old Jeans into Shorts: Those jeans you love with the holes in the knees can be cut into shorts, as short or as long as you want.

2 Create a Colorful Shrug: Use a pair of clean, brightly colored tights. Cut off the toes and put your arms through the legs so that the crotch rests against your back.

3 Make Fingerless Gloves or Arm Warmers: Take knee-high socks, cut off the toes, and make a small hole where the heel is. Then pull them over your arms on those chilly fall evenings.

4 Dye It: Have a white dress you love but can't wear to an upcoming wedding? All you need is a bucket, fabric dye, rubber gloves, and a little outdoor space.

5 Buy a Belt: A well-placed belt can turn any loose clothing into something with shape. A wide elastic belt across your waist always works, or a thin belt at your hips.

6 Make Bell Bottoms: If your skinny jeans are tired, slit them up each side and sew a triangle of additional fabric from the knee down.

7 Turn Around That Boxy Tee: Cut the neck out, shorten the sleeves, and cut off the bottom of that big old T-shirt from the office picnic you would otherwise never have worn. Let it fall off your shoulder a la *Flashdance*.

8 Use Safety Pins: For a hip and casual look, cut a shirt at the seam and reattach it with safety pins. Use black pins on a red shirt for a punk vibe.

9 Make a Wide Headband: Cut the neck off of your old turtlenecks and use the fabric to pull back your hair.

10 Embellish: Pin fabric flowers to a boring shirt or use fabric glue and add glitter or rhinestones.

Stock Your Own 911 Kit

1. **A Working Flashlight:** Put it in a location you won't forget when the lights go out and you are fumbling around. Remember the batteries.

2. **A Charged Cell Phone:** They work with or without electricity and can keep you informed and in contact with the outside world.

3. **A First-Aid Kit:** Keep adhesive bandages, antiseptic ointment, and hydrogen peroxide on hand along with large gauze bandages for more serious cuts and bruises.

4. **Water:** Emergencies like hurricanes and tornadoes can disrupt community water supplies. Have two gallons per person on hand.

5. **Extra Blankets:** If a winter storm takes out the heat in your area, extra blankets might be the only thing between you and a night shivering in all of your sweaters.

6. **Canned Food:** A major blizzard or storm could make it impossible to leave your house. Keep extra canned goods to supplement your diet. If you have an electric can opener, buy a manual one or invest in flip-top cans.

7. **A Bucket:** If a water main breaks due to natural disaster, your toilet won't flush. Unfortunately, you might have to be creative with what you do with the bucket . . . and its contents.

8. **Extra Cash:** When the electricity goes out, so do the ATM machines. Just in case it's difficult to get, keep a small stash someplace safe.

9. **A Cooler and Ice Packs:** During a power outage, transfer your perishables to a cooler with ready-to-go ice packs to keep them for as long as possible.

10. **A Battery-Powered Radio:** Stay in the know about what is happening whether or not you can use your Internet or television. It's old school, but it works.

Organize Your Kitchen Like a Chef

1 **Expand the Space:** Use what you can to make more space for chopping. Utilize the table and the tops of shelves as potential surfaces and stock extra cutting boards.

2 **Clean as You Go:** When you are finished with anything, clean it up and put it away. Even if you are midway through cooking, after you chop, rinse the cutting board and knife. Afterward, clean up the "station." It might make extra dishes, but it will keep you organized.

3 **Do Prep Work:** Have some food washed, rinsed, and cut up before you begin. Keep them organized in plastic containers that are labeled and dated.

4 **Utilize Squeeze and Spray Bottles:** Put oils and sauces you use often into easy-to-use bottles that you don't have to bother uncovering and closing up.

5 **Expose Your Salt and Pepper:** It might seem like a simple thing, but keeping your salt and pepper out in cups will keep you from shaking the shaker until you get the flavor right.

6 **Make It Stackable:** Use round takeout containers to store your spices. Label and stack them in your cupboard to make room for other things.

7 **Keep It Simple:** If you never use some of the knives that came with your knife set, get rid of them. Also throw out or move any pots or excess silverware that don't see the light of day.

8 **Brighten It Up:** To cook, you need good light. But if you'd like a romantic-lighting option, have a dimmer installed.

9 **Sort Your Food:** Keep similar types of foods together in the fridge and pantry so they are easier to grab.

10 **Keep It Close:** The objects you use most should always be within arm's reach. Arrange your space accordingly.

Play Hardball with the Men at the Office

1   **Never Cry:** Leave the room, hide under your desk, hide in a bathroom stall, but never unleash the waterworks in front of the boys club. It's what they expect you to do.

2   **Dress Well:** Dress like a woman, but like a confident, sophisticated woman.

3   **Know Your Shit:** In any meeting or group gathering, make sure you know what you're talking about. Guide conversations to your strongest speaking points.

4   **Don't Say Yes All the Time:** Men are good at delegating. Women, not as much. Make sure you know when you have to turn down another project to complete the work you have.

5   **Impress Them:** Never turn in half-assed work. It might be a double standard, but if you want to get ahead in a man's world, be the best.

6   **Talk Like a Man:** Even if you don't love sports, choose a team and follow it. Men like to talk about things they know. Many of them know sports. You should, too.

7   **Build Men Up in Public:** Complimenting without blowing sunshine is the best way to make the boys in your club feel like you like and support them. And they'll appreciate you for it.

8   **Talk Solutions, Not Problems:** Don't spend a lot of time breaking down the problems; move on as quickly as possible to how you plan to solve them.

9   **Keep Your Tone Breezy:** Emotional confrontations are a no-no. Keep your voice bright, casual, and certain, no matter what you're saying.

10   **Get Pregnant:** A pregnant woman is terrifying to men. You will win every argument. (Too bad it only lasts nine months.)

Shift Out of Relationship "Neutral"

1. **Go Away Together:** If you feel your partner is pulling away from you, see if you can convince him to go away with you. Sometimes a little alone time away from the daily grind will help you find your way back together.

2. **Talk:** Try to get to the bottom of things by talking it out. If he doesn't seem interested in letting you in, see if you can uncover matters with a little subtle spy work. You can't fix anything if you don't know what's wrong.

3. **Fix Things:** Once you have a sense of what is happening with your man, decide if it's worth attempting to fix. If it is, make those changes immediately and decisively.

4. **Do Better:** A relationship is a delicate thing and it takes two to protect it. Do your part to be a good partner and lover.

5. **Let Go:** Sometimes the best way to get him back is to let him go a little.

6. **Focus on Yourself:** It might feel counterintuitive, but turn your energies inward. What do *you* need? How can you fulfill yourself?

7. **Accept Each Other:** Try not to judge him. The tough time you are having belongs to both of you. Be compassionate.

8. **Therapy:** Seek professional help if you both agree to it.

9. **Be Prepared for Any Outcome:** Know this—no matter what happens, you will both be okay.

10. **Move On:** In some cases, ending the relationship is the best way to strengthen it in the long run. It's a risk, but it might be one worth taking.

Say Au Revoir to Social Media Faux Pas

1. **Posting Sexy Pictures:** You can be friendly and warm, but only go as far as you would in the office if you choose to have work contacts in your social networks.

2. **Posting Pictures of You Partying:** It's nice that you had a good time at the party, but don't relive it on your Facebook page. If someone else tags you, politely untag yourself as soon as you can.

3. **Making Social Plans:** Don't make plans for the night publicly over social media. Your boss or potential boss really doesn't want to know.

4. **Posting Personal Conversations:** Generally, keep banter to a minimum if your page is public.

5. **Linking Pages:** Something appropriate for Twitter might not be good for your LinkedIn page. Be separate and deliberate in your posting.

6. **Posting Company Information:** If anyone at work catches wind of a slipup *about work* on a site, you will only have yourself to blame.

7. **Confessing:** No need to tell everyone everything all the time. Keep private information private, no matter how sure you are that no one is listening.

8. **Posting While Drunk:** Be calculated with your information and stay in control. If you've been drinking, check your Google+ page tomorrow.

9. **Getting Too Political:** You wouldn't bring up politics at your interview, so don't go there on Facebook. It's tempting, but hold your tongue.

10. **Engaging in Risky Behavior:** Don't flirt, stalk, abuse, or hound anyone on a social networking site. It might come back to haunt you the next time you go into work, or start looking for new work. And it will last a lifetime.

Buy a Non-Sucky Gift for a Teenager

1 **Concert Tickets for a Band They Like:** Take them or if they are old enough buy them a few so that they can bring friends. Then offer to pick them up and drop them off.

2 **A Musical Instrument:** A guitar or electric keyboard is a very cool gift for a teen. Just make sure it's equally cool with the parents.

3 **A Pet:** Once again, if the parents are on board, a small pet like a lizard or a fish will be very cool to a teen. But a dog or a cat will be awesome!

4 **Retro Band T-Shirts:** Buy a T-shirt from a cool band they don't know. Pair it with an album.

5 **A Weekend Away from Their Parents:** Offer to take them to an amusement park or skiing. If you can swing it, let them bring a friend. If you are the parent, enlist someone else to take them if you want to make it (sorry) an even cooler trip.

6 **Gift Cards:** Give them money toward music, games, or apps. They will love it.

7 **Video Games:** If you know a game that they like is coming out in a new version, you can't go wrong. Look into it.

8 **Movie Tickets:** If they can't go alone, offer to take them with a friend.

9 **Driving Lessons:** Give them driving lessons. Offer to let them use your car or ask to borrow their mom or dad's—giving them a chance to practice is the perfect gift.

10 **Spa Treatments:** Teens often suffer from bad skin and general insecurities. Give the gift of a facial, a massage, or a manicure, depending on gender and interest.

Meet a Man, Get a Date

1 **Become the Hottest Girl in the Room:** Ever notice how the hottest girl is rarely the prettiest? So watch the girls that have every eye on them and mimic their moves.

2 **Show Vulnerability:** Don't permit yourself to be so hard and steely that guys will shy away from touching you for fear of cutting themselves.

3 **Defer to Him:** Let him have this conversation. There will be others that you can dominate. Focus on topics that make him feel comfortable.

4 **Touch:** When you are with a guy you like, touch him—arms and backs are best.

5 **Be Breezy:** Down the road, you are going to want to share your passionate views about the world, but for now, who cares? Death and taxes are your only commitments, and it isn't April 15 and you're feeling great.

6 **Look and Smell Good:** Yes, it's shallow, but in the beginning we all take notice of each other's appearances.

7 **Show Him That You Have Room for Him in Your Life:** Even if you have been single for so long you have mastered a power drill, that doesn't mean you don't need him. So act like it.

8 **Ask Compelling Questions:** Have a few great, memorable questions to ask. Just make sure they are neither probing nor testing.

9 **Don't Man-Hate:** It's one thing to love your womanhood; it's another thing to emasculate men. Try to avoid the latter.

10 **Be Open and Approachable:** Smiling and standing so that your face is open to the room will make you appear engaging and approachable.

Swim in These Magical Waters at Least Once in Your Life

1. **Beaches of the Fiji Islands:** From lagoons to world-class dives, if you like to swim, go to the Fiji Islands to do it.

2. **Pools of Oheo (Maui):** Frolic in one of Hawaii's most scenic destinations among the waterfalls along Hawaii's legendary Hana Highway.

3. **The Dead Sea (Israel):** Feel like you weigh nothing at all as you swim in the mineral-rich waters of the Dead Sea in southern Israel. They say these waters can heal any ailment.

4. **Bioluminescent Bay (Vieques Island, Puerto Rico):** Hundreds of thousands of phosphorescent organisms glow as you swim through them.

5. **Szechenyi Baths (Budapest, Hungary):** This complex features thermal baths thought to possess healing properties. Wander throughout the steam rooms, pools, and saunas.

6. **Lake McKenzie on Fraser Island (Queensland, Australia):** The blue waters and sandy bottom of this lake make it a popular swimming destination, one that is out of the way but well worth it.

7. **Seychelles Islands:** Off the coast of Madagascar, this island nation has some of the world's most pristine beaches, rivers, and lakes, into any of which you will be thrilled to have dipped your toes.

8. **Havasu Falls (Arizona):** Sapphire waters and roaring waterfalls make this swimming hole one of the world's most amazing.

9. **The Devil's Swimming Pool (Victoria Falls, Zambia):** Located a breathtaking 420 feet above the river below. Visually terrifying, but a rocky ledge beneath the water forms a protective barrier from falling.

10. **Gran Cenote (Tulum, Mexico):** This amazing snorkeling destination features an extensive cave system full of stalagmites and stalactites visible through crystal-clear waters.

Train a Dog in Ten Easy Steps

(1) Teach Him His Name: Cut a treat into very small pieces. Say his name, reward with a treat. Say his name, reward with a treat. Do this twenty times every hour. By lunch your dog will know his name.

(2) Make Her Sit: Never place food before a standing dog. If it's time to eat or get a treat, make her sit.

(3) Follow Through: If you order a command, do not stop until it's completed. It's okay if you have to guide the animal through it (i.e., gently push his bottom into a sitting position).

(4) Get Her to Stay: Say "Stay," then make her wait for a reward. Over time, extend the wait. Try walking away. If your animal moves, restart.

(5) Get Him to Come: Begin in a sitting position. Walk away using the "stay" command. Say "Come" and reward with a treat. Have a friend, child, or partner stand in another part of the house and call "Come," and reward. Then you again. Then the other person again.

(6) Add Distractions Incrementally: Turn on the TV and practice "Come." Go to the backyard and try it, then the dog park.

(7) Randomize the Reward: Don't reward with a treat every time once your pup knows the command. Sometimes reward with praise, and other times, don't reward at all.

(8) Be Repetitive: Train your dog a little every day if you can, or at least once a week. Always use the same command with the same inflection when you are working on training.

(9) Take It Seriously: Being able to call your dog anywhere is important, for both the people around you as well as your dog.

(10) Don't Hit: Most dogs do not need a heavy hand to be trained properly, just patience and a few good liver treats.

Calm Down for a Peaceful Life

1 **Picture the Eyes of an Animal You Trust:** Many therapists suggest that people suffering from anxiety disorders or panic attacks close their eyes and picture looking into the eyes of a pet or animal they love.

2 **Believe You Are Safe:** Anxiety is generally warning you against some future crisis. But in *this* moment, you are actually safe. Look around. Feel the ground beneath your feet and the clean air in your lungs.

3 **Take Up Exercise:** For a long-term fix, get moving and start releasing endorphins. When you are feeling good, anxiety is not a problem.

4 **Get Out of Your Head:** If you are not busy, get busy. Or distract yourself with a magazine, book, or TV show.

5 **Leave the City:** Anxiety can be exacerbated by crowded cities. If you live in one, take an evening or day to get into the nature and run around.

6 **Create a Safe Space:** Visualize a place in your mind that is calm and serene. When anxiety rears its head, go to your safe space and calm down.

7 **Learn to Relax Your Muscles:** You can't be anxious if your body is relaxed. See if you can't nip anxiety in the bud by relaxing your entire body.

8 **Meditate:** Begin a daily meditation practice. The increased oxygen in your blood will help, and you will get better at controlling your body.

9 **Find Faith:** Many would argue you either have faith or you don't. But finding something you believe in about the order of the Universe will help you make sense of your life.

10 **Talk to a Doctor:** If your anxiety has begun taking over, talk to your doctor and find a treatment that will help you to take back control.

Creative Baby Gifts Every Mom Will Love

1. **A Big Box of Colorful Cotton Balls:** Fill a plastic bin with craft store cotton balls in all the bright colors. Supervised babies will love to play in them.

2. **A Framed Newspaper Cover:** Frame the front page of your local newspaper from the day the baby was born for a gift he or she will keep forever.

3. **Babysitting Coupons:** A great gift for new parents is a coupon agreeing to babysit their tyke for a few hours or an overnight when they are older.

4. **A Performance:** This is especially great if you don't live in town. Record yourself performing a show, singing, dancing, and generally amazing the baby, and deliver it via DVD.

5. **A Bag of Silk Scarves:** You can buy them cheaply at thrift stores or find them new in bulk. A parent will be able to entertain a child for hours with colorful floating scarves.

6. **A Baby Faces DVD:** Go out and videotape the faces of infants. (Get permission from the parents first, of course.) Babies are fascinated by other babies and will love watching, especially if you play pleasant music overtop.

7. **A Personalized Bib Collection:** Buy white bibs and decorate them with fabric paints and markers.

8. **A Giant Ball Pool!:** Fill a baby pool with plastic balls so baby can explore without all the germs of a public ball pool.

9. **Rock 'n' Roll Baby Tees:** If you can't find a baby tee from the baby's parent's favorite band, have one made.

10. **His or Her Birthstone:** For a boy, get him birthstone cufflinks for when he's older. A girl gets a necklace or earrings she can't wear for a while. But their parents will love them and keep them someplace safe.

What Your Tummy Is Telling You That You Need to Hear

1 **Everyone Is Different:** Just as some people can drink a whole carton of milk and feel great, another person might get sick halfway through a glass. Take cues from your own body and not from your friends.

2 **Not Eating Is Not Good:** Your body needs food to survive. Not eating, even for short periods of time, will lower your metabolism and eventually force your body to shut down.

3 **Fatty Foods Constrict Your Blood Vessels:** After a fatty meal, your blood vessels actually constrict for several hours before returning to normal—that is, as long as your next meal isn't a fatty one.

4 **Stress Blocks Digestion:** Stress is designed to allow you to focus on survival during fight or flight—all systems shut down. But if you hold on to anxiety long-term, it will continue to compromise healthy digestion.

5 **It's More Than the Stomach:** Most of digestion takes place in the small intestine. It begins in the esophagus and works its way through nearly all of your organs before it's done.

6 **Your Stomach Size Doesn't Change:** Once you are an adult, your stomach pretty much stays the same size.

7 **Insoluble Fiber Is Your Friend:** Whole wheat, cabbage, and beets will help your body process food better than will soluble fiber like oat bran and citrus.

8 **Losing Two Pounds Can Stop Acid Reflux:** Often very minimal weight loss will help control acid reflux.

9 **It Isn't *When* You Eat, but *How Much*:** Your digestive system works the same before bed as it does in the morning.

10 **Calories Are Not Always Equal:** Three hundred calories of cookie is not the same as 300 calories of almond butter. The latter digests more slowly and keeps you satisfied longer.

Important Life Lessons as Taught by Daytime Soaps

1   **Great Love Never Dies:** No matter how many times your man has been "killed" and how many people verify the body, if it's true love, be ready for him to have been cloned and sent to live on a desert island.

2   **Say "I Love You" or Say Goodbye:** Miscommunication is the greatest destroyer of love. If your partner thinks you don't love him, even if you do, he will leave you for the hot redhead who was very very clear about it.

3   **Everyone Has a Secret:** Whether he fathered a child when he was a teenager or once was charged with murder, if you don't hear about it at first, just wait for it.

4   **Great Hair Does Not Equal a Great Heart:** The two are in no way linked and should not be mistakenly intertwined.

5   **Amnesia Is Your Friend:** If you can't remember that you tried to kill your lover, everyone can get over it, especially if the amnesiac-you is very sweet.

6   **Watch Out for the Twin Rule:** If there are two of you that look alike, one of you is evil and will try to steal the other's life.

7   **Be Sure You Can Answer "Who's Your Daddy?":** Even if you think you know who your child's father is, you should make sure you weren't roofied before you try to get a part of his liver to save the child's life.

8   **Don't Fight Like a Girl:** Even in stilettos, awkward pushing and grabbing looks awkward. Learn how to land a real punch.

9   **Wear Waterproof Mascara:** A good emotional cry can make anyone feel better about being abducted by aliens, married to their half-sibling, and then forced into piracy.

10   **At the End of Love There Is . . . :** . . . More love.

Charm Every Child You Meet

1 **Brighten Up:** Have a happy disposition and kids will respond to you simply because they are attracted to your smile.

2 **Listen and Respond:** Kids, like anyone, like to feel heard. So do your best to listen to them and respond accordingly. If you can't understand a small child, give it a few tries and then let him or her down gently by explaining that you're sorry but you don't understand, then move on.

3 **Get on Their Level:** Lower your body to their height so that you make a physical connection during basic conversation and any type of play. They will like you better for it.

4 **Use Distraction:** For an upset child, especially younger ones, distract them by changing the focus to something else engaging. The "look over there" technique can turn any crying child into a happy child.

5 **Avoid Harsh Responses:** Explain right and wrong to children without acting out a "wrong" behavior. If you don't want yelling, don't yell. They'll listen better and like you more.

6 **Be Affectionate:** Kisses and hugs can win over any child. Share them copiously.

7 **Learn to Play:** Exercise your imagination and play with kids whose company you enjoy. Kids love adults who like to play their games.

8 **Be Genuine:** Children can sense a phony a mile away. Say what you mean and stick with it.

9 **Calm Down:** Relax. These are kids, not rabid dogs. Calm your body physically. They will feel the difference and warm up to you much more easily.

10 **Become a Kid Again:** Think about the wonder with which they see the world and remember what a gift that was.

Round-the-Clock Ways
to Keep a Baby from Crying

1 **Don't Panic:** First of all, a crying baby is less noticeable to those around you than you think, at least in the short term. So stay calm.

2 **Get Yourself Under Control First:** If you are in the middle of a somewhat chaotic situation—handling groceries or out to lunch—situate yourself so that your hands are free and can deal with your child.

3 **Don't Worry about Others:** People appreciate that you're trying. And if all else fails, *looking* like you are trying will garner sympathy from most people.

4 **Use Distraction:** Point out pretty lights to your baby, tickle her cheek, blow on her face, or smile at her. Get her to refocus.

5 **Start with a Firm Schedule:** Get your baby on a fairly firm schedule so that in general, when he cries, you will know if he is in need of food, a nap, or something else.

6 **Check Comfort Levels:** Is your baby too hot or too cold? Is it noisy where you are, or particularly bright? Does he need something for teething? Try to make him comfortable.

7 **Leave Baby at Home:** Be pre-emptive by anticipating whether where you are going will be too tough on an infant.

8 **Go for a Walk:** If you are in a place where it is possible to pick your child up and walk around with her, give it a try. A change of scenery might be all she needs.

9 **Bring Treats . . . for *the Public*:** When you are someplace with relatively tight quarters, there may be nothing anyone can do. Bring a bag of candy to hand out. It will make people smile even if your baby will not.

10 **Bring Tools:** Have pacifiers, sparkly and rattle-y toys, snacks, spare diapers, and clean clothes at the ready in case of anything!

Landscape Your Lawn — Naturally

(1) Xeriscape: The practice used to be called "xeriscaping," meaning "dry landscaping." Look for ways to reduce any unnaturally applied water.

(2) Seek Professional Help: Local nurseries and landscape architects are great resources when you're deciding what to plant in your yard.

(3) Watch the Sun: Pay attention to sun movement across your yard. Which areas get the most sun (and will subsequently require more water — or a more drought-resistant species of plants)? Then plant accordingly.

(4) Look at Drainage Patterns: Look for the way water drains naturally in your yard. This will help to avoid erosion and also help you to create visually interesting valleys, crests, and plateaus in your landscaping.

(5) Consider Water Waste: Collect most of your water-loving plants into an area that may be reached by a single sprinkler. If a sprinkler is watering only one bush, it's wasteful.

(6) Choose Your Soil: Well-aerated soil that is high in organic materials conserves more water. Many plant species (other than most cacti) will appreciate a dense soil that holds moisture.

(7) Choose an Alternative Ground Covering: By using stones, brick, mulch, sand, and native plant species in place of turf, you will find you need far less water, not to mention less maintenance.

(8) Properly Irrigate: By replacing crude hoses and sprinkler systems with modern irrigation methods, a yard can thrive with limited to zero water waste.

(9) Consider the Space: As long as you aren't planning to organize a soccer league in your front yard, perhaps a more realistic rock garden will create a peaceful area where you can relax.

(10) Create a *Habitat,* Not Just a *Yard*: Although grasses, trees, and bushes alien to the climate in which you live tend to be your landscape's biggest water-suckers, minimizing water waste doesn't mean you have to sacrifice a beautiful landscape. Choose native plants that you love.

How to Talk so Your Colleagues Will Listen

1 **Be Confident:** A tone that is confident and decisive is much easier for those around you to trust.

2 **Focus on Solutions:** Don't harp on what could go wrong or complain about how something will fail. Instead focus your words on how it can be solved or what would have to be done to make sure it works.

3 **Say What You Mean:** Don't use passive aggression or convoluted arguments. Choose your statements accordingly.

4 **Keep It Emotion-Free:** Keep a steady, even tone or even lighten it up with an on-topic joke, but do not become frustrated or add emotion to your argument.

5 **Have a Plan:** Know in advance what you will say and what your goals are.

6 **Be Open Minded:** Listen patiently and without judgment. Maybe you will hear a better idea or discover something you hadn't thought of to build on.

7 **Maintain Flexibility:** If there is a better idea, don't be afraid to change course. Add to it and build on it as though it was an idea that belonged to you all.

8 **Use Your Voice:** Don't expect to be heard over e-mail or in a chatroom. Use your voice even if it means picking up the phone or seeking someone out for a one-on-one.

9 **Yours Need Not Be the Last Word:** It doesn't matter if you made your point in the middle, at the beginning, or at the end. Getting a point in anywhere is a feat you can be proud of.

10 **Be Clear:** Be precise and economical with your words. In the business world, time is money. Don't cost a fortune.

Make Everyone Like You

1   **Be Available:** When people call you up to do something, say yes. Make your friends your priority and they will like you for it.

2   **Be Friendly:** Be someone approachable and warm to everyone. Having a nerdy friend, contrary to what we thought in middle school, will not make you a social pariah.

3   **Don't Take Sides:** If your friends get into a fight, it's okay to tell them that you want to listen but that you intend to remain impartial.

4   **Don't Gossip or Badmouth:** Speak respectfully of people whether or not they are around. You can't stop others, but you can nod and smile without engaging.

5   **Enjoy Attention:** Be the girl who is a little loud, has a witty comeback, and an easy laugh. It's very endearing.

6   **Engage the Shy People:** If you see people who seem shy or uncomfortable, try to make them feel that you like them and are interested in them.

7   **Make No Judgments:** Keep your mind open and accept different lifestyles and behaviors.

8   **Be Nice to Everyone:** If you are having a bad day, stay inside. When you go out, be loving and warm. That way, even the guy pumping your gas will say, "What a nice lady. I *like* her."

9   **Prepare to Fail at This, but Remember It's a Noble Endeavor:** Chances are you will fail every now and then. Let it go and move on. Being happy and warm all the time is for cartoon characters, not real people.

10   **Ignore Anyone Who Doesn't Like You:** If you ignore them, then it's *as if* everyone likes you.

Tackle These Daily Must-Dos on Your Smartphone

① **Check Your E-Mail:** All smartphones are set up with a feature that connects you directly to your e-mail accounts; yes, all of them. You can know the moment each one comes in.

② **Navigate:** You can use your cell phone as a GPS. Even on foot, if you are looking for a place or an address, simply plug it into your phone and ask it to navigate you from your current location.

③ **Program Your TiVo:** Go to m.tivo.com to set up your TiVo over the phone.

④ **Get Phone Numbers:** You can call (800) FREE411 or (800) 373-3411 from your cell phone and never pay 411 another penny.

⑤ **Grocery Shop:** You can download apps from any of your favorite stores, even grocery stores, and get great prices and bargains when you do!

⑥ **Break into Your Car:** If your car is equipped with keyless entry, you can set up your phone to unlock it for you when you forget to bring your device, or accidentally lock it inside.

⑦ **Call Abroad Cheaply:** While international calls might not be on your plan, using a service like MyWebCalls.com will allow you to, for example, call France for less than two cents a minute.

⑧ **Make Original Art:** You can take photos and transform them with apps that can make them look old-fashioned or even like you painted them yourself.

⑨ **Get Rescued:** If you have to make an emergency call and you are out of the service area, dial 112. It should work almost anywhere.

⑩ **Be the First to Get an NFC Chip:** Currently in its testing phase, once added to your cell phone, you will be able to use it like a credit card or in place of an airplane or train ticket.

Rosetta Stone, Your Way

1 **Focus on Phrases:** Rather than grammar and individual words, memorize a phrase a day until you can say some basic things.

2 **Listen to It:** Play someone speaking the language into headphones every night before you go to sleep. A book on tape will work. You don't have to pay attention, just get comfortable with the cadence and sounds. Do this for a year.

3 **Say Words:** Start saying some of the words you've noticed sticking out. Just say them out loud and get comfortable with your pronunciation.

4 **Practice Twenty Minutes a Day:** Once you can say some of the words and are comfortable with the sounds, give yourself twenty minutes a day to actively begin studying the language.

5 **Meet Up:** See if you can swap thirty minutes of English instruction for thirty minutes of the foreign language at a café. You can post for a buddy on Craigslist or at an area university.

6 **Travel:** It will help to inspire you to keep learning if you travel to a country where your language of choice is spoken. It will motivate you to keep going.

7 **Use Sticky Notes:** Hang signs all over your house bearing the word and pronunciation in the foreign language—cabinet, refrigerator, book, television, bed, etc.

8 **Study in the Bathroom:** Have a textbook or dictionary in the bathroom, and while you are doing your business, practice the language and learn a few words.

9 **Translate a Poem:** Practice the language by translating a short poem a day from English.

10 **Move:** You could always move to a foreign country and surround yourself with only non-English speakers until, by sheer force of necessity, you learn the language.

Get Your Guy to Read This List and Help Him "Get It!"

1 **Truth #1:** The area *beneath* the toilet gets surprisingly disgusting after a few weeks without a good cleaning.

2 **Truth #2:** You actually *do* have to wash the handles of pots, pans, and utensils as well.

3 **Truth #3:** If she does your dishes, it is not because she likes doing dishes. Just FYI.

4 **Truth #4:** The smell test for wearability isn't enough if you've spilled spaghetti sauce anywhere on the article of clothing—yes, even if it's just a tiny drop.

5 **Truth #5:** Sometimes, just every once in a while, during a fight, your woman is actually wishing you would just tell her you love her and want her and are so happy to be with her.

6 **Truth #6:** You should know what a clitoris is and how it works. Look it up.

7 **Truth #7:** She likes to watch that TV show *because* it's cheesy and everyone looks impossibly pretty.

8 **Truth #8:** It *always* requires a little more foreplay than your erection pressed into her thigh. Sometimes she may be willing to forgo that extra work for a fun morning quickie, but please don't think that means *every time*.

9 **Truth #9:** Women like it when they're told, unprompted, that they look good.

10 **Truth #10:** Crying during movies is fun. There's really no explanation, so just go with it.

Get Everything Done and Done Well

1. **Don't Fool Yourself:** No one can actually drive the car and text at the same time no matter how adept they think they are at it. Multitasking is a cruel myth. Don't try it.

2. **Prioritize:** Be clear on what comes first, second, and third in your life.

3. **Be Flexible:** Just because you intend to always answer calls from family doesn't mean that when you are mid-meeting you have to take those calls. Sometimes they have to wait. Just make sure you return them as soon as you are finished.

4. **Keep a Running List:** The minute something new comes up, add it to your list, either in a notebook or your cell phone. Cross things off as you finish them.

5. **Set a Routine:** You get the added benefit of sense memory when your day is well scheduled.

6. **Set Boundaries:** Have a set time to go through e-mails, a time to return calls, a time to work, and a time to be with friends and/or family. Don't mix and match.

7. **Complete Tasks:** If you begin going through e-mails, respond. Do not leave threads dangling. Once you begin, you must follow through.

8. **Don't Become Overwhelmed:** Break down big problems so that they are manageable.

9. **Update To-Do Lists Before Every Task:** Cross off what's been completed and add new items. Also, take a moment to review the list from beginning to end.

10. **Color-Code Your List:** Keep them together in one list but put family items in blue, work in black, social in purple.

Build Good Fences,
Make Good Neighbors

1 **Smile and Wave:** At first a simple smile and wave is enough to open up a friendly relationship with neighbors. Over time, more might grow.

2 **Offer Them First Pick After You Spring Clean:** If you are making a big donation to Goodwill, see if they want to come by and check out the goods first. Bring something nice to the door they might truly want so it won't seem like you are offering them garbage.

3 **Invite Them to Dinner:** If there is a couple or family that intrigues you on your block, next time you see them ask them if they would like to come to dinner.

4 **Use Your Kids:** If you all have kids, ask your kids to go over and play with theirs. Or organize a play date.

5 **Ask to Borrow Something:** Whether or not you actually need it, go knock and see if they have a stick of butter you could borrow. When you go back to return it, bring them some homemade cookies.

6 **Go to Block Meetings:** If your neighborhood has a block association, become active in it.

7 **Spark Up Conversations:** When you see your neighbors outside, walk right up and say hello. Introduce yourself and ask how they are.

8 **Help Them Out:** If you see them coming home with groceries, help them unload. Pull in their garbage can after they've been emptied.

9 **Share Large Household Items:** See if they want to invest in a shared lawn mower or hedge trimmer.

10 **Throw a Block Party:** Organize a block party or show up if someone else organizes one. Bring a dish and some friendly repartee.

When Love Talks, Listen

1   **Pablo Neruda:** "Love is so short, forgetting is so long."

2   **Erica Jong:** "Do you want me to tell you something really subversive? Love is everything it's cracked up to be. That's why people are so cynical about it. It really is worth fighting for, being brave for, risking everything for. And the trouble is, if you don't risk anything, you risk even more."

3   **Winnie the Pooh:** "Some people care too much. I think it's called love."

4   **Song of Solomon:** "Many waters cannot quench love, neither can the floods drown it: if a man would give all the substance of his house for love, it would be utterly contemned."

5   **George Sand:** "There is only one happiness, to love and be loved."

6   **Mae West:** "Love conquers all things except poverty and toothache."

7   **Neil Gaiman:** "Have you ever been in love? Horrible isn't it? It makes you so vulnerable . . . It gets inside you. It eats you out and leaves you crying in the darkness, so simple a phrase like 'maybe we should be just friends' turns into a glass splinter working its way into your heart. It hurts. Not just in the imagination. Not just in the mind. It's a soul-hurt, a real gets-inside-you-and-rips-you-apart pain. I hate love."

8   **Langston Hughes:** "Folks, I'm telling you,/Birthing is hard/and dying is mean-/ so get yourself/a little loving/in between."

9   **George Carlin:** "If you love someone, set them free. If they come home, set them on fire."

10   **Maya Angelou:** "If you find it in your heart to care for somebody else, you will have succeeded."

Beauty Rest You Can Dream By

(1) **Cut Afternoon Coffee:** After 3 P.M. make it decaf.

(2) **Bathe Before Bed:** Take a hot relaxing soak and try to release all the stresses of the day.

(3) **Relax:** Literally. Focus your mind on relaxing your toes first and then your feet, then your ankles and legs until you have made it to the top of your head and feel the muscles release and let go.

(4) **Meditate:** Focus on your breathing. If your mind wanders, bring it back.

(5) **Get on a Schedule:** Go to bed at the same time every day and wake up at the same time every day. Then your body will know what to do.

(6) **Turn Off the Noise:** Limit background music, TV, and conversations. Invest in a lulling fan or a white-noise machine if you live in a noisy location.

(7) **Turn Down the Heat:** Make your sleeping temperature cooler than your awake temperature.

(8) **Read:** Read a magazine or a light book before sleeping. No work documents or important literature.

(9) **Get Up and Walk Around:** Kids have it right; when you can't sleep, don't just lie there. Get up and go for a walk around the block or around your house—not to the refrigerator or TV room, but just a slow, quiet stroll until you feel ready to lie down again.

(10) **Make Up the Details of a Pleasant Story:** Close your eyes and imagine yourself arriving someplace. Where are you going? What are you doing? Choose your outfit and notice the details of the scene. Being detailed in your observations will help your mind settle into sleep mode.

The Single Girl's Must-Own Library

1. ***Tropic of Capricorn*, by Henry Miller:** This masterwork from 1938 was banned in the United States until 1961 for obscenities. Guys. Love. This. Book.

2. ***The Kama Sutra*:** This Hindu text has become widely known for its practical advice on intercourse. It passes on info any guy would love any girl to know.

3. **Leather-Bound Classics:** Adding a series of leather-bound books to your collection will smell good and look fantastic.

4. **Dr. Seuss Books:** Dr. Seuss reminds guys of childhood. Guys are inherently immature. A collection of Dr. Seuss books might not make him randy, but they sure will make him happy.

5. ***Team of Rivals*, by Doris Kearns Goodwin:** He'll be impressed that you share a reading list with the president and might ask to borrow it when you're done.

6. ***Lennon*, by Ray Coleman:** If your guy isn't a Beatles fan, you might need to get a different musician's biography. But come on, what guy isn't a Beatles fan?

7. **The Bible:** Whether or not you believe in it, he'll just be impressed that you bothered to read it yourself and didn't just take someone else's word for it.

8. **Something in a Foreign Language:** It can be anything, but something like *The Little Prince* in French or *Don Quixote* in Spanish is a definite conversation starter, not to mention downright impressive.

9. ***Spiderman* or *Superman* Comics:** Guys like superheroes. A collection of comic books on your bookshelf is only going to intrigue him more.

10. ***Beyond Good and Evil*, by Friedrich Nietzsche:** There's just something about a nihilistic sex partner that a lot of guys find hot.

Don't Even Think about Looking in the Mirror . . .

1. **During a Long Workout:** Unless of course you are checking your form for safety. When running on the treadmill? You look bad. Why ruin a perfectly good workout by confirming it?

2. **After a Big Night of Drinking:** The bloating, the red puffy cheeks, that suspicious broken capillary on your nose? Just cover it up without looking too closely.

3. **After Watching a Horror Movie:** Just leave it alone. Haven't you already been through enough?

4. **When You're Looking Too Much:** Is it hard to take your eyes off yourself any time you spot your reflection? Maybe, Narcissus, it's time to take a break.

5. **When You're Over It:** Yes, it's a man's world. Once in a while decide that you don't care and cover up your mirrors for a week.

6. **When You're Camping:** You are dirty, you are having fun, and the squirrels and trees do not care what you look like. Anyway, au naturel looks good on you.

7. **When You Are Trying to Define Yourself:** Who cares if you don't *look* like a mother or a doctor or a chicken farmer? Neither your child, nor your patient, *nor* the chickens will mind!

8. **After Childbirth:** For the love of God, stay away from the looking glass. You will not like what you see.

9. **During Sex:** Well, to be fair, this is entirely dependent on the view. If things start to look too squished and bouncy, it's just going to ruin the mood. Turn over and look the other way.

10. **When You're Feeling Unattractive:** If you're in the throes of some major body image insecurity, walk away from the mirror and start by healing your soul.

What to Buy the Woman
Who Has Everything

1 **Think Sentimental Value:** Go to a thrift store, flea market, or antique store and buy her something from her past. A special box, a retro T-shirt, or an interesting piece of art might interest her.

2 **Get Spiritual:** Stones and crystals are inexpensive but lovely gift ideas. They often have a meaning that is easy to research—for example, rose quartz attracts love and citrine, success, so choose one that fits her.

3 **Select Jewelry:** Get her something simple and affordable that matches her style.

4 **Play the Nostalgia Card:** Search eBay for a game she loved as a kid, or find a yearbook from her high school.

5 **Ask Her Mom:** Call her mom to find out if there is a sweet drawing of hers from childhood or poems she wrote in school. Have one framed for her.

6 **Take Her Out:** Take her out for a nice dinner or out on the town. If you are looking for a cheaper option, host a girls' dinner with her other friends and make it a potluck in her honor.

7 **Pamper Her:** Get her a manicure or a fancier spa treatment. Those never go unappreciated.

8 **Pay Attention:** Listen to her when she mentions things in passing she might want and decide if any are worth getting her. She'll really appreciate not only the gift but that you remembered.

9 **Make It Yourself:** Choose a cool photograph and have it blown up and framed for her.

10 **Make It Easy on Yourself:** When all else fails, choose a store you think she might like, and pick up a gift card.

What to Buy the Man
Who Has Everything

1. **An Old Telescope or Camera:** Flea markets and thrift stores often have amazing old technical gadgets most guys would love to tinker or play with.

2. **Sports Tickets:** Take him to a game and buy him a hat and a beer. You will never meet a happier man.

3. **Give a "Special" Gift:** If the man who has everything is your partner, the gift of sexual favors never gets old.

4. **Name a Star After Him:** It's cheesy, but also kind of cool. And if he's an astronomy buff he'll love it.

5. **Make It Nostalgic:** Get him candy from his childhood (you can order from nostalgia shops online) and make him up a basket of everything from Nerds to Red Hots to Dots.

6. **Make Him a Mix:** Give him some new music, but consider *his* tastes, not yours. Busy guys especially appreciate being introduced to stuff they will love.

7. **Pamper Him:** When he gets home from work, have a bath ready for him with candles and music. When he gets out, present him with dinner.

8. **Go Sentimental:** Frame a picture of his parents, or a childhood shot of him and a sibling.

9. **Have It Made:** Get him a custom-made sports cap with his team's first logo on it. It will be something cool he will be happy to have.

10. **Get a Gift Card:** If all else fails, choose a fun store like Sharper Image and get him a gift card he'll enjoy.

Camp Like a Grownup

1. **Do It in Your Backyard:** Set up a fire pit and a tent, and "camp" where you have easy access to a toilet.

2. **Make It a Luxury Outing:** Some campgrounds are equipped for the high-maintenance camper. They offer personal-use restrooms *and* hot showers.

3. **Rent a Camper:** Like a personal hotel on wheels, take one someplace beautiful, plug in, and camp like a civilized person.

4. **Stay in a Cabin:** Who said that camping meant you had to sleep on a floor? Rent a cabin with a bed, a wood-burning stove, and running water, for heaven's sake.

5. **Forget Practical:** Find the most flowing fabrics you can, hire someone to hang them tentlike over a luxurious bed outside, and sleep like an Arabian princess.

6. **Be Prepared:** If you really want to go for it, visit a sporting goods store and buy the amenities that will make you comfortable. Waterless soaps, travel pads, and portable ovens take some of the rough out of roughing it.

7. **Accessorize:** Make sure your camping outfit includes a stylish hair scarf and a handkerchief to wipe away sweat.

8. **Go Au Naturel:** The doesn't mean you have to give up makeup; just don't do your normal heavy-on-the-liner routine. Keep it limited to mascara and foundation and a sheer gloss that'll make him say, "You look great without makeup."

9. **Avoid Strong Smells:** Bugs are attracted to perfumes. Bears like food. Make sure you read up on how to store food and leave the Chanel N°5 at home.

10. **Open the Doors:** For she who really doesn't have a camping bone in her body, open the windows, turn on a woodland-noises sound machine, and call it camping-ish.

From Culinary to Kinky:
Make Your Kitchen Fun Again

1 **Cook Like His Mother:** There is no great explanation for this, but almost without fail, a man will find you breathtakingly sexy when you can cook like his mother. So give her a call and ask about that "Chex Chicken" he won't stop talking about.

2 **Use Fresh Herbs:** They smell great and add unparalleled flavor to your dishes. The simple act of planting them in your herb garden will kick off this sensuality bouillabaisse.

3 **Make It Healthy:** Foods that are low in fats and carbs, not to mention foods that err on the healthier side, will inspire both of your libidos to kick into gear.

4 **Use Hands Only:** There is just something extremely hot about eating with your hands. The licking of fingers, the licking of lips, the licking of each other's fingers and each other's lips . . .

5 **Add Chocolate:** There are plenty of savory dinner ideas that include chocolate. Find a luscious mole recipe or make a hearty stew. Dark chocolate is an aphrodisiac, not to mention delicious.

6 **Add Almonds:** Almonds are thought to get the blood flowing where it counts. Feed each other almond butter on a cracker for a light, wake up-before-sex snack!

7 **Make Seafood Magic:** A lot of shellfish is known to inspire lewd thinking. Perhaps it is the shape and texture of an oyster. Then there are all the health benefits of fatty fish like salmon, which serve as master bedroom enhancers.

8 **Use It:** . . . Dinner that is, during sex . . . during the next round of sex . . .

9 **Make Something Up:** Only use foods that promise to invoke amorous tendencies and design dinner around them. Begin with oysters, then basil salmon followed by a chocolate avocado mousse with almond crème.

10 **Cook Naked:** Just make sure you use an apron in case anything hot splatters, or . . . never mind.

Shoes Every Woman Must Have

1. **Swarovski Crystal Stilettos:** When Niecy Nash unveiled her fabulous wedding shoe on *The View*, putting a foot in one became every American woman's dream.

2. **Glagla Tennis Shoes:** This French company makes a ventilated tennis shoe that comes in cool styles and bright colors and is machine washable so you don't need socks!

3. **Swedish Hasbeens:** These Swedish-owned miracles of clog goodness also come in several fabulous strappy wedge versions.

4. **Galoshes:** Chances are your mom will no longer help you get them on. But once you're in them, puddle hopping never looked so good.

5. **Birkenstock Sandals:** The best thing about these shoes has to be that by dipping them in water and wearing them wet, they mold to your foot.

6. **Retro Heels:** A great pair of Mary Jane heels or Marilyn Monroe polka-dot stilettos will glam up any outfit.

7. **Prada's 2011 Rope Bottom Sandal:** If you want your legs to look like they end on the other side of the world, you must own these shoes.

8. **Clog Boots:** One of the great trends of the preteen years of the millennium is a clog-shaped boot with leather to the knee.

9. **Christian Louboutin Black Pump:** Simple, classic, endlessly fashionable.

10. **Stiletto Manolo Blahniks:** Back pain, be damned! Put on a pair of these and it won't matter, because you'll be flying.

Stock a Palate-Pleasing Kitchen Pantry

1 **Keep White Wine:** White wine gives a bright flavor to anything you cook in a skillet. It is also a great base for a marinade.

2 **Buy Lemons:** A versatile food, you can use them to flavor fish or meat, as a dressing on a salad, and even, in a pinch, to wipe down your counter.

3 **Stock Up on Pasta:** They last forever, so stock up on several varieties. When you need a quick dinner, add garlic, some olive oil, and some fresh basil and/or tomato.

4 **Always Have Garlic:** Fresh garlic adds depth to meat, potatoes, and salads. Wrap a bulb in foil, bake on low for a few hours, and use it as a healthy butter-spread substitute.

5 **Spices Are a Must:** Keep a cupboard full of spices and learn how to use them. They'll improve any homemade meal.

6 **Always Buy Bread:** In a pinch you can always make a sandwich as long as you keep bread in the house.

7 **Make Sure You've Got Crushed Tomatoes:** Canned tomatoes have been linked to fertility issues in women, so stock up on the boxed version.

8 **Invest in Olive Oil:** Cook with it or use it on fresh cheeses, in your salad (with lemon), or on bread.

9 **Preserve Fresh Herbs:** Learn how to preserve your fresh herbs. Most can be dried or even frozen for the longest shelf life. If you properly tend a potted herb plant, it can last you through the winter. They'll make your house smell good and take everything you cook to the next level of delicious.

10 **Freeze Fresh Berries:** During peak season, stock up on berries, put them in a zip-top bag, and freeze them. Pull them out for a frozen snack, or let them thaw and use them in baked goods, on cereal, and for dessert.

Keep Any Kid in Line

1 **Use Compassion:** This is perhaps the first and most difficult step—find an inner kindness that transcends frustration, and cling to it.

2 **Know Where He's Coming From:** It might just be that this child is tired or hungry, or perhaps he has something more sinister in his past. Try to unearth what is at the root of his unhappiness.

3 **Don't Label Her:** She is not "bad" or "damaged" or even "impossible." She is a child. She will change and grow, so make sure there is plenty of room.

4 **Make Him Culpable:** He has to be held accountable for his behavior. Never excuse or minimize it. Reward good behavior and be very clear about what behavior should never be repeated.

5 **Never Threaten Without Following Through:** If you offer a consequence for a behavior, make sure you actually deliver.

6 **Pick Your Battles:** You will not fix this child overnight. At most you might contribute to his healing.

7 **If She Is Not Your Child, Get the Parents Involved:** If you are not the guardian of the child, attempt to get the parents involved in helping their child to change paths.

8 **Be Repetitive and Consistent:** In order to reinforce right and wrong behavior, repeat it and then be consistent about it. It can't *sometimes* be okay to hit someone and *sometimes* not.

9 **Use Patience:** You will need it. Take time-outs for yourself and remember to breathe.

10 **Get Help:** You can't do it alone. That doesn't make you a failure, it makes you human. It takes a village to raise a child. Go get a village.

Keep a Household Happy,
Even on a Snow Day

1 **Create a Schedule:** School days are partitioned into manageable forty-five-minute blocks. Feel free to divide your home day the same way.

2 **Prepare Meals Together:** Get your kids in on the lunch making. Take out all the supplies they will need to make their sandwiches and let them do it themselves. At dinner, assign helper roles based on ages.

3 **Have Downtime:** At some point in the day, if napping isn't an option, vote on a movie and watch it together.

4 **Retreat to Corners:** If moods begin to get touchy, give everyone some time for themselves. Smaller children can be given a project, and older ones can have some time in their rooms.

5 **Catch Up with Relatives:** Gather around the computer and Skype with grandparents and aunts and uncles. Or make phone calls together.

6 **Watch Home Movies:** How often do you watch all those videos you are always taking? Use some time during your day at home to watch them. Let everyone pick a favorite.

7 **Read Together:** Read a book with your kids. If they are old enough to help, let them read some of it aloud.

8 **Get Imaginative:** Encourage your kids to use their imaginations by giving them a bag filled with around-the-house objects and then time them for ten minutes while they write a play to perform for you, using the "props" in the bag. Do it twice.

9 **Tell Stories:** Have everyone tell a good story they know or heard or experienced. The funnier you can make them, the better.

10 **Get Moving!:** Lead a small yoga class or have a dance party to get out some of the frenetic energy from a day spent indoors.

Invoke Your Inner Wine Sommelier

① **Know Your Regions:** Most wine-producing areas are easy to learn about. For example, when buying California wines, look for ones produced in the Napa or Sonoma regions. They are renowned for flavor and quality.

② **Research:** The California Central Coast produces excellent Merlot grapes, so if buying wine from that region, stick with that wine. The more you know about grapes and where they grow best, the better you will know your wines.

③ **Know the Rules:** Wine connoisseurs will tell you that many recent wines produced during an odd-numbered year are best. This is particularly true for wine from both California and Bordeaux in 2007 and 2009.

④ **Learn the Reds:** When choosing a Pinot Noir and other lighter-bodied reds, look to wine producers of the Pacific Northwest, like Washington or Oregon. Spanish Tempranillos are more full-flavored and have a silky, not velvety feel.

⑤ **Learn the Whites:** Not everyone loves white wine. Pinot Grigio has a crisp taste that is refreshing and light. For more intensity, go with Sauvignon Blanc.

⑥ **Know Food Pairings:** Learn which wines are enhanced by which flavors. Chardonnay pairs well with seafood and basil sauces; Merlot with steak. Chiantis clash with creamy sauces.

⑦ **Explore the Southern Hemisphere:** The Marlborough region of New Zealand is considered to produce some of the world's oldest and finest Sauvignon Blanc wines. Argentina, Chile, and South Africa have also become widely known for their old-school vineyards.

⑧ **Learn the Italian Wines:** World renowned. You should know that Chiantis are fairly acidic, Montepulcianos are considered to make a nice, affordable table wine, and a good Zinfandel is a spicy wine with a deep red color that borders on black.

⑨ **Impress Your Friends:** For your foodie guests, consider buying "Old World" wines like Barolo or Piedmont from the Piemonte region in Italy.

⑩ **Ask:** If the salesperson is into a wine, chances are she knows what she's talking about.

Love Any Rainy Day

1. **Walk:** Dress appropriately with an umbrella or a rain slicker and take a rain walk.

2. **Puddle Jump:** Put on your galoshes and channel your inner five-year-old. Or better yet, take one with you.

3. **Take Pictures:** Waterproof your camera by shooting through a zip-top bag and see what amazing shots you can take reflected in puddles or through rain drops.

4. **Kiss:** Grab your guy and plant a long, slow kiss on him. What, it's raining?

5. **Play Touch Football:** Get your friends out for a roll in the mud, with a ball.

6. **Have a Sing-down:** Come up with as many songs as possible that have the word "rain" in them while standing in the rain.

7. **Build a Shelter:** Go to a nearby wooded area and compete with your friends or kids to see who can make the most waterproof shelter using nothing but what they can find in the immediate area.

8. **Mudslide:** Find a wet hill, climb into a garbage bag, and slide down.

9. **Have a Scavenger Hunt:** Keep the items on the list rain-related, like a wet towel or a dry piece of wood.

10. **Dance and Sing—Loud!:** Take a cue from Gene Kelly; find a street lamp and do a rain dance for the entire neighborhood.

Lose 10 Pounds in 10 Weeks

1 **Acknowledge Your Habits:** Begin by making a running list of your health habits so you know what tweaks to make.

2 **Change Your Most Fattening Habit:** Hone in on the biggest problem you have. If you don't exercise, add some exercise. If you love cheese, cut out dairy. If you drink too much beer, quit.

3 **Cut Portions in Half:** Leave half of everything on your plate or in your lunch bag. (This is not an excuse to order or pack double.)

4 **Walk:** Don't drive everywhere. If you go places within a mile of your house, walk to them. Or at least park at the farthest spot in the lot and walk from there.

5 **Re-walk:** Whenever you walk from point A to point B, turn around and go back, then retrace your steps back again to point B. It takes double the time, but it's good for you.

6 **Take the Stairs:** Give up elevators for good and choose the stairs. If you can, run or jog up, or at least walk up briskly.

7 **Cut Out Dessert:** Cold turkey and completely. Those are empty calories you don't really need.

8 **Turn Off the TV:** Don't zone out in front of your computer or television. Stand up, get outdoors, or dance in your living room. Just stop sitting.

9 **Do It with Friends:** Everyone puts twenty dollars in a pool and then whoever loses the closest to ten pounds in ten weeks wins or splits the pool. (*Don't compete to see who can lose the most weight; that can lead to unhealthy weight-loss behaviors.*)

10 **Cut Out Drinks:** Drink water only and watch the pounds fall away.

Dates You'll Really Want to Go On

1 **Floor Picnic:** Lay a blanket on the floor, turn on the some music, and enjoy a basketful of goodies.

2 **Movie and Dinner:** Sneak a delicious takeout dinner into the movies in a large bag (don't forget the wine opener!). When you are finished eating, spend the rest of the movie necking.

3 **Dance Party:** Create your own at-home dance club with a playlist of all your favorites. Dirty dancing is encouraged.

4 **Go High Class:** Dress up to the nines and go out to the chicest clubs and nicest restaurants in town. If you can't talk your way in without a reservation, walk out and try someplace else. It's all part of the unforgettable fun.

5 **Museum Walk or Gallery Hop:** Find out which nights the museums stay open late and take advantage of a romantic stroll through the art. An evening gallery-hop can be equally enjoyable.

6 **The Mall:** You haven't done it in years, so why not walk around the mall holding hands and drinking slushies? You can dream big while you window shop . . . .

7 **Cemetery Stroll:** Take an evening walk together through a nearby cemetery making up stories about the deceased. When something makes you jump, just make sure it's *into* his arms!

8 **Poor Man's Hot Tub:** Fill up a kiddy pool with hot water from the kitchen sink (use an attachment and a hose). Make a pitcher of cocktails and cuddle up under the stars.

9 **Outdoor Movie:** Hang a white sheet between trees and project a movie outside. Pop popcorn and share a sleeping bag while you watch.

10 **Stargaze:** Buy a book about the constellations and drive into the country. Take along a flashlight to read each other the stories of the stars in the night sky.

Become the Favorite Aunt

1 **Never Discipline:** That is a parent's job. Not the cool aunt's job.

2 **Indulge:** Have lots of candy, several movies, and plenty of toys on hand for when they come over.

3 **Love Them to Pieces:** From the minute you meet them, cuddle and kiss them.

4 **Put on Shows:** If they are younger, sing songs with them and keep them entertained with smiles and animated faces. Keep older ones entertained by playing games with them and asking compelling questions.

5 **Take Them Places:** Offer to take them to new movies or out for ice cream and occasionally let them watch a double feature and get a double scoop.

6 **Stay a Little Mysterious:** The more you see them, the harder it will be *never* to get on each other's nerves. Keep some distance so that you are sure they are *always* excited to see you.

7 **Don't Overdo It:** You are still the adult. Don't forget that they need you to protect them and make sure they get home in one piece.

8 **Have One-on-One Time:** If you have more than one niece and/or nephew, take them out on solo dates with you. But plan all of them at the same time so they all know that their time with you is coming.

9 **Never Ever Lie:** If you say you will do something with them, do it. If you promise them a treat or a prize, follow through.

10 *Be Cool:* The cool aunt is a cool person. So have a life that is made richer by your fantastic relationship with your nieces and nephews, not one that is only cool because of it.

Play Nice with Your Siblings

1 **Start Again:** Perhaps you won't ever solve past indiscretions and betrayals. Ask yourself if maybe it's worth it to start again from scratch.

2 **Pare Back the Emotion:** Sibling rivalry rears its head when all the immaturity of your childhood meets the rage of your adulthood.

3 **Stop Competing:** There is no finish line. In fact, the longer it takes you to realize that, the longer someone who might make a valuable teammate remains your competition.

4 **Value Your Memories:** Who else knows about that scary wall hanging in your grandmother's living room? Or the name of your childhood hamster?

5 **Appreciate Your Shared History:** If you let them in, you might find that you understand each other better than you understand almost anyone else in your life.

6 **Laugh:** Chances are, you guys have more to laugh about than most people because you've known each other longer and more deeply.

7 **Bond Over Relatives:** Call them and talk about your parents or children. Laugh about crazy uncles and cousins.

8 **Take Them to Lunch:** Maybe you can start with lunch. No family holiday or birthday. Just the two of you.

9 **Grow Up:** They are not still twelve, just as you are no longer ten. Be the adult you have grown into.

10 **Respect Them No Matter What:** Whether or not they return the favor, decide to respect them and treat them with kindness. Someday they'll come around, or they won't, but it won't be because you didn't try.

Relationship Warning Signs
Every Woman Should Know

1 **He Is Distant:** If he barely speaks and seems disinterested, that's a bad sign. Even if he never was much of a talker, not wanting to share his life with you could mean you both are feeling alienated.

2 **He Skips Family Events:** If you notice he no longer wants to be around you or the family, look into why. It could be serious.

3 **He Avoids You:** If you see that he leaves a room when you enter, it might be because he is hiding something.

4 **He Is Lying:** If you catch him in a lie, confront him. You might not like the reason he did it, but it will be better in the long run for you to know.

5 **Your Connection Feels Nonexistent:** You used to be able to anticipate his next sentence; now he's just another person in the house. Chances are, he feels it too.

6 **There's a Palpable Change in Physical Interest:** If your man is suddenly avoiding bedtime and feigning headaches, it might indicate a problem, especially if it came on rather suddenly.

7 **His Body Language Is Cold:** Is he angling away from you when sitting, bristling subtly at your touch?

8 **He's Watching Other Women:** If he seems free, almost single in the way he flirts or smiles, especially if this is out of character, it might be a sign that he is not wholly invested in your relationship anymore.

9 **He No Longer Answers the Phone:** If he always took your calls and he has suddenly stopped, there might be a disappointing reason.

10 **A Combination of Any of the Above:** It might be time for you and your partner to face each other and have a talk.

Dream Your Way All the Way to the Bank

① **Outline Detailed Steps:** No matter what your dream job is, figure out the clearest path to get there. Even if it includes items like "Go to school" or "Meet Steven Spielberg," simply break each of those down into manageable how-to's.

② **Don't Quit Your Day Job:** This isn't because you don't believe you can land your dream job; it's because it is unlikely that it will happen overnight.

③ **Shadow:** If you can contact someone at the place you want to work, see if he or she can arrange a tour or let you shadow someone for a day on the job. Make sure it's really worth all the effort.

④ **Go Back to School:** Find financial aid programs or see if the school you'd like to attend is hiring. Sometimes staff can take discounted or free classes during off-work hours.

⑤ **Keep Your Eyes on the Prize:** Keep focused as you get qualified or otherwise get closer to your goal. Write papers on your company's products or projects if you go back to school and generally do everything you can to keep learning about them.

⑥ **Get an Internship:** Call and e-mail as many people as you can until someone bites. Show up with a friendly demeanor and a resume.

⑦ **Make Friends:** Get to know people on the inside. Now you are there. Your dreams are in your grasp!

⑧ **Keep Climbing:** Even if you still have work to do to, don't cut yourself short. Complete degrees, finish tests, and complete general training.

⑨ **Be Passionate, but Know Your Stuff:** Make sure you approach your mission with heart, but also be thorough and complete in your training.

⑩ **Go for It:** Call your contacts, spread your resume, and land the job of your dreams!

Keep in Tune with
What Your Car Says about You

(1) SUV or Hummer: You like to get 4 miles to the gallon and feel above everyone else on the road—literally because you are, with those jinormous tires of yours.

(2) Mercedes-Benz: You are successful and you know it and you want everyone else to know it too. And we believe you because of your car.

(3) Restored Volkswagens: You can't let go of your hippie youth, but your law firm expects you for the meeting with the oil moguls you now represent.

(4) Hybrid: You are a little bit self-righteous and also a little bit of a trendsetter.

(5) Porsche: Who you are depends on what you look like. A hot Cameron Diaz type will likely stop traffic. But if you are of normal proportions you will look like a large person getting out of a small car.

(6) Honda: You like a good political debate, finished college, and likely have one or more additional degrees.

(7) Chevy: People in Chevys, they say, don't trust the Internet and like their meat bloody and their potatoes with butter. You are All-American and proud.

(8) Mini Cooper: You are well-mannered and making six figures.

(9) Schwinn: You are fit and wisely doing your part to cut down on traffic and save the world. You might also be unemployed, in high school, or out of high school but still living with your folks.

(10) Minivan: You are a mother. You have more than one child. You probably also have more than one car seat. And there is a very real chance you need a stiff drink.

Make Yourself Happy Now

1 **Smile:** Charles Darwin was first to suggest it and now Cardiff University in Wales has proven it—everything feels a little better when you're smiling. Just performing the action will change your outlook.

2 **Listen to Your Favorite Song:** A moment with your favorite song can turn any day from bad to good. Take five minutes and listen (if you don't have an MP3 player, feel free to look it up on YouTube.)

3 **Call Your Dad:** Or your mom or your mom's best friend who's practically your mom. Just take a minute to touch base and say hey.

4 **Write a Letter to Your High School Best Friend:** Remember that night you couldn't stop laughing and those hot guys asked you backstage? Write about that.

5 **Stretch:** A few stretches will release toxins and get your blood flowing. Follow up your stretches with a big glass of water to flush everything out.

6 **Read a Lovely Poem Out Loud:** Listen to the words and decide what they mean to you, even if you have no idea what they meant to the author.

7 **Sit in the Sun:** Even if you can only get it through a window, see if there isn't a patch available and let the vitamin D do its magical work.

8 **Eat a Burrito:** Foods high in vitamin B12, like beans, will give you a mental boost and make you feel good.

9 **Hug Someone:** Studies have shown that without human touch, we wither and die. Find the nearest person that wouldn't be weirded out, and share a hug.

10 **Listen to Someone Say "I Love You":** Call someone who loves you and listen to him say it.

Make Your Money Work for You

1 **Start a 401(k):** Most companies can help start you off with a retirement plan that includes a 401(k).

2 **Enlist a Professional:** Hire a trustworthy financial adviser to help set you on the right path.

3 **Invest in a Friend:** If you have a trustworthy friend starting a business, write up a contract and help with an initial investment that could pay off in spades down the road.

4 **Set Goals:** Decide what you are saving for so that you invest correctly.

5 **Go to the Bank:** Talk to a banker about your savings and checking account options. They might be able to suggest smart ways to keep your money safe and growing, especially when the market is unpredictable.

6 **Invest in Precious Metals:** While gold and other precious metals are currently at all-time highs, some people think they will be valuable to own no matter what happens in the long term to the dollar, and that they will continue to increase in value.

7 **Invest in America:** Buy bonds and let them mature before cashing them. It's a good way to support both your country's economy and your own.

8 **Set Up Trusts:** If you have enough money, set up trust funds for your children and husband. This way the money won't be taxed heavily if anything happens to you.

9 **Budget:** Know how much money you need every month so that you know exactly how much you have left over for savings and investments.

10 **Watch the Market:** Keep up with what is happening in the stock market so that you can be ahead of the pack. Also, watch the companies in which you are most heavily invested.

Work Smarter, Not Harder

1 **Make a Schedule:** Begin your day by returning e-mails while it's still too early to return phone calls. Save returning phone calls for after you return from lunch.

2 **Prioritize Your To-Do List by Speed:** Do the quick tasks first, followed by the most important. For complicated chores that are not pressing, break them down and do a little bit each day.

3 **Get Support:** Don't be afraid to ask coworkers to stick around and help you complete a task, or to come back early from a break.

4 **Do the Tough Stuff During Prime Time:** Figure out when you work the best. Is it the morning? After lunch? Organize your day accordingly.

5 **Stay Energized:** Get up every hour and walk around. Refresh yourself so that you can get back to work.

6 **Anticipate:** Plan your day, week, and month. Then be prepared for all of those plans to go out the window.

7 **Delegate:** Utilize coworkers when appropriate. Let someone else call the vending machine repairman.

8 **Keep Work Fun:** Listen to music during a big task. Reward yourself after it is completed, even if it's just extra-fancy creamer in your coffee.

9 **Stay on Task:** When you are at work, only browse the Internet on breaks. And only social network for personal reasons when you are at home.

10 **Ask for Tips:** Find the most organized person at work and find out what her methods are. You might be surprised at what you find.

Girlfriend Getaways Your Gals Will Love

1 **Manhattan's Soho:** Soho is where shoppers go to die happy. There isn't a single store in a ten-block radius that you can think of that you can't find.

2 **Las Vegas:** If you can't find something to do here with the girls, you can always do nothing sitting by a pool and drinking inexpensive cocktails . . . oh, wait.

3 **Kripalu Center (Lenox, Massachusetts):** This yoga center and spa is a great place to relax and enjoy a bit of girl time. You can also pick up some healthy cooking tips and get a great massage.

4 **Snowmass Village, Colorado:** This ski resort is a great place to take your more adventurous friends for the girls-only ski weekend of your dreams.

5 **Bagby Hot Springs (Estacada, Oregon):** Hike through the woods of Mount Hood National Forest to secluded hot springs in which you can lie like the nymphs you are, bathing suit optional.

6 **Montreal, Quebec:** Montreal is as French as it is English, which means it's almost like a little bit of Europe just over the border. With a plethora of wonderful culinary opportunities awaiting, pack up the girls for some serious *bon appétit*!

7 **Cancun, Mexico:** Cancun is no farther than flying between some U.S. cities. Scuba diving the Underwater Museum is a must. And then there are the beaches . . .

8 **Atlantic City:** While AC is definitely Vegas's well-tanned, little bit cheesy cousin, like Snookie, it has a certain charm once you get to know it. After all, this *is* the Jersey Shore!

9 **Napa Valley:** Take the girls on a train through the glorious Napa Valley. This is the way God intended people to live.

10 **New Orleans, French Quarter:** This historic district remains one of America's most exciting cultural and culinary treasures.

Instant Cures for "Are We There Yet?"

1. **Road Trip Scavenger Hunt:** Prepare a list of things people have to look for along the way to call out or photograph.

2. **Digital Camera Safari:** Name something for everyone in the car to look for along the drive, like cartoon character images or trains. Everyone then has to take pictures of as many as they see.

3. **My Cows!** The first person to call "My cows!" when passing a herd wins the herd. (A rough estimate of the number of cows, approved by another player, will suffice.) If you pass a church, call "my church" and marry an opponent's cows (at most you can double your herd). Call "my cemetery" and kill an opponent's cows, and "my hospital" to increase your cows by half.

4. **Sing-Down:** Choose any word and come up with as many songs as you can that have that word in the lyrics.

5. **Celebrity:** Players describe as many celebrities as they can within a minute's time without naming them outright.

6. **Name That Tune:** Hum the tune to a song and get your opponents to name it.

7. **Personal Trivia:** Ask questions about yourself that your friends may or may not know. Whoever gets the most answers right wins.

8. **Geography:** One person says the name of a place and the next player has to use the last letter in its name to start the name of the next place. No place can be used more than once.

9. **Cash Cab:** Bring along a bunch of trivia questions and ask them. To make it more fun, put a cash value on each question and let the losers pay the winner.

10. **Alphabet Game:** Start with "A" and work your way to "Z" by looking for letters in signs and on license plates. No sign or plate can be used more than once.

Go Ahead and Cry About . . .

1. **Death:** An experience this big deserves screaming, belly laughter, *and* a big brass band. But if all you can muster are tears, then by all means, let them flow freely.

2. **A Frustrating Illness:** If someone you love is struggling to find a diagnosis to an illness, it's okay to vent it with a good cry.

3. **A Big Loss:** You've done everything you can to nail the promotion but you didn't get it. Let yourself cry. Just do it after you've left the building.

4. **A Breakup:** When you lose a lover, no matter who leaves whom, it can be tough to not only reconcile the loss of the person but also the loss of the couple.

5. **Being Lonely:** Sometimes you just need to cry about it. Of course, it's important to remember that there are a lot of people who love you, too.

6. **Losing or Breaking Something You Loved:** You'd had that ceramic mug since childhood. It's okay to cry about dropping it.

7. **A Series of Small Things:** At the end of a very bad day, how could you *not* cry after you stub your toe to cap it off?

8. **A Ticket:** These small injustices just make all of us want to stand up and scream, "But I'm a law-abiding citizen!" So go ahead and use it as a chance to cry for everything unfair but unavoidable in life.

9. **Hungry Children Commercials:** Just knowing that suffering is happening around the globe is cause for sorrow. If once in a while a commercial starts the water-works, so be it.

10. **Missing Home:** Homesickness can strike even the most stoic and it can evoke strong emotions. Crying might just prove inevitable.

Never Let Them See You Cry About . . .

1. **Another Work Assignment:** This requires that you figure out how to break it down, delegate it, and finish it. No crying.

2. **Your Child's Failure:** Crying about this will only make it harder on your child. Your job is to be loving and prepare warm milk with cookies before bed.

3. **Your Friend's Breakup:** It's normal to feel sad when a couple you like breaks up. But let this one be about your friend and not how *you* feel.

4. **A Hangover:** Sorry, you did this one to yourself. Drink some water and pull it together.

5. **The Fact That It's Monday:** If you don't like your job so much that you are wishing five days a week out of your life, it's not time to cry. It's time to quit.

6. **Your Sports Team's Loss:** These people are making a ton of money to play a game. Someone was going to have to lose. For goodness' sake, find something worthy of your tears.

7. **The Pain of Getting a Tattoo:** If this makes you cry, don't do it and get up and go for a jog instead. Same endorphin release, less permanent.

8. **Your Crying Baby:** You really want to cry, too. You are so tired and you finally just fell asleep. But stay in control. She won't be a baby forever.

9. **A Bad Interview:** At least, don't cry in front of the interviewer no matter how badly it went. Crying will put the nail in the coffin. If you leave, your thank-you note might get you back on good footing. And anyway, you didn't see the other guys.

10. **Spilled Milk:** As they say, once it's poured out all over the table, you may as well fetch the rag.

Live with Your Man Without Killing Him

① **Communicate:** Be clear with each other about your expectations. If one of you is test-driving for marriage and the other is saving a few bucks, you are *not* on the same path.

② **Divvy Chores:** Decide what chores you plan to do. Include oil changes and grocery shopping as well as day-to-day housework.

③ **Have Roommate Meetings:** Don't forget that living together requires a different set of rules than dating alone. So designate one dinner a month where you guys discuss your living situation as roommates and forget for a moment that you are more.

④ **Have Date Nights:** Similarly, make sure you also set up one night a month that is meant for the two of you to go out together as a couple and *not* as roommates.

⑤ **Fight Well:** Set a goal for a discussion before you go on the attack. Also, be prepared to listen to his counterattack. And stay on track. One fight at a time.

⑥ **Keep Your Autonomy:** Living together is not marriage, which is why for many it is an attractive option. Keep your own bank account and your own furniture.

⑦ **Have a Financial Plan:** Either split everything 50/50 or make sure the person spending less compensates by doing more around the house.

⑧ **Live Within *Both* of Your Means:** Ideally, choose a place that both of you can afford and keep things as equal as they would be if you lived separately.

⑨ **Stay Checked In:** It's easy to become complacent about your relationship once you live together. Try to enjoy date nights and remind yourself to have regular sex.

⑩ **Co-Sign the Lease:** If only one name is on the lease, technically one person has all the power and controls who stays or goes in an apartment. Similarly, that person will be the one left stranded if the other decides to split.

How to Live with a Teenager Without Killing Yourself

1 **Don't Pressure Them to Talk:** Give them a break and let them talk when they're ready. That way, they won't wish you were somewhere else.

2 **Trust Them:** Until they give you a reason not to, let them live their lives . . . but stay on top of what they're up to.

3 **Watch Them:** Teens are better with physical cues. If they want you around they won't necessarily tell you, but they won't leave.

4 **No Matter What, You Are an Adult:** Don't try to be cool. Adults generally aren't. But let's face it, some are okay. Aim for "okay."

5 **Listen More, Preach Less:** They won't listen anyway. Lead by example. Be honest with them and live the life you hope they will live. Tell them *that* and let them deduce the rest.

6 **Give Them Space:** As long as you have no reason to believe you shouldn't, leave their rooms and computers alone.

7 **Don't Judge:** Try to hold back judgment. If their interests aren't anything you can relate to, be they online games or pop idols, don't put them down. In fact, try to learn about them and get involved.

8 **Trust Yourself:** Your intentions are good, even if they don't see it. Someday they will.

9 **Stay Involved:** Go to their school performances, sporting events, and activities so they feel valued. Even if they don't let you know they're grateful, they are.

10 **Keep Your Hand Out:** Let them know you are there in case they need you.

Beat a Cold Before It Hits

1. **Take Echinacea:** A lot of people swear by this little over-the-counter supplement to stop a cold in its tracks. Take it when you first feel a cold coming on. Just follow the instructions on the bottle.

2. **Get More Rest:** Getting enough sleep is crucial for keeping your body strong and illness-free.

3. **Fight the Battle in Your Mind:** Every night before sleep imagine your white blood cells stepping up like soldiers to battle and fighting all the germy germs trying to attack. Visualizing has been proven to help a body fight illness.

4. **Cheer Up:** Bad moods and depression have been proven to weaken our immune systems.

5. **Stay Hydrated:** Water cleanses you on the inside. Drink it and stay clean *and* healthy.

6. **Don't Run, but Don't Dawdle:** Overextending yourself can wear you down. But walking purposefully and regularly has been shown to boost your immune system.

7. **Eat an Apple a Day:** Actually, warming up a mug of apple cider has been shown to boost your immune system, and is especially effective when you start to feel the signs of a cold coming on.

8. **Boil Gingerroot:** Use three or four big chunks boiled for ten minutes, then strain and combine with lemon and honey to make a healing tea. The ameliorative properties of these three powerhouses will cure what ails you. Drink a mug before bed all winter long to feel strong.

9. **Eat Your Iron:** Spinach and broccoli are your best friends during cold season. They are the experts at helping your body fight illness.

10. **Wash Your Hands:** Don't go on an OCD rampage, but make sure you only ever touch your face with clean hands.

Vacation at Home and Actually Have Fun

1 **Museum Hop:** Even if you've seen them before, go back and visit some of the museums that bring culture to your city.

2 **Plan Day Trips:** Find nearby places to go that you've never been to. You'd be amazed how much is happening within a three-hour radius of your home.

3 **Leave It to Chance:** Pick up every brochure at your city's chamber of commerce and pull them out of a bag for a random mix of fun things to do.

4 **Find the Nearest Shore:** Enjoy a day of waterfront fun at a nearby watering hole, ocean, lake, or river.

5 **See a Show:** If there is no community theater, dance company, or music venue in your town, find a nearby university production, or in a pinch go see what the high schools are presenting.

6 **Stay Out Late Every Night:** This is your staycation. Why go to bed early when you can sleep in? Close the bars, restaurants, and clubs, and then stroll down by the river.

7 **Catch Up on Movies:** Go to your local multiplex for the first show of the day and stay until you've watched all the movies you want to see.

8 **Have a Tourist Day:** Is there a part of town where the tourists go? Check it out. You might even want to buy a souvenir. Also, forgo your car and use public transportation or cabs for *real* authenticity.

9 **Go to a Spa:** Just because you didn't invest in a resort vacation doesn't mean you can't indulge yourself with a few spa treatments. Since you're saving money, you may as well get two, or . . . okay, three.

10 **Hire a Chef and a Masseuse:** Pay a professional to come to your home one night and prepare a romantic dinner for you and your love. While you wait, get a couple's massage. Together it is the ultimate in staycation luxury.

Get Picky Eaters
(Under the Age of Five) to Eat

1 **Put New Foods on the Plate:** Always put something new on the plate. They don't have to eat it. It simply has to sit there.

2 **Don't Mistake Full for Picky:** Doctors will tell you that quite often a child needs fewer calories than you think. If they've eaten something, chances are they are finished for now and will eat again later.

3 **Be Casual:** Don't make eating time a tremendously unpleasant experience. Feed them what they will eat and supplement for the time being with vitamin drinks and juices.

4 **Don't Fight with Them:** At the same time each day, give them one bite of something new. If they cry or spit it out, stop and move on. Over time they will understand that they *have* to try one thing a day but that it is short and painless.

5 **Don't Starve Them:** Telling yourself they will eat something they don't like when they are hungry enough is dangerous and unpleasant for everyone.

6 **Trust:** Their eating habits will improve. But for now you just have to make sure they are eating *something*.

7 **Get Help:** Specialists at children's hospitals can help teach you how to feed a picky baby. And if something is wrong with your child, the earlier they are diagnosed, the better.

8 **Trick Them:** Mix healthy foods into foods they like, like pasta and pizza sauce, using a hand blender.

9 **Don't Give Up:** Just because you accept their diet doesn't mean you should stop trying to teach them to eat other delicious foods.

10 **Don't Introduce Unhealthy Foods to Them:** If you start off with healthier options, they may go for the unhealthiest of them, but at least square one isn't so bad.

Get Picky Eaters
(Over the Age of Five) to Eat

1 **Trick Them:** Mix the vegetables and nutrients into sauces and batters so that they have no idea that the spaghetti with extra meat sauce is actually *healthy*.

2 **Have "Try" Time:** As long as you make it fun and stress-free, most people are willing to *taste* anything. So ask them to take one bite of something at every meal in exchange for a prize, a sticker, or control of the remote.

3 **Get Input:** Ask them why they don't like the foods they don't like and what could be done to get them to like it. Most people understand that they *should* eat healthy.

4 **Work Together:** As you go, get feedback on what is working and what isn't.

5 **Get Unhealthy Options Out of the House:** Obviously the person has to eat, but limit how easy it is to choose the bad stuff. Snacks especially should be on the healthy side.

6 **Make Their Favorite Foods Better:** If they are craving McDonald's burgers, make them yourselves instead. Even if you take the recipe right off the Internet, anything made from scratch will ultimately involve fewer chemicals and fewer empty calories.

7 **Get Them Cooking:** Why not invite them into the kitchen to learn what goes into preparing a meal? In the beginning, you could start by having them make their favorite processed food from scratch, like mac-and-cheese or chicken nuggets.

8 **Be Patient:** It won't happen immediately, so allow for little accomplishments to garner big praise.

9 **Go for the Bad Good Stuff:** Slather peanut butter on celery or buy trail mix with milk chocolate pieces. Just get them to eat it.

10 **Show, Don't Tell:** Make sure you aren't making bad eating choices yourself. If you are, maybe it's time for a mealtime overhaul for everyone.

Write the Perfect Thank-You Note

1. **Choose the Stationery:** Use something that feels right for you. It doesn't have to be a cheesy Hallmark card unless as far as you are concerned Hallmark cards are far from cheesy.

2. **Get Creative:** If you don't have an available card, make your own. Find great postcards from your honeymoon destination and mail those as thank-you notes. The possibilities are endless!

3. **Handwrite It:** While it is easier to send an e-mail, a handwritten note leaves an impression.

4. **Time It Right:** There are plenty of etiquette rules for how long you have before you must send a thank-you note, but it all comes down to the sooner the better.

5. **Make It Personal:** Reference your relationship with the recipient and how the gift is meaningful because of her.

6. **Use Specifics:** You can talk about how you will use the gift, or, if you are thanking someone for dinner or another specific event, mention something funny or memorable that happened.

7. **Stay on Point:** This is a thank-you note, not a dissertation or annual report. Be warm, but concise.

8. **Include a Photo:** Send along a graduation photo, a wedding photo that includes the guest, or a baby photo, depending on the purpose of the original gift.

9. **Share the Work:** If you and a spouse or your entire family received the gift together, each of you write a sentence or two to keep the workload to a minimum for everyone.

10. **Stamp It:** The post office has stamps for all occasions. You can even make your own. Stash a set that you only break out for thank-you notes for a thoughtful touch.

Make That Layoff Pay Off

1. **At First, Do Whatever You Need to Do:** Go to the movies, cry to your sister, scream in the middle of an open field. Don't expect it to feel good.

2. **Don't Blame Yourself—At Least, Not Entirely:** While it doesn't hurt to get a sense of your culpability, it won't help to bog yourself down in feelings of self-loathing. It's a bad economy. Blame that.

3. **Don't Burn Bridges:** You want your employer to help you land your next job, so hard as it is, leave with your dignity. Don't take the company fish.

4. **Figure Out a Financial Plan:** Figure out what you can sacrifice. Also, see how long your benefits will last. Lay out a timeline.

5. **Wait a Month:** If you can, take a month completely off. Travel—even a drive to visit family might give you perspective. Or do nothing.

6. **Don't Be Afraid:** Fear is the enemy. Don't begin your job hunt anticipating failure. Just because everyone says it's a tough market doesn't mean you won't be one of the lucky ones who nails it on the first go.

7. **Put It Out There:** Make an announcement on social networking sites that you are looking for a job. Make personal calls to colleagues and friends who are well connected.

8. **Contact Headhunters:** Get your resume into as many e-mail boxes as possible. Ask friends to circulate it if they hear of anything.

9. **Be Prepared:** Be ready to send off your information the moment a lead comes in.

10. **Know You Can Do It:** In the meantime, do some freelancing, dream about a career change, and keep a hopeful and positive outlook. You will come out on top.

Stop Going to the Gym, and Instead . . .

1 **Lift Heavy Things:** When carrying groceries, lift them up high and hold them for an extra minute. Do this whenever you carry anything with some weight.

2 **Tighten Muscle Groups:** Whenever you walk, make sure you tighten your butt and your inner core. It will tone and strengthen them without much effort. You will notice a difference.

3 **Balance:** Buy a yoga ball and sit on it whenever you are watching TV or working at the computer, or even at your desk at work. You can also practice balance by standing and raising one leg at a time and holding the poses while watching TV.

4 **Raise Your Hand:** Hold each hand over your head while you are sitting in your living room doing nothing. Make sure your muscles are engaged. Keep your hand up. Change the height periodically to work other muscle groups. Add weight (like a full water bottle) for strengthening.

5 **Compete:** Get a friend or two in on it and use a pedometer to log how many steps you all take every week. Whoever takes the most gets a free meal compliments of the others.

6 **Walk a Dog:** Either get a dog to walk every day or borrow someone else's. Having a commitment to walk will get you going.

7 **Do a Morning Sun Salute:** Learn one complete Sun Salute from a yoga class or video and do it five times in the morning before you begin your day.

8 **Play Wii or Xbox 360:** If you have to play video games, make them games with remote features that let your body get in on the action.

9 **Be a Joiner:** Join a kickball league or your office softball team. It's not only good for you, it is a fun and social way to change your body.

10 **Bike:** Ride your bike to and from work as long as weather permits. If it's too far to do that, retire your car *after* work and make that bike time only.

Places Around the World Worth Seeing

1 **Angkor Wat (Cambodia):** The ruins of this twelfth-century temple and capital city boast enormous tree root systems hugging ancient buildings.

2 **Stockholm, Sweden:** Made up of fourteen islands that stand at the confluence of Lake Mälaren and the Baltic Sea, this city, Scandinavia's largest, enjoys nearly twenty-four hours of light in the summertime.

3 **Los Glaciares National Park (Argentina):** This spectacular ice field is the world's third-largest reserve of fresh water.

4 **Mount Everest (Nepal):** The world's tallest peak is worth the visit, even if you have no intention of making the challenging hike skyward.

5 **The Old Town of Český Krumlov (Czech Republic):** This stunning Bohemian city boasts winding cobbled roads and baroque architecture.

6 **Safed, Israel:** The center of Jewish Mysticism or Kabbalah, this is one of Israel's four holy cities. Artists as well as musicians have flocked to the area over the years. The city is known as the klezmer capital of the world.

7 **West Coast of Scotland:** Lush green islands and islets dot this magical coastline. Add that everyone is friendly and speaks English and it's a must-see.

8 **Machu Picchu (Peru):** This fifteenth-century Inca site, settled above the Urubamba Valley, has been voted one of the new seven wonders of the world.

9 **The Great Wall of China:** Begun in the third century B.C., this 1,500-mile structure might be visible from space, but to get the full effect you should just go to China.

10 **The Great Barrier Reef (Australia):** Located in the Coral Sea, this destination has been called one of the seven natural wonders of the world.

Spice Up Your Walk, Project Your Confidence

1. **Practice Your Posture:** Shoulders back, pelvis forward, stand up tall.

2. **Breathe:** A great walk begins with a calm, confident demeanor. So relax before you take a step.

3. **Use the Balls of Your Feet:** Don't come down on your heel when stepping. Instead, keep your weight light and springy on the balls of your feet.

4. **Line 'em Up:** You should walk by placing one foot in front of the other in a straight line. If you find you are thinking too hard about it, try taking wide steps, crossing one foot over the other, until you get the hang of it.

5. **Bend Your Knees:** Raise your legs by bending them higher than usual at the knee to make your strides appear longer.

6. **Keep Your Gaze Long:** Don't look down, but never totally make eye contact. A model doesn't smile when she walks, and she doesn't notice anything, or anyone.

7. **Keep Your Hands Relaxed:** Your hands should remain at your sides or on your hips as long as it works with your walk. But don't fidget or tense them, whatever you do.

8. **Wear Heels:** Models wear heels, and when walking like one, you should, too. You can practice with an old pair, but to get the full effect go for something painful and straight out of the box.

9. **Add a Bounce:** By bending your knees you should be able to accomplish this, but you can kick it up a notch by adding a swing to your hips. Watch yourself in the mirror because going too far, you might end up performing a caricature of a model walk.

10. **Think Long:** Lengthen your neck and extend your torso. Stand up straight, tighten your core, and walk long.

Promote Yourself — or Anyone — Online

1. **Amass "Followers," "Friends," or "Contacts":** Whatever they are called, reach out and create an audience so that your voice is heard.

2. **Create a Persona:** Describe someone you think would be the perfect spokesperson for your product. Then try to present that "character" online.

3. **Get Personal Without Getting Too Personal:** Be entertaining without being frank. Opt for what your audience would have liked you to have done that morning over what you actually did.

4. **Be Relevant:** Make sure your posts are compelling and interesting. Keep your audience engaged.

5. **Stay Deliberate:** Don't go online when you are drunk or feeling careless. If you are using it as a business face, take it seriously.

6. **Remember, Any Feedback Is Good Feedback:** If you have people commenting with negative ideas or challenging concepts, don't respond but don't delete them either. Move on to the next post.

7. **Keep It Short:** If you alert readers to a new blog post, don't repost the entire blog. Keep your output simple and direct.

8. **Learn the Rules:** Every social networking site has rules. Twitter and Facebook require different skill sets, but they are easy to learn. Know the basics of how to use them.

9. **Don't Panic:** If someone tags you or publicly messages you so that you feel compromised, do what you can — untag, unfriend, delete the post — then move on with a new post.

10. **Make the Most Out of It:** If something requires recognition, ask a few friends and associates to comment favorably and repost it so that it spreads further.

Fictional Role Models to Inspire You

1. **Annie Hall:** Charming even when plagued by neurosis, this lovely character shows us how to live surrounded by crazy people and not take any of it too seriously.

2. **Sarah Connor:** At the beginning of the Terminator series she's just a young woman trying to live her life. But when handed the future of the human race, she learns to kick ass.

3. **Claire Huxtable:** On *The Cosby Show*, Cliff's wife, played by Phylicia Rashad, is a level-headed mother of five with a full-time job as a lawyer and a gentle way with her off-the-wall husband. It's an impossible standard, but one it would be nice to live up to.

4. **Alice:** From *Alice in Wonderland*, this curious child shows no fear as she walks head-on into strange world after strange world.

5. **Princess Leia:** Protecting her people and the Alliance is her top priority. While matching wits with the boys, Leia battles the Empire and wins.

6. **Dana Scully:** This no-nonsense scientist approaches every situation with an open mind and a healthy dose of skepticism, as all of us should.

7. **Scout Finch:** This young narrator of *To Kill a Mockingbird* beautifully exposes racism in a small town and makes a hero of her young father, a widowed lawyer.

8. **Lisa Simpson:** This little girl with heart and passion can stir even the meanest, stingiest Springfield resident to do right.

9. **Hermione Granger:** The smartest girl in the room is also the smartest *person* in the room. Something to aspire to.

10. **Maude:** This character from *Harold and Maude* embraces life by accepting death and looking forward to whatever will come, with happiness, peace, and a healthy dose of excitement, romance, and fun.

Know That He Loves You—
Even If He Rarely Says It

1 **He's Available to You:** He answers the phone almost every time you call and texts you back immediately.

2 **He Has You on Speed Dial:** He calls you first when good things happen to him. He also vents when good things in his life go bad.

3 **He Likes "You" Time:** He spends most of his free time with you.

4 **You're on the Same Page:** He doesn't make you feel stupid for gazing at him, cuddling with him, or engaging in pillow talk—and mostly reciprocates.

5 **You're Welcome in His Life:** He likes to have you around his friends and family.

6 **He Makes an Effort:** He wants your friends and family to like him, so he behaves himself when he's around them.

7 **He Tells You His Secrets:** You are pretty sure he tells you things he doesn't tell anyone else.

8 **He's Only Got Eyes for You:** You sometimes catch him staring at you.

9 **He's on Birthday Patrol:** He takes your specials days seriously, like birthdays and anniversaries, even if he can't always remember the specific days they fall on.

10 **He Views the Two of You as a Team:** He celebrates you in small ways, like telling his friends about your accomplishments.

Please the People You Want to Please

1 **Be a Confident, Deliberate Decision-Maker:** Studies have shown that people feel more secure in the short term around those who make decisions without hesitation. However, in the long term they appreciate deliberate decision-makers. Find a happy medium.

2 **Stay Positive:** It's just much more fun to be around positive people.

3 **Be Breezy and Mean It:** Don't sweat the small stuff. Take a calm, casual approach to day-to-day problems as they arise.

4 **Be Loving, Not Smothering:** This doesn't apply only to kids and partners but to friends and coworkers. Show your support by trusting and appreciating those around you.

5 **Be Accepting but Not a Pushover:** Take suggestions and be willing, but don't end up becoming someone who can't say no. There is a fine line. When said with a smile, a simple "I just can't take that on right now" can get you out of an awkward situation.

6 **Lighten the Mood:** If you are the girl who laughs in the face of tension, people will love having you around. That doesn't mean you don't take it seriously. It just means you'll get it done—and if you don't, the world will go on.

7 **Be Honest and Objective:** People don't enjoy a liar, and they really dislike those who lose perspective.

8 **Don't Get Defensive:** If opposition arises, stay cool. Get to the bottom of it without panicking or passing blame.

9 **Make Sure You Are Trying to Make the Right People Happy:** If there are toxic people around you, let them go. Cultivate your healthy relationships.

10 **Accept That You Can't:** . . . make *everyone* happy.

Sit Alone in a Bar with Allure and Charm

1 **Change Your Attitude:** Think of a bar as a much more fun coffee shop, but by all means, do not bring your laptop.

2 **Choose a Crowded Bar:** At a crowded bar it might just look like your friends are in the bathroom and the fact that you are alone might go entirely unnoticed.

3 **Don't Go with an Agenda:** Most of the people at a bar are generally out to have a nice time. Be open to anything.

4 **Sit at the Bar:** Don't put yourself in a corner. A girl at a bar can be sexy and mysterious if she plays it right.

5 **Get to Know the Bartender:** When you are out with friends, get to know the bartender. Then, if you ever want to go out alone, you will feel like you know someone.

6 **Write a Letter:** Ask yourself who, of all of the people you know, you would share this drink with. Then write that person a letter, telling him what you would say if he were with you.

7 **Bring Reading Material:** Have a book or a magazine to read, but glance around once in a while so you don't look unapproachable or aloof.

8 **Look Busy:** Bring a sketchpad or a journal and engage in an activity that is genuinely enjoyable to you while enjoying a drink.

9 **Make Up a Story:** If you'll feel better about it, pretend you were on a bar crawl and you lost your friends. For good measure, add that you think they are supposed to eventually end up here.

10 **Don't Get Shitfaced:** On the other hand, a drunk girl alone at a bar is uncomfortably close to pathetic.

Flirt with Confidence and Class

1 **Giggle:** Engage with people by keeping dialogue light. Giggling is a great way to signal that you aren't taking things too seriously.

2 **Touch Your Face and Hair:** While listening, rub your lower lip. Occasionally push back your own hair. And tap your cheek or neck when you're *really* focused.

3 **Flip Your Hair:** Moving your hair around allows you to show off your features in many ways and from different angles. Pull it up, re-part it, or flip it over your shoulder.

4 **Touch Him:** Touch his arm, pat his back, or ruffle his hair, any opportunity you have.

5 **Lean In:** Body language has a lot to do with how you make someone feel. Angling yourself inward will make you look like you are really paying attention.

6 **Make Eye Contact:** Don't stare him down or start in with crazy eyes. Just casually look away and then coyly look back.

7 **Don't Just Look Interested, *Be* Interested:** Don't fake it. Try to really listen and hear what the object of your flirtation is saying. Ask pertinent questions while nodding and inflecting agreement.

8 **Laugh with Abandon:** If he tells a good joke, laugh at it, loudly.

9 **Be Complimentary:** Occasionally point out his assets and compliment him however you can. Keep it light and be genuine.

10 **"But Enough about Me . . . ":** Talk about yourself by getting him to talk about you. Get his opinion about little things in your life. Ask him what class he thinks you should take this summer or where he thinks you should go on vacation.

Get Yourself Out of a Hair(y) Situation

(1) **Fried Hair:** Some hair has kinks and curls that get more intense as you age. Use a flat iron to smooth it out and make it shine.

(2) **Frizzy Hair:** Olive oil is a great natural moisturizer. Mix some with egg whites and coat your hair. Leave it in for ten minutes and rinse thoroughly.

(3) **Dull Hair:** When you need to wake it up, add a dab of product to the roots of your hair to give a lift.

(4) **Dandruff:** Cover your head with a scarf or wide headband to avoid flaking onto your clothing. And then figure out what's causing it for a more permanent fix.

(5) **Flyaways:** Not every hair type needs to be washed every day. In fact, most are good with a wash no more than twice a week—and then using limited shampoo. Some hair just looks healthier if it's washed less.

(6) **Smelly Hair:** Spray a nice-smelling leave-in conditioner onto your hair if you don't have time to wash it. In a pinch, rub a little conditioner onto your roots, where most bad-hair smells originate.

(7) **Grown-Out Roots:** Nothing like a little mascara in a shade that matches your dyed hair color as closely as possible to cover your roots in a pinch. Just don't get caught in the rain unless you use a waterproof version.

(8) **Flat Color:** Comb the juice of a lemon through your hair and sit in the sun for an hour to wake up your color.

(9) **A Bad Cut:** If you don't want to cut it even more, remember that curls are more forgiving. So make sure you crimp or curl your hair until it grows out.

(10) **And When All Else Fails:** Got a hat? How about a scarf? Put it on.

Find Where the Cute Boys Are, from Age 18 to 80

1 **Join a Club:** But consider the club—choose something where you can expect to run into men, like athletic activities or other manly pursuits.

2 **Get a Dog and Go to a Dog Park:** It's amazing what a dog will do for your self-esteem and for your love life. Meeting guys at a dog park is a cinch.

3 **Go to a Home Improvement Store:** Decide on a DIY project and go pick up supplies. Don't be afraid to get a few tips from the attractive man shopping next to you.

4 **Visit a Hotel Bar:** A man who travels for business often doesn't have time for relationships. But if he meets a great woman, he might reroute his work trips to start passing through on a regular basis.

5 **Take the Train:** Rather than driving for short-distance road trips, take the train. You never know whom you will meet.

6 **Mix It Up:** Go to singles mixers or organize them yourself.

7 **Say Yes:** If a friend wants to fix you up, say yes. If you are asked out, say yes. If someone invites you to a party or an event, say yes!

8 **Get Introduced:** Tell people that you are looking to meet single men. As long as you are not giving off a desperate vibe, people are usually happy to comply.

9 **Go to Happy Hour:** A lot of men go out just after work. Choose bars near downtown or other work centers and get there by 5 or 6 P.M.

10 **Buck Routine:** If your life's routine is such that you don't ever find yourself in the path of single men, change your patterns and habits.

Learn from the Best and Worst Tabloid Scoops

1 **Think Twice Before Naming Your Child Apple or Pilot:** If you give your baby a ridiculous name, people will make fun of you—if not to your face, then behind your back.

2 **Don't Hide the Nanny:** You can give up the act. No one really believes that you work that much, look that well-rested, *and* are raising your kids single-handedly.

3 **You Are *Not* the U.N.:** Building a family should not be contingent upon your travel itinerary. You don't need to collect a new child from every city you visit— they are not snow globes.

4 **Take Away the Car Keys:** No matter how old your child is, you shouldn't go out clubbing together.

5 **Use a Car Seat and Common Sense:** Babies never belong on your lap while you are behind the wheel, nor should they be dangled from balconies.

6 **Be Tactful:** If you curse out your preteen in a voice mail, on her Facebook wall, or in a tweet, someone else will likely learn about it in the amount of time it takes to hit "Send."

7 **Choose Your Partner Wisely:** No matter what, even after twenty years, it is *never* okay to fall for your twenty-one-year-old stepchild.

8 **If You're Going to Have an Affair . . . :** Even if everyone loves your hot, smart, cool partner, they will forgive you as long as you fall in love with the only person in the world who is hotter, smarter, and cooler.

9 **Remember That Everyone Has Cellulite:** And most people look rough without makeup. But it shouldn't stop you from going to the beach or grocery shopping on a bad hair day.

10 **Don't Dress Your Cute Girl Like an Ugly Boy:** Maybe if you dressed her like a *cute* boy people wouldn't be so judgmental. But, in general, people are more comfortable with traditional gender roles.

Love Your Work — While Loving Yourself

1 **Get Out of Your Chair:** At least once an hour, stand up and walk around. If you can, leave the building or at least the floor.

2 **Laugh:** The lighter you can take things, the less you will internally fall apart.

3 **Take Mental Health Days:** Give yourself time off when you begin to feel like you need a break. Do something cleansing that will help to renew your spirit.

4 **Give Yourself a Mantra:** Something like "It's not Pearl Harbor" will work when it seems like the world is crumbling, and it will keep you sane.

5 **Have a Workout Plan:** Try to exercise every day, or excuse yourself to exercise at the office gym if you feel burnout setting in.

6 **Make Sure You Are on the Right Path:** Write down your career goals and intentions and see if they match where you are right now. If not, consider changing to a new field.

7 **Volunteer:** Having other places where you achieve a sense of purpose can be important. And on top of everything else, it will feel good.

8 **Have an Escape Route:** You will take things at work less seriously if you know that you can always leave. Know what you'd do if you had to get out.

9 **Create Rituals:** Have something you do each day to renew your spirit. Wash your face with something delicious-smelling in the bathroom at eleven. Say a silent prayer at three.

10 **Be Responsible:** Don't blame anyone else for your life. It will only make everything seem even more out of control. Own it, fix it, and move on.

Outrageous Ways
to Lose Five Pounds Fast

1 **The Caveman Diet:** This gluten-free diet, also known as the Paleolithic diet, is high in fruits, meat, and nuts and encourages you to eat locally grown foods.

2 **The Vision Diet:** The idea follows a theory of color, professing that red, yellow, and orange motivate hunger and blue diminishes it. Therefore, wearing blue lenses will help you lose weight.

3 **The Chewing Diet:** Chew your food thirty-two times before swallowing and lose weight. The theory goes that when you chew your food more thoroughly, your appetite shrinks.

4 **The Raw Food Diet:** With this creative diet, which eschews heating foods beyond a certain low temperature, you may spend a lot of time making uncooked food seem cooked.

5 **The Baby Food Diet:** You only eat little jars of baby food. Bland and lacking anything to sink your teeth into, you'll eat more fruit and vegetables while keeping portions small.

6 **The hCG Diet:** In this one, you inject pregnancy hormone and decrease your caloric intake to lose weight. Experts advise that just decreasing your caloric intake will do the same thing without having to inject yourself with someone else's hormones.

7 **The Morning Banana Diet:** You eat a banana for breakfast with a glass of room-temperature water to boost metabolism, and eat a normal lunch and dinner. No snacks or desserts. That's it.

8 **The Master Cleanse:** These fad diets usually involve days of drinking a concoction of lemon juice, maple syrup, and cayenne pepper, and not eating for a week each month.

9 **The Grapefruit Diet:** Eating half a grapefruit before every meal will help you eat less of the meal, or so they say, but the fine print indicates that the "meal" can only be around 800 calories.

10 **The Breatharian Diet:** More of a spiritual practice than a diet, people who follow a breatharian way of life see no need for food at all. Instead, they seek nourishment and energy from air and sunlight. Do not try this unless you can perform photosynthesis.

Remind Him How Much You Love Him

1 **Keep Track:** Every time he does something great, write it down. Go back and read it every now and then. And once in a while, read it to him.

2 **Do It His Way:** Not always, but every now and then go where he wants to go and do what he wants to do.

3 **Have "His" Sex Nights:** Sometimes make the sex entirely about his pleasure. This can be a birthday treat or on a night when he seems like he could really use it.

4 **Watch and Tell:** The moment your man impresses you, take notice and let him know it.

5 **Be Generous with Apologies and Thank-You's:** When you are spending your life with someone, it is easy to lose sight of culpability and kindnesses. So reflect on both and be verbal about your discoveries.

6 **Quit Badmouthing:** Women often relate to one another by venting frustrations. However, when you talk your man down, careful you don't start to believe it.

7 **Give Yourself Time-Outs:** If you find yourself in a bad mood, don't take it out on him. Let him know that you are having a bad day and need a little time.

8 **Give Him Room:** Encourage his hobbies and friendships outside of your union. You almost always have him to yourself. It's okay to share him once in a while.

9 **Say It Simply:** Leave him notes in his car or on his pillow, or send him midday text messages and random e-mails, all essentially saying the same thing—"I love you."

10 **Kiss Him Hello and Goodbye:** Make a point of walking straight into his arms before you leave or come home and vice versa. Both of you will appreciate the gesture.

When It's Cheaper
to Buy the Whole Album

(1) ***Blood on the Tracks* (Bob Dylan):** From "Simple Twist of Fate" to "Meet Me in the Morning," this album does no wrong.

(2) ***Black Eyed Man* (Cowboy Junkies):** This melodic masterpiece features the haunting vocals of Margo Timmons and the music and lyrics of her brother Michael.

(3) ***Thriller* (Michael Jackson):** Who can't hum along to any one of these classic tracks? A nearly perfect record, this is one for the ages.

(4) ***Rumors* (Fleetwood Mac):** Two couples in the band were breaking up during the making of this album, producing one hit after another, proving that one person's pain is another's great album.

(5) ***Live at Leeds* (The Who):** You feel like you are at a classic Who concert with Keith Moon still on drums. And the songs are a greatest-hits bouillabaisse peppered with the best of the B-sides.

(6) ***Exile on Main Street* (Rolling Stones):** This double LP is a masterpiece, mixing genres and transcending any rock 'n' roll sound prior to it.

(7) ***Abbey Road* (The Beatles):** One of the most successful Beatles records, this one features an incredibly eclectic sound with songs as disparate as "Octopus's Garden" and "Come Together."

(8) ***The College Dropout* (Kanye West):** This smashing debut album is arguably the most important rap contribution in recent memory.

(9) ***The Love Below* (Outkast):** While some might argue that omitting the first album *Speakerboxxx* from this listing is all kinds of wrong, the fact is, it was Andre 3000's work on the second that created one perfect song after another.

(10) ***Control* (Janet Jackson):** This '80s megahit put Michael's little sister on the map. Five tracks made it into the top ten. And all are great.

Never Get Caught Sleeping on the Job

1. Wear Dark Sunglasses: Tell your coworkers you recently had corrective surgery on your eyes, and then start wearing dark sunglasses so no one will know if your eyes are open or closed.

2. Hide: Find a supply closet or an empty office to take a quick break. If you can't lock the door, make sure you are obscured by a table or some supplies.

3. Set an Alarm: Be sure you choose a time when no one will seek you out. Then set an alarm so you don't get caught.

4. Sneak Out: If you can leave work and run home for a quick nap, what's stopping you?

5. Work with Your Back to the Room: Set up your office so that no one can see your face while you are working. Even better, put yourself in a corner where a person would have to make some effort to find you.

6. Prop Your Head: Use the wall to prop up your head and grab a nap. Keep an open book on your desk to enhance the deception.

7. Get Someone to Cover for You: Explain to a trusted coworker why you need a break. Have her serve as a buffer between you and the rest of the office by answering your calls and contacting you immediately if you are needed.

8. Take a Meditation Nap: Keep your eyes closed for thirty minutes, focusing on your breathing and relaxing your muscles. If anyone catches you, you're not really asleep.

9. Visit a Nap Café: If you are lucky enough to live near a place where you can pay to sleep for a few minutes, by all means skip lunch.

10. Go Under Your Desk: Crawl under your desk and cover yourself up so that you cannot be seen.

Love Your Lipstick All Day Long

1 **Choose the Right Shade:** When buying lipstick, test the color on your lips, not on your hand, to see if the shade works with your skin tone.

2 **Respect the Shade:** Light colors will complement heavy eye makeup, but dark colors need their space.

3 **Blend the Lip Line:** Your lip liner should not appear independent from the rest of the lip. Rather, its job is to keep the color from feathering.

4 **Use Liner as Lipstick:** Use a lip liner as your lipstick. Some of them are rich in color and they will stay on longer and go on easier.

5 **Line Them Twice:** Lay color over your lips with the lipstick, then line them afterward to help you avoid an obvious ring around the lips.

6 **Stay in the Lines:** Don't line outside the border of your own lip. You are fooling no one. Instead plump your lips by hydrating or biting them gently or using a lip balm or lip plumper.

7 **Go with Staying Pow(d)er:** Applying powder over your lipstick will alter the color from shiny to matte and, depending on the powder, might lighten the shade. However, it will also hold the color on your lips longer.

8 **Exfoliate:** Take your toothbrush and brush your lips once a day. Just a gentle once-around should do the trick. It will keep your lipstick from peeling off and your lips from cracking.

9 **Try Out Different Tools:** It doesn't matter how you apply your lipstick as long as you get it on your lips. Try brushes or even your finger, and stick to what works best.

10 **Blot:** Put your index finger in your mouth as if you were going to suck on it, then pull it out through your lips. This will keep the lipstick off of your teeth. Afterward, blot your lips with a tissue.

Train Anyone to Do Anything

(1) Pinpoint the Behavior You Want to Work on: Don't tackle too many things at once. Start with one behavior and work from there.

(2) Keep It Simple: Don't nuance it. If, for example, you want to train your roommate to have dinner waiting when you get home, don't expect Chicken Cordon Bleu. Take what you get and keep your expectations low.

(3) Be Clear with Your Instruction: Let the person know from the outset exactly what you want. Do not mince your words. There's a reason we train a dog to "sit" and not "sit leaning a little to the left with your left paw extended just so . . ."

(4) Use Repetition: Always ask for the same behavior and reward the success of it in a predictable way. Similarly, punish the failure.

(5) Reward or Punish Immediately: Don't let time elapse. Reward a completed behavior immediately. Similarly, punish in a timely fashion.

(6) Don't Ask for It Until You Know You Will Get It: If you plan to use a cue like "Get me a cup of coffee," make sure you know you know the individual is ready (and willing) to complete that behavior. You weaken the command by using it when you probably won't see follow-through.

(7) Use Positive Reinforcement: We are animals. That's why we will always choose a candy bar over a burning coal. Make sure good behaviors are treated as such.

(8) Use Negative Reinforcement to Stop a Negative Behavior: Similarly, when the individual does the wrong thing, let him know. Don't pout, don't use passive aggression. A simple "Don't do that" is all you need.

(9) Watch the Clock: Try to keep a schedule. All animals, even human ones, like repetition and predictability.

(10) Be Patient: Training anyone or anything takes time. They'll learn. Give them a chance.

Stop Doing Everything Yourself

1 **Cultivate Trusting Relationships:** It takes time, but watch what those around you do and learn to respect their abilities.

2 **Select What to Let Go:** Go over your workload and choose the thing that you believe would be best and easiest to hand off to a coworker.

3 **Believe in the Person You Select:** Choose someone you know is up to the task, then have faith when you ask her to take over the job.

4 **Explain the Task:** Give specific parameters and make her responsibilities crystal clear.

5 **Choose a Question-Asker:** Give the project to someone you can rely on to check in with you when she needs to. It will ease your mind that something you forgot to mention will not ultimately be overlooked.

6 **Don't Be Too Needy:** She will require the freedom to successfully take over and execute the job, but if you'd like for her to check in, ask for a general synopsis and not a play-by-play.

7 **Relax Your Grip:** Be flexible with your vision. Once you hand it off, you will defeat the purpose of having delegated it if you continue to closely monitor progress, comment on the work, and generally get in the way.

8 **Offer Feedback:** However, periodically you might want to check in and offer helpful ideas as someone with whom the idea took its early form.

9 **Remember, Micromanaging Is the Enemy:** You don't have to give up the power, just a little of the control. So, learn to be better at taking in an overall view and leaving the details to the others.

10 **Give Credit Where It's Due:** It's the gracious thing to do, and your coworker whose hard work paid off will respect you for it.

Get Runway Curls

1. **Get a Curly Cut:** If you have waves, getting your hair cut so that it follows the natural curl pattern will help you to get gentle curls and great wave.

2. **Go for a Trim:** Get regular trims if you want your curls to be healthy. The drier and messier the ends, the frizzier the curls.

3. **Condition Your Hair:** Wash your hair less and keep it conditioned, especially if your hair is naturally curly.

4. **Apply Product:** The right product can do wonders for a great head of curls. Leave it in and let it dry. Don't use a dryer or it will frizz.

5. **Dry Hair *with* the Cuticle:** You can use a towel as long as you dry your hair gently without rubbing against the cuticle. Let the towel absorb the water without rough friction against the scalp. Press, rather than rub.

6. **Use a Round Brush:** With a hair dryer, straight, wavy, or curly hair can get smooth body and shiny curls.

7. **Use a Curling Iron:** Flat irons are for straightening. Use a curling iron to get curls.

8. **Try Curlers:** Hot rollers are good; leave-in curlers are better. But both work.

9. **Use Hairspray:** Give yourself great hold with a soft hairspray that leaves your hair bouncy and touchable.

10. **Go to a Japanese Salon for a Perm:** People in Japan have been getting perms for the last twenty years, while Americans have largely stopped. Their technology has progressed while ours has mostly stagnated.

See the USA the Only Way

(1) **Pull Over in Joshua Tree National Park (Southern California):** Located south of Los Angeles, once you have driven into the park and made it a good way down the straight road, pull over and get out. You have never "heard" such deafening silence.

(2) **Cross to the Florida Keys:** The Seven Mile Bridge connecting the Florida Keys to the mainland lightly skims the water, so that you feel as if you are driving right on it. And you are.

(3) **Road-Trip on Route One (California):** The Pacific Highway, or Route One, features majestic cliffs that fall straight down into the blue waters of the Pacific. Stop at the Henry Miller Library in Big Sur and Hearst Castle outside San Luis Obispo.

(4) **Trek Through Yellowstone National Park (Wyoming, Montana, and Idaho):** Old Faithful will shoot its water sky-high in this, one of America's most picturesque parks.

(5) **Cruise the Going-to-the-Sun Road (Glacier National Park, Montana):** Everything from pristine lakes to untouched wilderness surrounds this magnificent park.

(6) **Drive Balmorhea State Park and Big Bend (Texas):** This drive, about 200 miles north of El Paso, takes you from the Chisos Mountains and down the Rio Grande.

(7) **Chart the Maine Coast:** New England towns dot your journey as you wind your way along this craggy coast. Go in autumn, when the leaves are themselves an attraction.

(8) **Wind Through Shenandoah Park, Smoky Mountains (North Carolina):** The Blue Highway offers views you had forgotten still existed in this busy world.

(9) **Take a Pit Stop in Sequoia National Park:** If driving among the giants is a wonder to behold, get out of the car at some point and walk.

(10) **Snake Down Hana Highway (Maui, Hawaii):** You'd probably have to fly to get here, but once you arrive, this drive will take you around breathtaking twists and turns along some of what are arguably America's greatest coastal views.

Forgive and Forget . . . If He's Worth It

1. **Get Help:** Go with your partner to therapy. If he won't go, go alone. You will need the help of a professional.

2. **Make Sure You Both *Want* to Heal:** If a betrayal was committed because someone wanted out of the relationship, letting your partner go might prove inevitable.

3. **Find New Ways to Trust:** For example, you might not trust him when he goes on business trips, so you might ask him to call you more then he used to when he goes.

4. **Don't Air Your Dirty Laundry:** Don't tell everyone you've ever met what happened. It's no one's business and you don't need endless and varied advice.

5. **Allow Time for *Everyone* to Heal:** A betrayal doesn't just belong to you and your partner. It also belongs to people who love you who find out about it. To those who deserve them, give appropriate apologies.

6. **Be Patient:** With yourself, with your partner, and with your relationship.

7. **Understand Each Other:** Don't get too indignant. All is fair in love and war, after all. Make sure you own your part in any betrayal and respect each other's flaws.

8. **Restart:** Pretend you are just meeting for the first time, before you judged each other or held each other accountable. Don't forget a betrayal, but try to let it go.

9. **Go Away Together:** If you can, take some time away from your life in a neutral setting. Be together without expectation.

10. **Be Prepared to Let Go:** The attempt to heal is noble, but you might find that too much damage has been done and you must walk away. Be brave enough to admit it and follow through.

Eat Meat Without Risking Your Health

1 **Substitute:** Supermarkets are now inundated with tons of healthier meat options. Try swapping out fatty beef for lean bison, or use lean free-range turkey in place of chicken pumped full of hormones and antibiotics.

2 **Grill:** As long as you go light on the seasoning, rubs, and sauces, what you put on a grill will come off lower in calories and richer in flavor than anything you fry in a pan.

3 **Skip the Salt:** Ever wonder what the flavor of meat actually is? Why not try cooking it with fresh herbs, garlic, and lemon and leave out—or at least cut back on—the salt.

4 **Oven, Meet the Meat Course:** Baked meats that are not cooked in butter or oils are automatically better for you. The best part is, you can cook your veggies along with it!

5 **Wok It:** Stir-frying meat cuts back on fat and shortens the cooking time. Add vegetables and brown rice, and you will become your family's favorite Chinese food chef!

6 **Marinate:** Choose flavorful and healthy marinade recipes from the Internet. Let your meat soak in one overnight and then enjoy the flavor explosion.

7 **Cook It Slowly:** If you have the time, set a roast in your oven at its lowest setting and let it cook all day. It will be so succulent and juicy no one will notice how healthy it is.

8 **Add Healthy Side Dishes:** "Beef" up your meat meals by adding hearty, healthy sides.

9 **Fake-Fry:** Bread the meat with a healthier option, like crumbled rice cereal or corn cereal, and dip it in egg white to bind. Then bake it crispy.

10 **Know Where It Comes From:** You want to be sure the animal you are eating had a healthy life, preferably free of antibiotics, before you consume it.

Bejewel Yourself

1   **Get Inspired:** Look through magazines and figure out what you like or don't like about the jewelry you see.

2   **Investigate:** Find stores in your area that carry beads and chain. You don't have to buy anything; just get familiar with what's out there.

3   **Incorporate Metal Pieces:** If you want to create molds to cast metals like gold and silver, you will first need to carve them from wax. Then find a place that makes molds and also casts them.

4   **Find Your Chain or Wire:** If you plan to make bracelets, rings, and necklaces, you might need gold or gold-filled chains and wires. Figure out where to go for these materials, or order online.

5   **Design Online:** Plenty of online sites let you design your own jewelry without all the legwork. You can shop for beads, stones, and charms right there and have them made up easily.

6   **Do Some Easy Beading:** Go to a bead store and choose stones you like that look good together. String them up and attach to a clasp of some kind.

7   **Use String:** Kids will tell you—you can do some very fancy bracelet work by knotting colorful string intricately.

8   **Take a Class:** Classes will often lead you to the right tools and resources to get going on your jewelry-making adventure, especially if you find a teacher who is in the know.

9   **Limit Yourself:** A great beginner technique is to decide that you will simply attach one stone to a chain or cord so that you avoid overdoing the design.

10   **Try Wire Wrapping:** Instead of having to solder or otherwise bind metal, use a precious-metal wire and wrap it around string to form basic pendants and rings.

Don't Dial Your Ex!

1   **Write Him a Letter:** Step away from all electronic communication devices and instead break out a pen and paper. Then rip it up or burn it.

2   **Talk It Out:** Call a friend and vent. Leave it to her to give you some perspective. Just make sure you choose someone who has your best interests at heart!

3   **Get Busy:** Don't just find something else to do for the moment; find something else to do with your life. Start taking classes—at the gym or a community center. Or volunteer. Just get out of your own head and get too busy to call.

4   **Become Super Self-Absorbed:** A person who loves herself will not do things that are bad for her. So go ahead—do something good for yourself, even if it involves blowing $100 on a facial.

5   **Flirt!:** Even if you are pretty sure you are about as good a flirt as a potato bug, peruse a dating site and "wink" a few times. Or "like" a few of your cuter friends' status updates. Just make sure you are interacting to the best and flirtiest of your abilities.

6   **Go to a Movie:** Or a play, or underwater, or anywhere else you can't use a phone for a while.

7   **Bake:** Get your hands dirty. This way you can't call—or touch anything that isn't improved by powdered sugar.

8   **Tie Yourself Up:** Literally tie a string around your finger to remind yourself *why* you shouldn't type in his number and hit "Send."

9   **Use Positive Reinforcement:** Start treating yourself. Every time you don't call, enjoy a guilty pleasure, from cookies to reality TV.

10   **Delete Him:** E-mail, phone number, and Twitter page. Just gone.

What to Eat When You Feel Rotten

1. **Shepherd's Pie:** Nothing makes you feel better than this hot, meaty mixture smothered in brown gravy and topped with mashed potatoes, then baked for twenty minutes at 350°F.

2. **Spaghetti and Meatballs:** Make your grandmother's meatball recipe and add it to your homemade spaghetti sauce.

3. **Stew:** On a cold, dark day, set up your slow cooker in the morning so by day's end you can sit down and eat.

4. **Dessert Dinner:** Not recommended for every day, this treat is only when things are really blah. Go ahead and indulge in a sundae or a hunk of cake and ice cream. You'll eat a salad for dinner tomorrow.

5. **Chicken Soup:** To make it from scratch, boil a whole chicken, bones and all, skimming the fat as you go. Remove the carcass and add your favorite veggies, salt and pepper, and if necessary, one bouillon cube.

6. **Tuna Casserole:** "Casserole" pretty much translates to "kitchen sink." This recipe is basically tuna, noodles, and anything else you want to add. Then bake it at 350°F for forty-five minutes.

7. **Noodles and Butter:** Egg noodles smothered in butter is a simple and delicious dish to eat when your stomach is upset.

8. **Carrot Ginger Soup and a Hunk of Crusty Bread:** Boil carrots, onion, one parsnip, a sweet potato, garlic, and a chunk of grated gingerroot. Use a hand blender to purée. If you don't like the texture, strain it through a sieve. Add sour cream (or fat-free Greek yogurt) and serve with your favorite peasant bread and butter.

9. **Egg on Toast:** Spoon a soft-boiled egg over a slice of toast and cut it up.

10. **Mashed Bananas and Warm Milk:** Can't sleep? Try this late-night snack. It will soothe you before bed.

Break Up, Don't Break Down

1 **Have an Emotion:** Sometimes it's tough to be emotional in our culture. After a bad breakup let people know so that they'll cut you some slack.

2 **Be a Cliché:** For two weeks you may proceed with any of the following crazy behaviors: watching sad movies and sobbing, listening to Sinéad O'Connor on repeat, and eating ice cream from the container.

3 **Then Get a Haircut:** If you've done this before and hated it, you can dye it, perm it, or get a weave instead.

4 **Take Care of Yourself:** Don't fall apart by not eating or overeating. Don't give up your workouts or take them to the extreme. Be diligent about your behaviors and keep an eye on dangerous ones.

5 **Get Help:** Enlist a friend or hire a therapist and ask her to help monitor your choices for a little while. Check in before making big decisions, especially if they're life-altering.

6 **Assess Your Life:** This might be a great time to decide if maybe it's time for you to get a better job in a new city or move closer to family.

7 **Channel Your Emotions:** Go back to music or art, take a class, or begin writing a novel. Don't deny the sadness; harness it.

8 **Use a Surrogate "Him":** With a tape recorder or a journal, record everything you hate about him, everything you want to say to him, and what you'd like to do to him.

9 **Maintain Dignity:** This is best done by not ever reaching out to him directly and instead focusing on your own healing.

10 **Come Out Better:** By the end of your grieving, be a much better you. It truly is the best revenge.

Ride Out a Storm with Class

1 **Build a Fire:** If you have a working fireplace, what could be cozier than starting it up and gazing at the dancing flames, no matter how nasty the weather gets?

2 **Watch It from Your Porch:** From blizzards to rainstorms, there is nothing more fun than sitting outside (under shelter of course) and watching what Mother Nature can do.

3 **Cuddle Up with a Book:** Pick something dark and stormy like *Wuthering Heights* or *The Legend of Sleepy Hollow*.

4 **Tell Ghost Stories:** Turn off the lights and tell each other the scariest stories you know. See if you can time the big reveal to a particularly loud crack of thunder.

5 **Put Together a Drum Circle:** Take out your dad's bongo set or just use a book and a spoon and pound out the rhythm of the storm.

6 **Crawl into Bed:** Get everyone under the covers and huddle there until the storm passes.

7 **Take a Nap:** Listen to rain as you drift off.

8 **Play a Game:** So there's a storm outside. Light some candles and play a board game by candlelight. Or turn on a few flashlights and play Spotlight I Spy or Spotlight Charades.

9 **Have a Sing-Along:** The best way is to use an acoustic guitar or piano, but if you don't play, just pick songs you love to sing and belt them out louder than the thunder.

10 **Make Love:** What's sexier than a storm?

Boost Your Creativity, Better Your Life

1. **Cloud Watch:** Watch the clouds overhead and look for faces, shapes, and messages.

2. **Make Believe:** Pretend something. Anything!

3. **Imagine a Historical Version of Your Street:** Walk down your street and imagine what it looked like 20 years ago, 50 years ago, 100 years ago, 1,000 years ago. Later, you can look it up and see how right (or wrong) you were.

4. **Read Fiction:** Pick up a book and be transported to another place and time.

5. **Once in a While, Don't Be You:** If you are flying alone or out by yourself, start up a conversation as someone other than yourself. What's "your" story? Do "you" work? Have a family? What's "your" name?

6. **Star Gaze:** Our ancient ancestors made up stories in the stars. If you go someplace where they are bright enough, you can do the same.

7. **Tell Cemetery Stories:** Walk through a cemetery with a friend, partner, or child and make up stories for the names on the tombstones.

8. **Play a Children's Game:** Seek out your favorite eight-year-old and play Barbie dolls with her, or engage in a game of "House," where maybe you play *her* baby.

9. **Create Worlds:** On a long drive or before bed, challenge your partner by asking him to imagine a faraway world. Who lives there? What does it look like?

10. **Alter Your Journal, Slightly:** If you keep a daily journal, modify one experience each day so that it comes out the way you hope it will, or wished it would have.

Really Enjoy a Family Road Trip

1 **Schedule:** When it comes to kids, when *aren't* schedules helpful? Break the trip up into manageable activities.

2 **Stop, a Lot:** Look into kid-friendly activities along the way and make sure they get out and look around.

3 **Play Games Outside of the Car:** If you stop at a rest area, have at least one relay race in the grass to get people moving. Offer a good prize (bring it with you) so that they will enjoy the challenge.

4 **Play Games Inside of the Car:** There are tons of age-appropriate games to play with your kids in the car, from I Spy to the Alphabet Game.

5 **Bring Activities:** Have board games, lap tables for drawing, Etch-a-Sketch, et. al, with which your kids can entertain themselves.

6 **Bring Snacks and Hydrating Beverages:** Hand out snacks like trail mix and water and healthy juices to keep hunger and outbursts to a minimum.

7 **Have a Sing-Along:** With or without the radio, let each person choose a song you can all sing along with.

8 **Alternate Music/Movie Choices:** Allow each child to choose the movie or music. Even better if each has his or her own e-toy so everyone can be happily occupied.

9 **Turn Fights into Games:** If a fight breaks out, have a plan. Make each child argue the *other* person's side of the fight. Whoever wins gets a prize.

10 **Lead a Fun Relaxation Game:** Have everyone (except the driver) close their eyes and take them on a magical journey in their minds. End by having them relax all of their muscle groups. If you're lucky, maybe they'll fall asleep.

Tell a Joke That Actually Makes People Laugh

1 **Religious Joke:** I asked God for a bike, but, it turns out, that isn't how it works. So I stole a bike and asked God for forgiveness.

2 **"Walks into a Bar" Joke:** A three-legged dog walks into a bar and says, "I'm looking for the man who shot my paw."

3 **Silly Joke:** What do you call a one-legged girl? Eileen.

4 **Word-Play Joke:** Two peanuts were walking down the street. One was assaulted.

5 **Gross Joke:** How do you get a tissue to dance? Put a little boogey in it.

6 **Math Joke:** What did the 0 say to the 8? "Nice belt!"

7 **Fashion Joke:** What does a mosquito use to keep her hair in place? Bug spray.

8 **"Walks into a Bar" Joke #2:** A duck walks into a bar, orders the seafood, gets ready to leave, and says to the waiter, "Put it on my bill."

9 **Lawyer Joke:** Two lawyers were walking down the street when they spot a gorgeous woman. "Boy, I'd sure like to screw her," says one. The other replies, perplexed, "Out of what?"

10 **Food-for-Thought Joke:** What did the cannibal order for dinner? A pizza with everyone on it.

Mantras to Breathe By

1 **English Proverb:** Waste not, want not.

2 **The Universal Prayer:** May good befall all / May there be peace for all / May all be fit for perfection / May all experience that which is auspicious.

3 **The Serenity Prayer:** God, grant me the serenity to accept the things I cannot change / Courage to change the things I can / And wisdom to know the difference.

4 **Latin Proverb:** A broken friendship may be soldered, but it will never be sound.

5 **Hindu Chant:** Om and Victory to the self within, victory, victory to the self within.

6 **Buddhist Saying:** The greatest effort is not concerned with results.

7 **Dr. Seuss Quote:** Unless someone like you cares a whole awful lot, nothing is going to get better. It's not.

8 **Nursery Rhyme:** If wishes were horses, beggars might ride.

9 **Mantra from the Dalai Lama:** When you lose, don't lose the lesson.

10 **Shakespeare Quote:** Journeys end in lovers meeting.

How to Say "I Love You" First

1 **Make Sure It's Love and Not Lust:** If your relationship is only a few weeks old, it is probably too early for a gesture this grand. Similarly, don't blurt it out during sex or in the middle of a fight.

2 **Dip Your Toe In:** Do a little investigating to gauge how he feels. Does he answer your calls? Is he engaged when you are together? If yes, proceed to the next step.

3 **Build Up to It:** Begin dropping the word "love" around him casually. "I *love* your shirt!" "I *love* the way your arm feels around my shoulders."

4 **Anticipate His Response:** Have some idea what he will say—or will want to say after you drop the L-bomb—and prepare for it.

5 **Eliminate the Fear Factor:** Tell him not to reply so that he can have a little time to digest your words and you don't have to suffer through him reacting awkwardly.

6 **Prepare for the Worst:** While it might be a necessary risk to move your relationship to the next level, if you say it and he doesn't say it back, understand that it might be the end of your relationship as you know it.

7 **Keep It Light and Breezy:** Ask, "If I said 'I love you,' would you a) want to kiss me? b) want to jump out the window? or c) want to get back to watching baseball?"

8 **Choose Your Timing:** Avoid bringing this up during stressful times or when he is otherwise distracted.

9 **Choose Your Location:** Find a special place to tell him how you feel.

10 **Give It Space:** Afterward, let him process it. Try to leave him alone until he is ready to contact you.

Perfect an Updo
(Without the Help of a Stylist)

1 **A Little Dirt Never Hurt:** That saying couldn't be truer than when you are prepping your hair for an updo. Hair holds better if it hasn't been washed in a day or two.

2 **Know Your Look:** Enlist a friend to photograph you with your hair pulled tight, loosely styled, and with a few tendrils around your face. Which looks best?

3 **Choose a Style:** Find a photo of a hairstyle you like. Don't set your expectations so high that you expect it to come out exactly the same—it is for inspiration only.

4 **Dry It:** Some of the more severe looks can begin with wet hair; however, in most cases it is best to begin with a dry head.

5 **Prepare Your Tools:** Nothing is more frustrating then when you have the perfect twist in hand but no clips or pins anywhere close. Get them ready to go.

6 **Practice:** If you have time, get comfortable in advance twisting your hair and pinning it.

7 **Straighten It:** For maximum shine and the healthiest look, begin by straightening your hair.

8 **Curl It:** Once it is straight, as counterintuitive as it sounds, your next step is to curl it. Curly hair holds its shape better and also looks fuller.

9 **A Little Dab'll Do Ya:** Some stylists suggest putting a little mousse or gel in your hair before you begin, for hold.

10 **Twist and Pin:** If the look you want is more severe, you could start with a ponytail and twist the rest of your hair around the base. For looser looks, separate hair into sections and then twist and pin them as your chosen look dictates. Note: If your hair is short, use extensions or twist and pin the pieces directly against your head.

What You Need to Know about Baseball to Score

1 **Foul Balls:** Foul lines begin at home plate and extend to the end of the field. If the ball flies outside these lines, it's foul.

2 **Strikes:** When the batter swings and misses, or doesn't swing at a good pitch, it's a strike. A foul ball is *also* a strike unless it would be the third. In that case you get a do-over.

3 **Outs:** You are out after three strikes, or if you hit the ball and someone catches it mid-air, or tags you with it as you're running to base, or tags the base you're running toward before you get there.

4 **Scoring:** The batter stands at home plate. When he hits the ball, he runs to first base, followed by second and third. When he makes it back to home plate, he scores one point.

5 **RBI:** This stands for "runs batted in." If there is a runner on a base when a batter hits the ball, the runner heads for the next base. If she makes it home and scores a run, it's credited to the batter's statistics as an "RBI."

6 **Designated Hitters:** In the American League, designated hitters bat for pitchers. In the National League, pitchers bat like everyone else. When the two leagues meet in the World Series, the designated-hitter rules of the home team are used in any given game.

7 **Impolite Behaviors:** It's okay if players spit and scratch themselves inappropriately. But leaving a game before it's over is often considered very rude by the man you came with.

8 **Calorie-Free:** Hot dogs and beer are healthy when consumed at a baseball game.

9 **Innings:** A game is comprised of nine innings, during which both teams bat. If a game is tied after the ninth, it goes into "extra" innings.

10 **The Seventh-Inning Stretch:** In the middle of the seventh inning, the fans stand up to stretch and sing "Take Me Out to the Ballgame" as the teams change sides.

Kitchen Counter Skin Care Remedies

1. **Orange Facial Tonic:** Zest two oranges and mix with one-third cup of apple cider vinegar. Add 3 cups of water and 1 tablespoon of baking soda. Mix together and let stand for a week, then strain and use as an astringent and to increase circulation.

2. **Avocado Face Masks:** This fatty nourishing fruit is great for moisturizing. Mix with several drops of almond butter—or prepare with an egg white, olive oil, and apple cider vinegar for very dried-out faces.

3. **Chocolate Face Mask:** This mask mixes honey and oatmeal with cocoa powder and cream. Yum.

4. **Honey and Cinnamon:** Honey is a naturally antibacterial, and cinnamon works as an anti-inflammatory. Use this delicious mixture to reduce pimples.

5. **Sugar Exfoliant:** Mix it with rosewater and scrub your feet to really soften them.

6. **Yogurt Cleanser:** Combine 7 ounces plain yogurt with 1 tablespoon of lemon and 1 tablespoon of honey to clean and exfoliate.

7. **Oatmeal Cleanser:** Oatmeal calms sensitive skin. It has also been known to clear up rosacea. Make your own by adding water to the oatmeal of your choice, then apply to your face in a gentle circular motion.

8. **Milk Powder Facial:** Mix milk powder, turmeric, honey, and lemon juice in equal parts to form a paste. Apply to your skin, avoiding the eye area, then rinse and glow.

9. **Egg Mask:** This natural firming mask combines egg whites and cornstarch with white clay (from any crafts store) and your favorite essential oil.

10. **Aloe and Honey Moisturizer:** Mix aloe and honey together, refrigerate overnight, then apply to your feet and hands for an instant moisture dousing. It is gentle enough to use on your face.

Enjoy a Lifelong Friendship with Your Folks

1 **Talk to Them as the Adult You Are:** Don't whine to them when things don't go right. Speak to them as you would to a peer.

2 **Behave Like an Adult:** Your folks will be better able to respect you if you aren't always needing them to rescue you from your childish choices. So stop making them.

3 **Set Boundaries for All of You:** Establish how often you will speak to each other (be it once a day or once a month). Also decide what information you will share and what you hope to know. Then discuss it.

4 **Be Kind:** Your parents will appreciate and enjoy you all the more if you are kind to them.

5 **Consider Them as People:** You know how your parents don't have sex or use the toilet? Well, they do. Get over it.

6 **Don't Try to Change Them:** Accept that they are who they are. If someone is going to change them, it ain't gonna be you. So love them unconditionally, if only on major holidays and birthdays.

7 **Separate from Them Financially:** Taking control of your own finances will go a long way toward establishing mutual respect.

8 **Separate from Them Emotionally:** Your parents are not out to destroy your life or humiliate you. Repeat.

9 **Take Responsibility for Your Own Life:** It's time to stop blaming mom and dad. You are off the leash. Now take ownership of your choices.

10 **Lighten Up:** When you are around your parents try not to take everything they say personally. So your mom doesn't like your hair. Be honest. How much do you like hers?

Desserts Without All the Calories

1 **Frozen Fruit Bars:** Freeze your favorite juice by pouring it into an ice cube tray that is then covered in saran wrap and pierced with a toothpick in the center of each cube, or use fruit bar molds to make these easy and refreshing summer desserts. Add honey, low-fat cream, or real fruit bits to give them a kick.

2 **Chocolate Fondue:** By replacing milk chocolate with good-quality dark, fruit dipped in this rich chocolaty pond is downright healthy.

3 **Watermelon Skewers:** Place watermelon, cantaloupe, blueberries, and mango on a skewer. For those with a real sweet tooth, drizzle these treats with honey to liven them up.

4 **Sugar-Free Pudding:** Find a flavor you love and stock up so you'll have it on hand when the mood strikes.

5 **Meringue:** This healthy, fluffy dessert is made from egg whites (goodbye fat and cholesterol), granulated sugar, and a dash of vinegar, baked at 350°F for about twenty minutes.

6 **Banana Boats:** A great substitute for the traditional s'mores. Split the banana peel and stuff a few marshmallows and lots of dark chocolate inside the banana. Wrap in foil and heat over a campfire or in the oven until the chocolate melts.

7 **Ricotta and Cherries:** Heat fresh cherries on the stove with a tablespoon of sugar. Pour the mixture over light ricotta and finish with a sprinkle of almonds over top.

8 **Frozen Berries and Cream:** Freeze summer-fresh berries in zip-lock bags and take them out whenever you are in the mood. Smother them in a low-fat cream you whip yourself.

9 **Avocado Chocolate Mousse:** A ripe avocado, a dash of cinnamon, a tablespoon of cocoa, two egg whites, and half a cup of brown sugar whisked and refrigerated will make this a decadent yet guilt-free concoction.

10 **Tofu/Vegan Cheesecake:** Use a no-bake vegan cheesecake recipe from the Internet. Maple syrup usually gives it that delicious and sweet kick, and tofu gives it the right consistency.

Souvenirs Worth Declaring to Customs

1 **Go Where the Tourists Go:** Find the "old town" or most touristy part of a city. It will almost always have souvenir shops full of inexpensive items you can buy. Just be sure to focus on items that allude to the culture of the place you are visiting.

2 **Find a Market:** Find out when and where the local markets operate—that's where you'll find hand-crafted goodies at locals' prices.

3 **Look for Local Art:** Is there some craft or artwork native to the area? Find shops with small souvenir-sized versions of the real (expensive) thing.

4 **Visit the General Store:** In rural areas, stop at a "country" or "general" store for funky pieces unique to the area.

5 **Bring Home the Bacon:** Most places have some kind of native cuisine. Depending on where you are traveling, you can purchase nonperishable food items or have some shipped home.

6 **Look for Amateur Artists:** Find the local artists—the ones who aren't famous yet—and invest in an affordable sculpture, print, or painting. It might be worth a mint one day!

7 **Personalize It:** Have a portrait done by a street artist with the local scene in the background.

8 **Seek Out Music:** Go out and hear a local band, then buy a CD of their music if you enjoyed the show.

9 **Visit Museum Gift Shops:** If you buy from a museum, not only are you making a financial contribution to help maintain the institution, but you can get some great regional items to bring home.

10 **Pick Up Post Cards:** For a great, inexpensive, and personalized gift, buy post cards and put them in cool old frames you find at flea markets and fairs. Then give them out to friends.

Know When You're in Love with Love and Not Him

1 **You Lack Impulse Control:** When it comes to your man, you can't stop yourself from calling him, you show up unannounced, and check in multiple times a day.

2 **You Can't Stop Thinking about Him:** If a guy is on your mind all the time, there is a point at which it becomes unhealthy for both of you.

3 **You Dig:** When you are with him, sometimes you find yourself digging to get him to tell you how he feels about you. No answer is good enough. You keep needing more and better responses.

4 **You Break Up and Then Get Back Together:** In an effort to regain that early rush of excitement, you test boundaries and push him away.

5 **You Don't Really Know Him:** Take a minute and ask yourself if you could answer some basic questions about your guy. If you don't know the answers, it isn't love.

6 **You Want to Control Him:** If you fight to control his moods, choices, and behaviors, you do not love him. You are addicted to an idea into which you hope to fit him.

7 **You've Done This with Other Guys:** If this isn't the first time you've felt this out of control in a relationship, it's probably you and not him.

8 **You Are Depressed:** If you suffer from depression, you might be prone to love addiction.

9 **You Use Sex to Change Your Mood:** Do you typically go into sexual encounters hoping to feel better? That's a sign it's about something other than bonding with another human being.

10 **You Relationship Hop:** If the thought of being single terrifies you, maybe it's time for you to try it and find out why.

Pamper Yourself for Real

1 **A Celebrity Facial:** Next time you visit L.A. or New York, choose a spa where the celebrities go and drop some extra cash on an elaborately sumptuous facial.

2 **A Diamond Massage:** Diamonds are considered a healing stone, known to bond relationships and attract abundance. Why not employ someone to rub your back while they trail a row of them down your spine? All the uber-wealthy are doing it.

3 **A Five-Star Restaurant:** If you are in a city that features a restaurant of this caliber, give it a try. It will be worth it.

4 **A Five-Star Hotel:** Spend a year setting aside enough money to pay for it, and then give yourself one night at the hotel of your dreams.

5 **A Gem Rental:** Whether or not you own your own, splurge for a night on a necklace, earrings, bracelets, and rings fit for royalty.

6 **A Rolls:** So what if you can't buy one? Go to the dealership and go for a test drive. Just make sure you dress the part.

7 **First Class:** Go ahead and upgrade so that you can experience what the fuss is about over flying first class.

8 **Order Everything on the Menu:** Can't decide what to eat? Maybe just once, splurge by trying out everything on your favorite menu. Wrap up the leftovers to go and treat a food bank to something extra special.

9 **Hot-Air Balloon Over Provence:** This exquisite French wine country is the pinnacle of romance. Enjoy something over-the-top decadent by seeing it from the air.

10 **Shower (or Bathe) Outside:** For top-of-the-line extravagance, overlook the ocean or another beautiful view. Make sure you indulge in fragrant soaps, shampoos, and oils.

Speed Up Your Metabolism
Without Really Trying

1 **De-Stress:** When a body is in a state of stress, its systems fail to function normally. Find your inner peace and watch everything, even your metabolism, work out the kinks.

2 **Kick It Off:** Eat something nutritious when you wake up and again after long periods of sitting still. You don't have to eat a lot, just enough to tell your body you are ready to go.

3 **Look to Sunshine to Wake Up:** Getting sunlight helps turn on your metabolism. So drink your morning coffee outside and soak it up.

4 **Ice Your Morning Caffeine:** Drinking iced coffee or tea in the morning helps your body utilize both the stimulation of the caffeine and the energy of heating the beverage to boost your metabolism.

5 **Eat Frequently:** Eating small meals throughout the day will keep your body from thinking it's hungry, which makes it slow down your metabolic rate accordingly.

6 **Eat Kiwi:** This superfood is known to boost your metabolism almost as much as exercising.

7 **Order a Shirley Temple at Dinner:** Studies have shown that the body burns up alcohol first, storing the other calories you consume as fat.

8 **Drink Water . . . Cold:** Did you know your body burns calories warming up the water you drink? Not only that, but making sure you consume enough water each day helps keep your systems in check.

9 **Add Spice:** A teaspoon of cinnamon added to your diet every day will increase your metabolism. So will hot peppers, at least temporarily.

10 **Raise Your Heart Rate:** This doesn't mean you have to go to a gym or run a race. Your heart rate goes up the minute you stand up. So keep moving.

"Play" with Your Food

1. **Get Creamy:** Whipped cream applied, whipped cream licked off. Delicious.

2. **Hot and Cold:** Fill two mugs, one with hot tea and the other with ice water. Go down on each other alternately, using the liquids to heat or cool your mouth as you go.

3. **Sensate Focus:** Blindfold your partner and rub foods and liquids of varying sensations all over his body. Make him guess what each one is by smelling and feeling them, and then finally, by tasting small bites.

4. **Eat Dinner:** Using him as a plate, lay out your whole meal on his body and indulge until you are completely satisfied.

5. **Fruit Roll-Ups Fashion:** Have him dress you in a dress made out of Fruit Roll-Ups. (Or make your own.) Also create a pair of boxers for him. Then eat each other's clothes off.

6. **Feed Each Other:** Instead of eating a normal meal, feed each other. Even better: feed each other with your hands.

7. **Body Shots:** After he licks up salt on your thighs, pour a shot of tequila between your breasts and let him drink it as it flows across your navel. Then have him suck the lime wedge you are holding in your mouth.

8. **Carrots, Cucumbers, and Yams—Oh My!:** Wash thoroughly, then cover one in a condom and gently insert.

9. **Hot Pepper Sex:** A little of the capsaicin from a hot chili will add an amazing tingle to an already sensitive and aroused private part. Have a high-fat milk on hand to lessen the burn if you go too far.

10. **Hot Ice:** A little ice cube a la *9½ Weeks* can be thrilling. Kick it up a notch by using a chocolate Popsicle instead.

Give Your Back a Break

1 **Get a Massage:** Sometimes all you need to fix your back is a good rub. It might be worth it to try a chiropractic massage.

2 **Invest in a Good Mattress:** Finding a bed that properly aligns your body while you sleep can be the difference between a good and bad back.

3 **Eat Dark Green Vegetables:** High in vitamin K, veggies like kale and broccoli help your body deposit calcium into your bones, making them stronger and less injury-prone.

4 **Use Your Small Purse:** It's time to retire your enormous bag and swap it out for a lighter, less-easy-to-overfill version. Less weight on your shoulders, back, and neck equals less pain.

5 **Change Your Shoes:** It is possible that your back pain is directly related to what you are wearing on your feet. Avoid stilettos and other shoes that compromise your body's natural alignment.

6 **Watch Your Posture:** Your grandmother was right—stand up straight and sit up straight.

7 **Try Acupuncture or Acupressure:** It is said that where Western medicine can no longer help, Eastern medicine holds the answers. Many people swear by these ancient healing arts toward the elimination of back pain.

8 **Support It:** Wearing support belts or knee braces or even tightening your core muscles while exerting yourself are all ways to keep your back supported and pain-free.

9 **Get Over It:** Some schools of thought insist that back pain is often psychosomatic. If you are under stress or experiencing depression, do what you can to feel better. Your back pain just might improve.

10 **Try an Ounce of Prevention:** Keep your core muscles strong to support and protect your back.

Rekindle an Old Friendship

1 **Research:** Is there someone you can ask to learn how your ex-friend is doing? If not, look online and see if she has some kind of public persona you can check out.

2 **Remember:** Remind yourself why things went wrong. Decide if you even *want* to be friends again.

3 **Pinpoint:** Figure out what has to happen from your perspective for the relationship to begin again. Similarly, anticipate what she will need.

4 **Test the Waters:** Extend a Facebook friend request, or just a short note saying hello. See how she reacts. Don't obsess about it. Just stay casual. She may not want you back.

5 **Meet to Talk:** Open up a dialogue by sending out an apology and asking if she'd like to repair the relationship. Listen to her answer and see if you have it in you to meet her expectations.

6 **Give Yourselves Time:** You may need to go back to your corners to consider all the information. If you both are ready, issue apologies and hugs and begin again.

7 **Don't Try to Pick Up Where You Left Off:** Think of her as a new friend. Enjoy her from scratch.

8 **Be Wary of Old Triggers and Patterns:** You don't want to restart any of the behaviors that led to your fallout in the first place.

9 **Reach Out:** Continue to reach out to her as long as you both feel comfortable.

10 **Let It Be:** Allow the friendship to grow or diminish as it will. It's okay if it's time to move on.

Plan a Picture-Perfect Day in the Park

1 **Play Chess:** If there isn't a chessboard there already, bring your own. Open yourself up to challenges and spend the day plotting your moves.

2 **People-Watch:** Sit by a fountain or under a tree and watch the people stroll by. Make up biographies for people who stand out. Maybe even strike up a conversation with one of them to see if you got it right.

3 **Watch a Play:** If there are performances taking place, find out about them and go watch from your perch on a blanket.

4 **Picnic:** Bring a basket and some food to share with your family or friends. Keep it easy (cold food only) so that the picnic is fun.

5 **Go Boating:** Find a park that allows you to rent rowboats or paddleboats and go for a ride.

6 **Play Ball:** Book a diamond in advance or hijack an empty one and organize a game of softball, baseball, or kickball with friends.

7 **Explore:** Go looking to get lost. Sneak off trails (but be careful about ruining fragile vegetation) and discover something new.

8 **Sing:** Bring a guitar and some rhythm instruments and have a sing-along. If you can get enough other park-goers to join in, it will increase the festivity factor.

9 **Go for a Lovers' Stroll:** Take your honey's hand and walk around the park. Stroll in and out of the trees and ramble over the hills, purring sweet nothings to each other as you go.

10 **Have an Alphabet Scavenger Hunt:** Split your group into teams and have everyone find one item that starts with each letter of the alphabet, then reconvene for a celebratory picnic.

Decorate Your Digs in Vintage Décor

1 **Grain Sacks:** These can be made into throw pillows for beds or sofas that would cost you hundreds in the retail world.

2 **Old Books:** Old books in good condition will give your bookshelf a little "street cred" and look attractive to boot.

3 **Cool American Furniture:** Pieces from the '50s and '60s take on new life once you reupholster their dirty cushions.

4 **Mirrors:** A great mirror can decorate the wall and visually expand a small space. Be on the lookout for art deco frames.

5 **Old School Clocks:** Add a new battery and most can be made functional—and the big round faces look sharp. Use them to make any white wall on-trend.

6 **Frames:** Chunky metal frames and intricate wooden ones add an artistic element to cool vacation photographs.

7 **Amateur Art:** Dig through the framed original artwork that has been tossed from someone's basement. There is bound to be a gem or two you will love hanging on your wall.

8 **Mason Jars:** You can use them to hold flowers, pens, marbles, or just leave them empty for a simple but excellent decoration or gift.

9 **Wooden Crates and Military Trunks:** Use these as great ways to store magazines and off-season clothing. They look good and open up space.

10 **Fabric:** Find great patterns and frame a few for a kids' room, or use them to reupholster chairs and benches. If you are feeling especially craftsy, make scarves or even clothes out of them.

Make New Friends in a Minute

1 **Master a Warm Handshake:** When you greet someone and shake hands, place your other hand on top. If it's appropriate, go in for a hug. People will find you warm and accessible.

2 **Remember Him:** Associate a new acquaintance with a TV show that has a character sharing his name, or perhaps a popular song that includes it.

3 **Use Her Name:** Hearing one's own name puts everyone at ease, so use hers regularly in your conversation. But don't force it, or it will come off as creepy.

4 **Be Curious:** Ask questions and genuinely listen to answers. See if you can ask follow-up questions. Everyone likes to feel interesting. Just try to mean it.

5 **Invite People:** When an activity comes up that has room for others, invite acquaintances to join you to get to know them better.

6 **Verbalize Positives:** Let people know what you like about them; compliments go a long way with most people.

7 **Tease Kindly:** Teasing, when done right, has an intimate quality that makes people feel at ease. If you can find a way to get one in that is gently funny and will get a laugh, do it.

8 **Say Yes:** You can't agree with everything, but in general people like to be agreed with and supported in decisions. Table your judgmental side and listen to their point of view.

9 **Relate and Share:** When a new friend shares personal information about her life with you, see if you have a story that shows you can relate with her. Don't one-up her, but create camaraderie by identifying.

10 **Present Yourself Well:** Avoid bad or overbearing smells, and look presentable. For better or worse, people like to be seen with people they are proud of.

Get a Preteen Girl to Put Down Her Cell Phone

1 **Take Her to the Theater:** Find a dance or stage performance she will enjoy and take her to see it.

2 **Give Manis and Pedis:** Let her pick her colors and then have a mini spa at home. Let her soak her feet in rose water and rub her tootsies. Then do the hands.

3 **Go Horseback Riding:** Find a farm that offers horseback riding tours and stroll through the paths on horseback.

4 **Go to the Movies:** Let her pick the movie and bring a friend. Then sit three rows back.

5 **Take Her to a Concert:** Any all-ages show will work, even if it's a smaller venue and she doesn't know the band. She will have a great time. Just make sure you have enough money to buy her a T-shirt.

6 **Take Her for a Spa Day:** Get facials or get your hair done together by a professional.

7 **Go Shopping:** Just keep a budget in mind. Then help her try on clothes and suggest great looks for her.

8 **Ask Her to Read to You:** If the preteen is your child, let her read out loud to you before bed. It will be something special both of you will always remember.

9 **Organize a Drama Day:** Get a few of her friends to get in on it and lead them in improv and theater games they will love. End by splitting them into groups and having each film a movie they will show each other when they are done.

10 **Throw a Season-Finale Party:** Have a *Gossip Girl* season-finale party, or one for another show she loves. Have finger sandwiches, candy in girly colors, and colorful juice drinks.

Get a Preteen Boy to Turn Off His Video Game

1 **Take Him to a Game:** Buy tickets to almost any sporting event. If the professional sports are too expensive, find a college game or a AAA league.

2 **Play a Game:** Let him show you one of his online worlds. Or play a board game together.

3 **Go to the Movies:** Let him pick a movie and then go along with him and his friends to see it. Sit three rows back.

4 **Go on a Hike:** Take him and his friends hiking. If they move more quickly than you, set boundaries. Tell them they have to stop when they hear you call out and wait for you to meet them. Just don't forget to call out.

5 **Organize a Team Sport:** Get a group of kids together to play kickball or baseball.

6 **Take Him Fishing:** Even if you bring a book, he'll love being quiet and out on the water. Just make sure one of you knows what you're doing.

7 **Ask Him to Teach You Something:** Boys have many varied interests. Have him teach you about one of them. You might find that your faked enthusiasm becomes very real.

8 **Ask Him to Read to You:** If the preteen is your child, have him read a book to you out loud each night before bed. It's something he will always remember sharing with you.

9 **Go to a Science Museum:** Take him and a friend to a science museum for the day. Follow them around and see it through their excited eyes.

10 **Throw a Party for His Friends for the Big Game:** Tell him to invite five friends and then provide tailgating food. Give them ginger ale in bottles.

Pour Traditional Japanese Tea

(1) Choose a Venue: Traditional tea ceremonies are generally conducted in small rooms called *chashitsu*; however, they can happen anywhere there is a place to set out the tea before guests, including outdoor areas.

(2) Know the Seasonal Variations: The changing seasons affect some of the traditions in a tea ceremony. Since most tea ceremonies are held between May and October, this list will follow the variations traditional during late spring, summer, and early fall.

(3) Choose Your Tea: Most ceremonies use thick teas called *koichas* or thin teas called *usuchas*. Of course, it's safe to use a black or green tea if you are unsure.

(4) Organize Your Tools: You need a tea bowl, a cloth to wipe it down, a tea pot or caddy, a scoop for the tea, and a tea bowl and whisk.

(5) Prepare the Tea: Using your tools, prepare the tea in front of your guests. You can enlist an assistant to serve as host for the remainder of the ceremony so that you may join your guests.

(6) Bow: When you are handed your cup of tea, you must bow to the server.

(7) Right Hand: Take the cup with your right hand and then pass it into the palm of your left hand.

(8) Turn It: Turn the cup three times clockwise before taking your first sip.

(9) Slurp It Up: When you have finished your tea, it is traditional to share a loud, flourished slurp so that your host knows you truly enjoyed it.

(10) Wipe the Cup: With your right hand, wipe the place where your lips touched the cup and then turn it counterclockwise once before returning it to the host.

Why It's Worth It to Go Back to School Now

1. **Learning Is Actually Fun:** You might not remember, but you will have an unparalleled sense of accomplishment after a day of learning.

2. **You Can Reinvent Yourself:** This time around you can use school as an opportunity to try something different on for size and indulge in personal growth.

3. **You Are Stuck:** If you are having a moment of paralysis, get moving again by going back to school. You will never say that furthering your education was a waste of time. Endless games of solitaire, on the other hand . . .

4. **You Need Inspiration:** Exposing yourself to new ideas can open up avenues of change in your life and get your blood flowing again.

5. **You Want to Keep Your Childhood Promises:** What did you want to be when you grew up? Are you there yet?

6. **You Can Compete:** With more education, you can beat out others for the job of your dreams and win the opportunities you deserve.

7. **You Can Make More Money:** Maybe you aren't bringing in the big bucks. People with higher degrees earn a third more money than people with a bachelor's. And people with a bachelor's make double what people with only a high school diploma make.

8. **You Can Get Connected:** Going back to school means having the chance to meet people in the field you are interested in pursuing. You can learn how to get where you want to go more easily and more directly.

9. **You Can Use Your Smarts:** Do not underestimate the value of life experience. Go back to school older and wiser and be the star student this time around.

10. **You Can Set an Example:** Live the dream you have for your children and inspire them to follow you.

Throw Yourself an Unexpected Wedding

1 **Elope:** You hardly need any time to prepare. Just go to city hall with two witnesses.

2 **Go Meta:** Have the most wedding-y wedding ever! Wear an enormous white dress (buy one cheap at DavidsBridal.com) and ask all of your guests to do the same.

3 **Celebrate Each Other:** Find some other way to let your friends and family know that you celebrate each other every day.

4 **Do the Opposite:** Instead of wearing white, wear black. Get married by the drummer in your band and have your mom walk your groom down the aisle.

5 **Throw a Domestic Partnership Party:** Get your DP and then celebrate it with family and friends.

6 **Make It "Jeans Optional":** The more casual the party, the less wedding-like it is.

7 **Have It at a Restaurant You Both Love:** The TGI Fridays where you met, or a McDonald's with an awesome kids' space—just bring your officiant and invite your peeps.

8 **Do It at a Bar:** Close the bar to the public and pay the bill at the end of the night. Put out pretzels and bowls of M&M's.

9 **Make It a Performance:** A wedding is basically a play that everyone has seen before with different actors. So make yours a performance your guests will love.

10 **Make It a Movie!:** Get a few of your talented friends together to make a movie about a couple trying to make it to the altar. Premier it at a theater you rent out and end it with you and your partner taking the stage and saying your vows!

Make Every Minute Count
for Someone Else: Volunteer

1 **Find the Right Place to Volunteer:** Start by checking out *www.volunteermatch. org*, or any local, national, or international organizations doing compelling work.

2 **Do Your Homework:** Carefully choose the organization you'd like to help. It will make any experience more meaningful.

3 **Be Prepared:** Volunteering is not always glamorous. Pulling weeds and doing dishes or filing and data entry can be par for the course.

4 **Have a Good Attitude:** You may find that reading to the elderly or teaching kids, is more rewarding when you do it with a smile on your face.

5 **Bring Your Friends:** Sharing your volunteer experience with others can help you build strong bonds and create meaningful shared experiences.

6 **Use Your Skills:** Teach what you know and put your skills to good use. You might also help organize a fundraiser.

7 **Bring Your "A" Game:** Volunteer work can lead to paid work. If other volunteers or employees of the organization see your enthusiasm and hard work, you might end up at the top of their lists for open positions.

8 **Go the Extra Mile:** If you're told to bring a lunch, pack extra drinks, fruit, or snacks for other volunteers, and anyone else that looks like they could use it.

9 **Share Your Experience:** Write a thank-you note to the organization or the person who got you involved, blog about it, and tell others what you learned . . . and how they can do it, too.

10 **Anticipate Your Comfort Level:** Some volunteer work can test your personal and emotional strength. You may need to lift heavy objects or confront your own prejudices and stereotypes.

Forget the Hair of the Dog:
Hangover Cures That Work

1 **Drink Water Before Alcohol:** Hydrate well before going out drinking, while you are drinking, as well as the morning after. A bad hangover is mostly the result of a dehydrated body.

2 **Go for a Walk:** Contrary to popular belief, nursing a hangover won't make it go away any more quickly. Better to get out of the house and distract yourself if you can.

3 **Nux Vomica:** Before you drink, take the homeopathic remedy nux vomica. Many people swear by it. However, use caution. Homeopathic remedies are rarely FDA approved.

4 **Drink Clear Liquor:** Vodka, white wine, and gin are less likely to induce bad headaches the way red wines and malt liquors can.

5 **Take a Non-Acetaminophen Painkiller:** Tylenol and other acetaminophen-based painkillers are hard on your liver. So stick to aspirin and ibuprofen.

6 **Eat a Coconut or a Banana:** Eat fruits that help you replenish liquids. Anything high in electrolytes or potassium will help.

7 **Eat:** Even if you are feeling sick to your stomach, you need to elevate your blood sugar. So eat whatever you can keep down.

8 **Take a Shower:** It will wake you up and help you feel better more quickly.

9 **Don't Believe the Hype:** Drinking more booze will not stop a hangover; it will only delay it. Sorry.

10 **Laugh:** Focus on how much fun you had the night before. If your dignity is wounded the morning after, it only makes the headache worse. Call a friend to confirm that it was *funny* when you walked into the sliding glass door, and that the hosts of the barbecue hold no grudges as long as you pay for the damages.

Make Your Eyes Pop

1 **Cleanse Your Palette:** In other words, wash your fa... makeup or facial products.

2 **Moisturize:** Put a comfortable amount of SPF 15 moisturizer on y... hydrate. Avoid the delicate skin around your eyes.

3 **Use a Primer:** Keep oil from melting away your eye shadow as the hours tic... Once your primer is in place, give it a minute to dry.

4 **Line Your Upper Lid:** Using the tool you are most comfortable with, whether it's a pencil or liquid, make a smooth line on your eyelid above your lashes. (The color is your choice, but black or gray are most typical.)

5 **Line Your Lower Lid:** Using a pencil, line your eyes beneath your lashes, and then use your finger to smudge it.

6 **Base Shadow:** Choose a lighter color, like a cream, to sweep across your lid up to your brow bone.

7 **Opt to Make It Smoky:** Using a darker eye shadow and a brush, carefully pull the color upward from your lash line. At the crease, allow the color to blend into the base.

8 **Blend It In:** Make sure the color is blended from liner to base. There should be no hard lines.

9 **Touch It Up:** Use a cotton swab dipped in eye-makeup remover to fix any little mistakes.

10 **Add Mascara:** For the final touch, brush dark mascara over your lashes until they are full and your eyes pop. Curl lashes if desired for a framing finish.

e they are coming for a game

an bow out gracefully.

arrive, turn on some music and offer

s a choice of games the night of the
what games will be played.

ght, you must be prepared to call the game
ouncement and let guests know where to

5 **Organize.** r guests if they should sit in a circle or in a
group. Also, have ᴜ ᵤ aking everyone into teams. Counting off or
assigning team captains are ᴄ ᵢsy methods.

6 **Have the Tools Ready:** After you have everyone's attention is *not* the time to begin
rummaging around for pens. Be prepared to hand out tools immediately.

7 **Assign One Person to Go Over the Directions:** Make sure it doesn't turn into a
chorus. Only one person explains the rules.

8 **Keep It Moving:** If a game isn't working, be prepared to stop it and move on to
a different one.

9 **Offer Prizes:** It's always an exciting touch when the host gives the winners prizes.
Even something silly and small will be a hit.

10 **Have Fun:** Keep it light. Pay attention and stay in control of sore losers and competitive fights. Make calls quickly and be a fair and impartial judge when you
have to be. And laugh. A lot.

Make Some Extra Bank
and Have Fun Doing It

1 **Have a Bake Sale:** Prepare items to sell. Make sure you consider the cost of baking materials when setting your prices. Donate 50 percent to charity and people will buy.

2 **Have a Garage Sale:** Gather unwanted items from your home. Also see if neighbors have anything they'd like to donate. Price everything, post it on Craigslist and at *www.Garagesales.com*, and wait for your windfall.

3 **Sell Books:** Go to a used-book store and sell your books.

4 **Write an Article:** Research and write a compelling story in your area. Reach out to local or national publications and see if they are interested in buying it.

5 **Babysit:** Let your friends know you are available to babysit their kids for a fee. They'll probably appreciate the break.

6 **Walk a Dog:** Offer to walk a dog every morning for a busy friend or neighbor for some extra cash.

7 **Be a Scientific Test Subject:** Find a place that tests new medications. You are more likely to make $500 to $1,000 for being a part of an FDA study, but you'll deserve it if the side effects have you vomiting.

8 **Raise Money for a Charity:** Raise money for charity and be transparent about keeping 10 percent of the proceeds for your efforts. It's a common practice in many charities.

9 **Cut Your Hair:** Shiny, healthy, untreated human hair is worth quite a bit, so grow your hair until it is as long as you can get it, then cut it all off and make some real money. Try Hairwork.com or BuyandSellHair.com to list the hair you are selling.

10 **Bet:** Make a hundred-dollar bet with someone over something you're not likely to lose. If you lose, go double or nothing.

Take Kids Out to Eat and Still Enjoy Your Meal

1 **Wait Until They Can Obey Orders:** Don't bring walking children before they're at an age where they can understand cause and effect. You need to have some control.

2 **Go on Good Nap Days:** If your child is tired or sick, skip it. Do it another time when things aren't as volatile.

3 **Dress Up:** Make sure all of you look nice when you go. People are more apt to forgive a cute, well-dressed misbehaving toddler than one with mud on his shirt.

4 **Prepare:** Before you go, sit the child down and explain where you are eating and what is expected when you get there. Have punishment and rewards planned for both good and bad behavior.

5 **Go Early:** People can generally handle things a little more casually before formal dinner hours.

6 **Order When You Walk in:** Make sure your child's meal comes out quickly. Mealtimes are always challenging in part because everybody is hungry.

7 **Distract with Quiet Activities:** Bring things to keep your child occupied, like drawing materials, muted games, or TV shows (but only with ear buds).

8 **Be Polite:** If your child does act up, smile and apologize even to the rudest people. If nothing else, *you'll* feel better about how you handled it.

9 **Have a Plan:** In anticipation of a meltdown, give your server your credit card when you first arrive and let him know you might not make it, but you're going to try. If things go south, get dinner to go and get out.

10 **Be Helpful and Gracious:** If your child makes a huge mess, do something to help clean up and leave a tip showing that you appreciate the extra help.

Stop the Swell

1 **Know Your Triggers:** Cut back on the foods that make you bloat—but only after you take time to notice what they are.

2 **Take the ALCAT:** This easy-to-look-up food and chemical sensitivity test basically has you cut out all foods and then slowly re-add them to your diet until you figure out what makes you feel good and what makes you feel bad.

3 **Hydrate:** Drinking water helps with everything, including bloating, so make sure you are getting enough.

4 **Limit Your Sodium Intake:** Especially around your period, make sure you cut back on how much salt is in your diet.

5 **Take a Walk:** Moving around can help increase your blood flow and stimulate circulation.

6 **Cut Portions:** Overeating can lead to bloating, so try halving portions to see if that helps.

7 **Eat Slowly:** Eating too fast can cause your stomach to distend. Make sure you carefully chew and swallow each bite.

8 **Take a Cooking Class:** Avoiding excess salt and other bloat-causing foods is harder if you eat out or eat too many processed foods. Learn to cook so you know what's in your food.

9 **Drink Ginger Tea:** Ginger is a great belly soother. Boil this root and drink the tea to ease discomfort.

10 **Take Apple Cider Vinegar:** One tablespoon of apple cider vinegar three times a day will help your body beat the bloat.

Romance Your Way Across the USA

1 **Niagara Falls (Niagara, New York):** If the vibrating, heart-shaped bed in *Superman II* didn't do it for you, then perhaps you should stick to the breathtaking views.

2 **Glen Canyon, Utah:** Located in southern Utah, this part of the Colorado River is truly a stunning testament to the power of nature. With rafting tours and spa resorts, it is also incredibly romantic.

3 **The Berkshires (Massachusetts):** At the base of the Taconic Mountain range, this wonderful part of New England has some of the most romantic bed-and-breakfasts in the country. In the summer the Boston Pops plays at Tanglewood, and in the autumn the leaves are the main attraction.

4 **The White Mountains of New Hampshire:** This mountain range boasts romantic ski resorts and cozy inns around every bend.

5 **Sanibel Island (Florida):** Enjoy blue waters and white sand beaches, or ride any of the twenty-two miles of bike paths with your love and then collapse under the Florida sun.

6 **The Grand Canyon (Arizona):** One of the world's great honeymoon capitals, this natural wonder is an unforgettable destination to share with someone you love.

7 **Monument Lake Resort (Colorado):** Described as an area so peaceful and quiet "you can hear the fish bite." Go someplace beautiful where you and your honey can truly be alone.

8 **Lake Shasta (California):** Rent a houseboat for two on this magnificent lake in northern California.

9 **Mammoth Cave National Park (Kentucky):** Rent a cottage near the stunning visage of these wondrous caves.

10 **Big Sur, California:** A wonderful place for a lover's hike that ends looking out at a sunset over the Pacific.

Pick a Perfume That Does All the Talking

1. **Consider That It Reveals Your "Style":** Your scent says as much about you as your shoes or bags. So when choosing one, marry it to your style.

2. **Expect It to Linger:** When you leave the room, your perfume stays behind. It also remains on clothing and in cars. Choose wisely.

3. **Remember It Can Set the Mood:** Your perfume should enhance your "aura" and help you to set the mood as much as lighting and attire.

4. **Wear It Before You Buy:** A good perfume will change once it's on your skin, so put some on when you arrive at a store. Decide whether or not to buy it at the end of your shopping trip.

5. **Choose a Signature Scent:** Even if you wear different fragrances, make sure they all share one or two specific elements.

6. **Consider Timing:** At work wear bright scents from the citrus family or try something earthy to keep you and those around you alert. Save flowery and romantic scents for evening.

7. **Have a Friend Help You:** If you are not 100 percent confident in your own nose, enlist a backup when you go perfume shopping.

8. **Break Down the Scent:** Ask or look up what scents have been combined to create specific perfumes. Investigate the inspiration behind them as well so that you are clear about what has gone into making it.

9. **Consider Others:** Don't just go with perfumes you like; look into the psychology of smells and choose scents that elicit a sense of power or beauty or both.

10. **Remember, Less Is More:** Start light if you are new to wearing scents. Over time you can add more until you begin getting only the occasional response. If everyone is noticing, you've gone too far.

Make Someone Happy Now

(1) Celebrate Someone's Half Birthday: It will be unexpected and it will make her feel even more special than if it were actually her birthday.

(2) Show Your Pride: Give someone a few specific reasons you are proud of him and happy to know him.

(3) Pick Up the Tab: Go out for lunch and when no one is looking, pay the tab unprompted and without discussion.

(4) Send Flowers: Do it for no good reason and include a note that says "I just wanted to say hi."

(5) Donate: Make a donation in the name of someone you care about. Choose something you know she cares about and have confirmation sent to her on your behalf.

(6) Do Someone Else's Work: Finish up a lingering project or take care of a few simple items on your boss's or coworker's to-do list, and then let him know it's taken care of.

(7) Compliment Your Boss: Without looking like a kiss-up, let your boss know that you think she is doing a good job. If you can be specific, even better!

(8) Communicate Boldly: Tell your partner you love him . . . in lipstick on the bathroom mirror.

(9) Bring Bagels: Tomorrow, when you buy your breakfast, pick up an extra dozen bagels or doughnuts for your coworkers and go ahead and toss in two kinds of cream cheese.

(10) Treat the Mailman: Leave a bottle of water and a snack in your mailbox.

Score Free Stuff Without Breaking a Sweat

① **Flirt:** Flirt heavily with bartenders, waiters, and other people in service positions. You might find that every bill has a savings column.

② **Be Prettier Than Average:** Prettier people get more stuff free. It's a sad truth about our culture. So, as your mother would say, put on a little lipstick and work it.

③ **Announce Your Neediness:** Don't be afraid to let people know when you are broke. If they like you, they will give you a hand.

④ **Make People Feel Like They Owe You:** If you are helpful and eager, people will want to repay you for your help and kindness.

⑤ **Be the Fun Friend:** If your friendship is worth it, people will want to have you around. This might net you free drinks at the bar and even free trips.

⑥ **Know Where to Look:** Some websites will give you the lowdown on who is giving what away, like TotallyFreeStuff.com and the Freecycle.net.

⑦ **Ask for It:** Come right out and ask for free stuff. Whether you're out to eat or requesting samples or overstock, you'd be surprised how much you can get if you are okay with getting a few no's as well.

⑧ **Write a Blog:** Gain a following and then ask for products to test to share with your readers. You can get everything from vacations to kitchen gear if you know how to ask.

⑨ **Be in the Right Place:** Go to a grocery store just after close and you might be able to grab close-to-expired food items before they get thrown out. Same goes for restaurants and bakeries.

⑩ **Befriend People with Stuff to Give:** If your friends have things to give away, ask them for some of it. If they don't want to share, get in with a crowd that has more to offer.

Make It Chic — on the Cheap!

(1) Make Your Own Wall Hangings: Cut out great photos from old calendars and frame them for incredible and inexpensive wall art.

(2) Get Wild in Summer: Pick wildflowers where you know you are allowed to, or ask neighbors if you can have trimmings from their gardens.

(3) Fill Modern Fruit Bowls: Use a glass vase to hold lemons, limes, or oranges. The bright colors look fresh and make lovely and creative centerpieces.

(4) Change It Up: Switch your curtains from one window to another. Mix and match two different patterns as long as they are the same length.

(5) Get Out the Scissors: Cut an old but brightly colored flat sheet into strips and use them as a tieback for curtains. This small touch can really make your windows pop.

(6) DIY "Wallpaper": Apply liquid starch to several fabric samples or one old sheet and hang it on a white wall. Place existing framed photos over top.

(7) Make a Mosaic: Using free paint-color cards from any hardware store, make a faux mosaic "tile" design on an empty wall.

(8) Create a Natural Centerpiece: Gather pretty rocks, pinecones, and twigs on your next walk in the woods. Place them in a shallow dish and bring nature indoors.

(9) Light Up the Outdoors: Place candles in Mason jars. Wrap the jars with wire and hang them from a tree for a starry-night lighting scheme.

(10) Move the Big Furniture: A large bookshelf placed in the center of a room will divide it into two distinct spaces. For a semblance of more space, move things around and see how you like them.

Get Noticed by the CEO

1. **Share:** If you come across an interesting article about office life that might be helpful, share it with the CEO.

2. **Make Suggestions:** At staff meetings, come prepared with at least one thing to say. Hold on to it until it fits the conversation and then slip it in.

3. **Be an All-Around Pleasant Employee:** Have a friendly but professional demeanor. Laugh easily but take your work seriously.

4. **Be a Supporter of the Company:** If there is a softball team, join it. Become your company's target audience and share insight into what the company can do better.

5. **Organize Events:** Helm one event a year. It can be small, like an anniversary toast, or something big, like the Christmas party. Either way, it will get you noticed.

6. **Look Good:** It might ring of sexism, but there is some truth to the fact that attractive people get noticed, and in the long run they excel. If you look better than everyone else, you will be noticed.

7. **Reach Out:** Seek appropriate advice from your CEO. If she's just come back from a place you'd like to travel, pretend you are going and ask for suggestions.

8. **Support His Ideas Publicly:** There is a fine line between appreciation and asskissing. But you are fairly safe if you stick to loving his ideas, rather than loving *him*.

9. **Learn the Key to Bringing in and Maintaining Customers:** Find a secret or a cutting-edge tactic and use it to get your CEO's attention.

10. **Bring Cookies or Other Goodies:** If you have mad skills in the kitchen, show off in the lounge after work one day and invite the CEO.

Give Him a Night He'll Never Forget

1 **Follow the Treasure Trail:** Use your tongue on this aptly named trail of hair from the belly button to his penis with a gentle circling motion.

2 **Don't Forget the Ears:** Earlobes make for a veritable minefield of tantalizing nerve endings. And while you're there, whisper a few irresistible sweet nothings.

3 **Nipples (His, Not Yours):** We forget that male nipples can be as sensitive as ours. So take your time kissing, licking, and sucking in reciprocation.

4 **Kiss:** Slow, deep kisses are sometimes all your need to drive him wild.

5 **Tease:** Tie him up and take control. Just when he thinks he has you, pull away fast.

6 **Take It Off Slowly:** Let him look (but don't touch!) while you slowly remove your clothes, one inch of skin at a time. Then take his off—with your teeth.

7 **Get on Top:** When you're on top you're in control. Gyrate your hips slowly and lean in to let your breasts lightly touch his chest.

8 **Find His G-Spot:** Start by gently rubbing the area around his anus to stimulate it while you are having sex. When he is about to come, dip your finger inside and gently apply pressure to his prostate. Awkward though it sounds, it will be the best orgasm of his life.

9 **Lift the Gate:** Keep you panties on and tease him by gyrating against his erection. Then, just when neither of you can stand it, push aside the fabric at your crotch and let him in.

10 **Use Your Words:** The dirtier the better. Describe your lovemaking or tell him a dirty story based on a forbidden fantasy, like a threesome or an illicit affair.

Get Over Your Ex After It's Really Over

1 **Write a Dialogue:** Write out an imagined conversation someplace quiet when you are alone. Try to channel your ex and choose words you think he really would say.

2 **Simplify:** Try to form a one-sentence explanation for why your relationship ended. Miring yourself in complex details is a good way to drive yourself crazy.

3 **Look at It from His Side:** If you can't think of a good reason not to be with *him*, see if you can understand why he decided not to be with *you*. If nothing else, it might inform future relationships.

4 **Know What You Need Explained:** Try to determine exactly which ends still require tying up. If you can't resolve them for yourself, wait until time has passed and contact him for answers.

5 **Own Your Culpability:** Figure out your role in the breakup and offer the appropriate apologies.

6 **Figure Out What You Want:** Make a list of everything you want from a man and then go out and find him.

7 **Let Him Go Symbolically:** Burn up his pictures and mail back items of his that you still have. Remove him from your life as completely as you can.

8 **Take Him Off the Pedestal:** How much of your missing him is directed at the relationship, and how much is directed at the man? Maybe you miss him less than you miss the idea of him.

9 **Let Your Friends In:** They might be able to help you heal. Let them remind you why you are better off now.

10 **Forgive:** If you can get to a place where you accept that your ex is only human, you might find a way to forgive him and move on.

Play All Day at These Dream Jobs

1. **Ice Cream Flavor Developer:** You get to think things like, "I bet stuffing a piece of dark chocolate with fudge and then putting it in chocolate ice cream with a creamy caramel ribbon running throughout would be good," and then try it.

2. **Hollywood Stylist:** You get to shop for fabulous clothes with the money of very, very rich people who will look great in them no matter what.

3. **Doll Clothes Designer:** Someone makes Barbie dresses. Why not you?

4. **Celebrity Photographer:** Imagine, you, Brad Pitt, and nothing between you but the camera's lens.

5. **Tour Director in Fiji:** Greet the tourists and show them the very best places to lie around and do nothing while drinking cocktails . . . and get paid for it.

6. **Park Designer or Landscape Architect:** You get to choose the flowers and decide how many dead ends the garden maze will have.

7. **Master Sommelier at a Five-Star Restaurant:** Right now someone is tasting all kinds of amazing wines and spirits and very likely loving every second.

8. **Resort Caretaker:** People actually live at luxury hotels and resorts. While they probably don't get all the perks of the guests, they probably get quite a few roll-over perks, which, let's face it, doesn't suck.

9. **Water-Slide Tester for Resorts:** Your job is to make sure they are fun. The downside is that sometimes you might run into slide burn, but . . . no, still worth it.

10. **Chocolatier in Belgium:** You'd have to move to Belgium, but it would be delicious.

Travel Abroad Like a Local

① **Learn a Few Words in the Native Language:** You don't have to speak fluently, but knowing a few simple phrases of the language will endear you to the locals and help you figure things out.

② **Find the Expats:** Every city has some Anglophonic population living in its midst. Ask at your hotel where you can uncover them. Then pick their brains about what to do in town and how to avoid tourist scams.

③ **Be Deliberate:** Fear is in your mind. Stay calm. Ask "Can you please help?" in the native tongue while indicating any automated machines or maps you encounter. Panicking will only make you look like the tourist you are.

④ **Keep Your Voice Down:** You can always spot a tourist talking loudly and looking out of place. Respect the environment, and shhh.

⑤ **Be a Copy Cat:** Look around at the population and do what you can to look and act like them.

⑥ **Buy a Few Things to Wear:** A few locally bought pieces to add to your outfits will help you blend in.

⑦ **Match Your Sports Logos:** Make sure you are not wearing your Cleveland Indians T-shirt if you want to fit in. Find out what sports are played in town and then buy the corresponding attire.

⑧ **Open Your Mind:** Try the local food. No McDonald's for you!

⑨ **Ask Around:** Get your travel tips from locals, not tourist pamphlets.

⑩ **Visit Friends:** If a friend moves to a foreign place, make a point of visiting. Or solicit friends of friends in a pinch. Give them time to settle in, then let them show you the sights.

Keep Your Mechanic Honest: Learn How to Keep Up Your Car Yourself!

1 **Learn How to Change the Oil:** Not all oils are created equal. Check your owner's manual to know which kind your car takes. Drain it and replace it with clean oil. Use the dipstick to check the levels once a month.

2 **Learn How to Check the Tire Air Pressure:** The PSI, or pounds per square inch, tells you how much air your tires need. Check the manual so you know before you hit the pump.

3 **Learn about the Kind of Fuel You Need:** Does it really matter? Yes . . . and no. Gas burns more quickly or less quickly depending on the octane level. High-performance cars will see a difference, whereas cars that call for regular-grade gas will see no added benefit from higher octane.

4 **Learn What to Pay Attention to:** Oil changes, warranty information, and fuel levels. Know how old the plugs, brake pads, and filters are. And know when you last bought new tires.

5 **Learn How to Change a Tire:** Don't find yourself in a desperate situation if your tire needs sudden changing. Practice once in your driveway with someone who knows the ropes.

6 **Learn How to Listen:** If your car is tapping or clicking, a valve is likely sticking. A high-pitched squeal might indicate that a belt is slipping.

7 **Learn How to Read Your Dashboard:** Understand all the numbers and what they are for before you start your engine.

8 **Learn How to Add Fluids:** Lift up your hood and see where oil, windshield wiper fluid, and antifreeze/coolant go.

9 **Learn How to Jump a Battery:** Red is positive (a plus sign), black is negative (a minus sign). Attach the cables accordingly, and start your engine.

10 **Learn How to Select a Mechanic:** Mechanics often specialize in specific makes of cars. Find one that knows yours and build a relationship.

Buy a Bit of Nostalgia

(1) **An Old Bicycle:** Both decorative and functional, there is nothing like a cool old bike and an excellent outfit to keep you hip and on-trend. Who knew?

(2) **Record Player:** Music still sounds great on vinyl. Better yet, all the best music is still recorded on it and sold at small record stores around the country.

(3) **Roller Skates:** No need for inline skates; jump back to these '80s icons. Lace up a pair of white ones with the pink pompons for good measure.

(4) **Board Games:** Even though there is a new Clue game out there, nothing's better than playing with the Miss Scarlet you remember.

(5) **A Juke Box:** This old-fashioned technology can still be found. Even better, you can fill it with any songs you like.

(6) **Iron Skillets and Other Kitchenware:** A well-used iron skillet works better than new versions, as do many of the old gadgets used for cooking back in the day— as long as you keep them well-conditioned. And some of it just looks stylish hanging on your wall.

(7) **An Old Radio:** Put it on a shelf for decoration or have it rewired so you can run it on batteries and keep it handy to use during emergencies.

(8) **A Tiffany Lamp:** Sure, it might be pricey, but stained-glass lamps were a popular style. You can probably find something similar that doesn't have the name and is just as colorful and beautiful.

(9) **A Fan:** Make sure it is properly wired and then use it to make your house both breezy *and* stylish.

(10) **Old Toys:** You can find old train sets, dolls, and even games like marbles and pick-up sticks. They will take you back and make you feel great.

Say "I Love You" Without Saying Anything

1 **Touch:** A quick squeeze of his adorable butt cheek when he passes by or a hand on his arm while he is talking can remind him how much you love him in an instant.

2 **Make Yourself Available:** It's important to make sure that when you have free time, you attempt to plan at least some of it together.

3 **Once in a While, Stop Teasing:** Teasing is a great way to keep humor in a relationship. But letting him know that you take him seriously will remind him that you value him as well.

4 **Take Time to Notice:** Jot down moments in a journal when you notice you are especially proud of him. Then occasionally, remind him of those times.

5 **Wine and Dine Him:** Every now and then it's okay to treat him like a prince.

6 **Make It about Him Sometimes:** Once in a while do something together that isn't your favorite activity for the pleasure of making him happy.

7 **Check in on His Parents:** Provided you have met them, developing a personal relationship with his family shows how important he is to you.

8 **Do Some of His Chores:** You don't have to feel like a 1950s housewife for grabbing his pile of dirty clothes and tossing it in with your own when you have additional room.

9 **Pick Up the Slack:** The best part of being a couple is that you have a teammate. When your man is extra busy, it's okay to do more than your share.

10 **Be Romantic:** While he's in the shower, write "You're Sexy" in the steamed-up mirror or leave him a note on his pillow before you leave to go out of town.

Go Basic, Not Botox

1. **Get a Facial:** With the right products and a gentle facial massage your skin can go back to its glory days.

2. **Add Color:** An easy way to take years off your look is to brighten your hair color and skin tone as it begins to fade with age. A safe organic hair dye and bronzer are good bets.

3. **Try a Radiofrequency Treatment (Thermage):** This FDA-approved procedure claims to be a "mini facelift." The skin and muscles are heated to firm and energize them. Afterward, facial swelling is common and treated with painkillers.

4. **Employ a Masseuse:** Massage keeps your skin firm and helps to reshape your body.

5. **Go to Yoga:** Stretching and tightening your body with yoga is a great way to elongate your muscles and feel and look younger.

6. **Become a Picky Eater:** Avoid foods that cause bloating or breakouts. Try white-fish and nonstarchy vegetables. Cut out refined carbohydrates and saturated fats.

7. **Pull Your Hair Back:** A tight, high ponytail will achieve some of the effects of a facelift.

8. **Apply Makeup:** A carefully shaded shadow on the sides of your nose can elongate it if your nose is broad. Blush will elevate cheekbones and eye shadow can raise the brow bone. Learn makeup artists' tricks and skip the knife.

9. **Lose Weight:** You don't need to shrink to the size of an ingénue, but losing weight will keep you looking younger, longer.

10. **Give Your Face a Workout:** If your problem is loose skin, facial exercises won't help you. However, strengthening the muscles in your face will keep it taut, and gently massaging the skin will help it stay elastic.

Become a Hip-Hop Heavyweight

1 **Go Old School:** Start out with some of the historic tracks from bands like De La Soul and A Tribe Called Quest—these "conscious" rappers sang from the heart and are a good entry point to more challenging stuff.

2 **Rap *Is* Music:** Many bands play their own instruments and others sample great music that came before.

3 **Listen:** If the lyrics are too hard to digest, focus on the music that's in the beat. See if you can spot the classic '70s songs that are being sampled!

4 **It's Like Telling a Joke:** The best hip-hop is setting up for a "punch line." Focusing on that will help you start to see the humor and fun in many of the songs.

5 **Don't Mistake It for Poetry:** Analyzing the lyrics as you would a poem is like trying to taste a fine wine the way you taste a great piece of fruit. They're related but different.

6 **It Differs:** There's a surprisingly wide spectrum of artists and subgenres. If you don't like the first artist you hear, there are thousands more to choose from.

7 **Move to the Beat:** Some people find the repetition in the beat incredibly easy to move to. So don't just sit there.

8 **Be Impressed:** Imagine the artist is making it up off the cuff. Many of them do. It's an amazingly skillful art.

9 **Listen to the Story:** Some hip-hop lyrics are filled with profound stories. Listen past the swear words and you might love what you hear.

10 **Watch the Movies:** *Breakin'*, *8 Mile*, *Wild Style*, and *Krumped* are great glimpses into the world of hip-hop from varied perspectives that can help you build a foundation for understanding.

Trim the Fat from Your Resume

1 **A Short but Fascinating Account of Why You Should Get This Job:** No one will read it. Keep your resume short, legible, and concise.

2 **Your Expectations:** Especially if they are simplistic, obvious, or general. "Furthering your career" doesn't really mean anything, so don't say it.

3 **Typos:** Even though you are not trying to get a job as an editor, having a typo on your resume looks sloppy. Ask a friend—no, ask two friends—to read it over and check for grammar and spelling mistakes.

4 **Lies:** Yes, even white ones. If you didn't finish your PhD program, own it. If the process goes far enough, they'll figure it out anyway.

5 **Arrogance:** You are great. You know it. Your mom knows it. But if you try to make them know it via resume, they won't want to meet you, much less hire you.

6 **Dates:** It doesn't matter when you worked where. Lay out past jobs in the order that is most compelling and leave off dates. You can be more specific when they ask you direct questions.

7 **A Second Page:** And yes, that includes the other side of the paper. A resume is one page.

8 **Achievements That Aren't Really Achievements:** Winning the award for most punctual or best cheerleader is a better anecdote for an interview when you can sheepishly admit that it doesn't mean *that much*.

9 **Something Frilly:** Okay, maybe this doesn't apply to *your* resume, but some folks think that a floral border or bright-colored paper will jazz up their resume. It won't. Stick to a neutral color. Take it seriously so they take *you* seriously.

10 **Salary:** Just leave it until you meet to discuss it in person.

Just Dance . . .
Even If You Don't Know How

1. **Sway:** Begin just by swaying your shoulders back and forth. You don't even need to be in time with the music to do it successfully. Just look engaged.

2. **Don't Start on the Dance Floor:** Stay off the dance floor until you feel ready. It's okay to watch at first until you feel the vibe.

3. **Listen:** Close your eyes and see if you can find the beat. Try to tune out everything but the drum.

4. **Tap:** Once you hear the rhythm, see if you can tap it out with your hand. Then move the beat down to your foot. Hint—tapping with your heel accesses what is a stronger muscle for most people and is often more accurate when matching a beat.

5. **Practice in Front of a Mirror:** Watch better dancers and see if you can spot anything simple that they're doing that you might be able to copy.

6. **Loosen Up:** When the music comes up, let your muscles turn to jelly. Bend your knees, relax your hips, then begin to move gently to the beat. No spastic jerking.

7. **Use a Side Step:** Now it's time to get out there. You don't have to own the floor. Just join in. A simple side-to-side is all you need. Keep listening to the beat and match it.

8. **Pay Attention to Yourself:** Are you tightening up? Loosen up your shoulders and your knees.

9. **Don't Forget Your Hands:** Hands can be problematic on a dance floor. What do you do with them? Put them on your hips or clap them.

10. **Smile:** If you look like you're having fun, no one will care about the rest.

Hit the Easy Button for an Organized Life

1. **Bank Online:** Register your recurring bills with your bank's online banking service. Schedule weekly automatic withdrawals, as well. By converting everything into online statements you eliminate paper and streamline your financial chores.

2. **Clean Up Your Kitchen:** Discard kitchen appliances you haven't used more than twice in the last year and eliminate duplicates. No one needs a hand blender *and* a freestanding one. When you get a new mug, get rid of an old mug, etc.

3. **Donate Your Clothes:** Line up your hanging clothes facing the same direction. Then, all year, anytime you wear something, put it back hanging the opposite way. Anything still facing the original direction goes to charity.

4. **Put Valuable Items in a Safe:** Keep warranties, important receipts, titles, and any valuable jewelry safe and organized.

5. **Hire an Accountant:** At tax time, don't do it yourself. An accountant can clarify your money situation and help to provide financial organization.

6. **Clean Up Your Bookshelf:** Keep ten books that are sentimental and any you are currently reading. Keep ten more that you plan to read. Discard the rest.

7. **Go Through Your Old Letters:** Discard any cards or letters that aren't from your parents, children, or spouse, including the witty holiday and birthday cards.

8. **Change Your Internal Clock:** When scheduling your day, allow a thirty-minute buffer between appointments, especially if you're often late. You'll feel better organized and more sane.

9. **Empty Your Wallet:** Discard *all* receipts and unused credit and business cards immediately, and save them someplace better in case you need them at a later date.

10. **Embrace Organizational Technology:** Buy a P-touch or software for your computer and label all of your files clearly. It is so satisfying and, while it doesn't make you organized, it does demonstrate that organization is possible.

Relearn the Lessons Kids Already Know

1 ***The Lorax* (Dr. Seuss):** This story gently teaches about environmentalism and living a life respectful to the planet, and it is also brilliantly funny.

2 ***The Big Orange Splot* (D. Manus Pinkwater):** Mr. Plumbean lives on a "very neat street," until a can of bright orange paint lands on his roof. He creates the house of his dreams, igniting a chain reaction that turns the very neat street into a canvas for self-expression.

3 ***Alexander and the Terrible, Horrible, No Good, Very Bad Day* (Judith Viorst):** Alexander's day is full of tragedy, but ultimately he discovers his mama is right: we all just need to hang on 'til tomorrow.

4 ***The Giving Tree* (Shel Silverstein):** This loving book about generosity is full of useful adult lessons.

5 ***Charlotte's Web* (E. B. White):** This tremendous story about change and loss is tempered by a sweetly powerful story of friendship.

6 ***Oh the Places You'll Go!* (Dr. Seuss):** This tale both encourages and warns the reader that while the future is bright, no life comes without its share of bumps in the road.

7 ***Corduroy* (Don Freeman):** Even a bear missing a button needs someone to love him. In fact, it is our flaws that make us the most lovable.

8 ***The Ugly Duckling* (Hans Christian Andersen):** We all have beauty within us and the ability to transform into our best, truest, and most beautiful selves.

9 ***Harold and the Purple Crayon* (Crockett Johnson):** We all create our own lives, so make your as creative as possible, even if you only have a purple crayon.

10 ***Free to Be . . . You and Me* (Marlo Thomas and Friends):** The title says it all.

Give Back and Make It Count

1 **Find Out Who's in Need:** The woman who sleeps at the bus station, a friend who just lost a job, your cousin with the degenerative illness? Noticing need is how you begin.

2 **Pick One:** You could respond to any of the million envelopes you get in the mail and send some much-needed money. Or choose something a little more personal.

3 **Find Your Passion:** Do you love animals? Kids? Want to cure cancer? There are lots of organizations to choose from. Narrow it down to local, national, or international to make the choice easier.

4 **Ask Your Friends:** You have at least one friend who spends all of her time doing charity events or projects. Ask her about the organization she loves and what its needs are.

5 **Donate:** Besides money, many charities need household goods, clothes, diapers, etc. Choose any organization serving the homeless, abused, or otherwise in-need.

6 **Go with God:** Your congregation needs to keep the lights on and the clergy on staff. They also know of families in need, homebound seniors, and others who could use your generosity.

7 **Be Selfless:** There's nothing wrong with anonymous giving. The money is appreciated and spent whether your name is attached or not.

8 **Get Active:** If your charity of choice is struggling to make ends meet, help out with a fundraiser. Engage in a letter-writing campaign, a dinner, a gala, or even a car wash. Just be sure to plan it *with* the charity, so it is involved and on board.

9 **Talk about It:** Once you find your charity, share the love. Talk about it with your friends and get them to give!

10 **Increase Each Year:** Continue to give, increasing your gift to account for inflation and increased programming and services.

Halloween Costumes
That Are Treats, Not Tricks

1 **Alice in Wonderland:** You can't go wrong with the protagonist of this beloved American tale. Run away with Alice to Wonderland in her classic blue dress, long blonde hair, and white knee socks.

2 **Wheaties Box:** Imagine . . . *you* as a champion. Poke your head through a board painted to look like a box of Wheaties. Finally . . . you're famous!

3 **Elizabeth Swann:** Get your guy to don dreds and go as Captain Jack, while you go as the tough but lovely Elizabeth Swann from Disney's *Pirates of the Caribbean.*

4 **Sandy from *Grease*:** Go as Sandy or as a whole gang of the *Grease* pink ladies with your girls. Costumes from any era—specifically the '50s—are always an easy hit.

5 **Jessie from *Toy Story*:** Yehaww! Braids, a cowboy hat, and a pair of chaps are all you need to go as this awesome spitfire.

6 **Sports Characters:** Who didn't want to be or date a high school cheerleader? If you aren't so sporty, wearing a soccer jersey, shorts, and knee-high socks over shin guards will be both funny and cute.

7 **Super Heroes:** Wonder Woman is a classic, as is Cat Woman. But what about the girl Wonder Twin (Jayna) or Rogue and Storm from *X-Men*?

8 **Classic Characters:** Be a ghost or a witch and see how many children you can scare!

9 ***Star Trek*:** Dress everyone in your family in a different color "Trekkie" shirt! Or make your own by ironing on the logo to shirts you already have. Live long and prosper.

10 **A Goddess—Greek, Hindu, or Otherwise:** From Athena to Devi (for whom you could make extra arms out of nude stockings stuffed with cotton), these women were all-powerful, beautiful, and recognizable—the Halloween costume trifecta.

Settle Your Stomach

1 **Stay Still:** If you are experiencing motion sickness, stop moving for a minute and take deep breaths.

2 **Apply Pressure:** Pressure points on your wrists and beside your ears can help stop nausea.

3 **Eat Saltines:** Pregnant women swear by them. They will raise your blood sugar, which might be the problem.

4 **Suck on Ginger Candies:** Actually anything ginger (tea, ale, etc.) will ease a jostled belly.

5 **Drink Mint Tea:** Many people believe drinking a warm mint tea after meals will quiet nausea and other digestive ailments.

6 **Use Willpower:** Turn your thoughts to something else and change the way you feel. It can be done if you set your mind to it.

7 **Apply Pressure:** Have a partner place a hand on your stomach, or hug a pillow to it.

8 **Go Outside:** Sometimes a distraction is all you need. Open a window if you are in a car, or if you can, take a walk in some fresh air.

9 **Rule Out Allergies:** If you find you are sometimes sick after meals, consider that what you are eating might be causing it.

10 **Keep Food Simple:** Broths, bread, and noodles are easy foods for your body to digest. Keep your meals simple until you are feeling better.

Talk to Anyone, Anytime, Anywhere

1. **Be Friendly:** Smile casually but with a friendly, approachable air.

2. **Assess the Situation:** What do you have in common? Are you together at an airport? In line at the grocery store? Think of an opening line that you both can relate to.

3. **Start with a Statement:** Make an observation and consider the reaction. A quiet or nonexistent response might signal that the person doesn't feel like chatting.

4. **Ask a Question:** Keep it light. If you are traveling, you might ask where he's heading, or while waiting in a line, ask how she is doing on time.

5. **Look for Cues:** In a checkout line, ask about a product she is buying. If she is working or reading, ask what it's about.

6. **Prepare Banter:** Think of questions in advance so the next time you are in a situation in which you want to talk to someone you will know what to say.

7. **Ask, "How Are You?":** A simple, "Hey, how's it going?" is a good lead-in to a conversation. Try it the next time you're out.

8. **Find an Easy Topic:** Most people have mutually shared experiences, like weather, culture, and news. Find something about one of those to bring up and discuss.

9. **Dig a Little:** After there is some flow to your conversation it's okay to let the questions become more personal. Best is to have a similar personal story to share that might inspire a little more depth to his story.

10. **Practice:** Talking to people does not come naturally to everyone. The next time you go out, say hello to someone you pass. Over time it gets less scary.

Get Rid of a Zit, Fast

1   **Apply Toothpaste:** A dab of toothpaste on the zit overnight will dry it out by morning.

2   **Apply Aspirin:** Crush up one aspirin and add enough water to make a paste. Apply to affected areas for ten minutes and then wash off.

3   **Apply Alcohol:** Not the drinking kind, the rubbing kind. Wet a cotton ball and pat the affected area to dry it out and reduce swelling.

4   **Floss It:** Wash the area, then very gently roll a piece of dental floss back and forth over it until the pus comes out. Immediately dab with rubbing alcohol.

5   **Ice It:** An ice cube is an easy way to reduce the swelling and minimize redness. Wrap in a clean towel and press to the pimple.

6   **Moisturize It:** If skin is dry and flaky, it will clog pores. Use a water-based moisturizer to make sure your skin is hydrated.

7   **Use an Eggshell:** To decrease swelling and redness, empty an egg and try to remove the delicate white skin against shell. Place this on your zit to decrease swelling and minimize redness.

8   **Use a Hot Compress:** Dampen a washcloth with warm water. Hold it to the aggravated area, rewarming the washcloth as needed. This will pull the infection forward.

9   **Don't Pop It:** Popping your zits leaves scarring and will further irritate the area. Steer clear of this very bad approach.

10   **Wash Your Face and Hands:** Avoid getting zits by keeping your face clean, only touching your face with clean hands, and using the hands-free feature on your phone to keep the skin from contact with it.

Fall in Love for the Long Haul

1 **Fall in Love . . . with Yourself:** Start right now. Quit worrying about how he feels about you, and start feeling the love for yourself.

2 **Change Your Outlook:** Just because all your other relationships to this point have ended doesn't mean this one will. So be positive.

3 **Care Less:** Let's just say it—nagging never helped a woman get closer to her man. So ease up on him and let him live his life.

4 **Set Limits:** On the other hand, when you are in a new relationship it is important to exhibit a modicum of self-respect by letting him know exactly how far he can go.

5 **Remember the Last Time You Were Wanted:** If you can recall the last guy who would have done anything for you, you can recall what you did to earn it. Then mimic those moves.

6 **Tease Him:** Both in the bedroom and out, make sure that you give just enough and then pull it back. Soon he will be breathless with longing.

7 **Stop Doing Everything You Have Already Tried:** Clearly, if it hasn't worked up to now, it isn't working. So retool your approach and see if a new path doesn't land the desired outcome.

8 **Let Him Go:** There are a lot of old expressions that back this one up, but the thing to remember is that sometimes not having you is the best way to convince him to want to have you.

9 **Create a Happy Future Today:** Rather than using your words to relay how great your lives *will be* together, just make your lives great *now*.

10 **Know When You're Fighting a Losing Battle:** If your guy is young or is surrounded by single friends, or if he's never committed to anything beyond a childhood pet hamster, maybe you have to take the hint and throw in the towel.

Bring the Best for Brunch

① **Quiche:** Use a savory piecrust and mix eggs with your favorite quiche fillings. Bacon and tomato, spinach and cheddar, or mushroom, ricotta, and sausage are all popular options.

② **Frittata:** Basically quiche minus the piecrust—mix cheese and vegetables with beaten eggs and bread crumbs. Bake until cooked through and brown under the broiler.

③ **Salmon Benedict:** Poach eggs by boiling water and rice vinegar (to bind the egg.) Place them over toasted English muffins topped with smoked salmon. Add hollandaise sauce to taste.

④ **Brie-Stuffed Pancakes with Berries:** Pour the pancake batter, then add sliced brie and fresh berries. Flip to brown and top with maple syrup.

⑤ **Brioche or Challah French Toast:** Make a wash with egg, cream, cinnamon, and vanilla. Let infuse overnight in the refrigerator. Dip a thick-cut slice of bread in the wash and fry in butter.

⑥ **French Toast Bread Pudding:** Use the same brioche recipe but cut up a loaf of bread and coat it in the egg wash, leaving it overnight in the refrigerator. In the morning, bake it at 350°F until it's crispy.

⑦ **Homemade Granola:** Make granola, then offer your guests yogurt, cream, milk, or vanilla ice cream along with fresh fruit to prepare their own.

⑧ **Corned Beef Hash:** Use thick-cut corned beef, onions, and diced potatoes. Fry together until cooked and top with poached eggs.

⑨ **Chilaquiles:** Put leftover chicken over crispy tortilla strips. Make a chili sauce, heat, and pour over top. Add a fried egg.

⑩ **Bloody Mary and Mimosas:** Offer your guests virgin or regular bloody marys and mimosas (substitute club soda for booze in both as desired).

Turn Him from Messy to Tidy

1. **Sit Him Down:** If you're just on different pages about housework, the first step to closing the gap is to discuss it without rancor.

2. **Teach Him:** Some people just didn't grow up with the kind of parents that you did and don't know how to wash dishes. So, without being snotty about it, show him the ropes.

3. **Reward Him:** Every time he does scour the toilet, sidle up to him with a heartfelt thank-you. Just make sure he knows what your "gratitude" is for.

4. **Remind Him:** His mess might just be a simple case of forgetfulness. A reminder might be all it takes.

5. **Barter with Him:** Trade him the remote for doing the laundry. Sexual favors and other chores also work.

6. **Ply Him with Statistics:** Remind him that men who help with housework tend to be 30 percent more virile than men who don't.

7. **Wait It Out:** Everyone has a different threshold for messiness. Yours just might be lower. See how long it takes before he wonders where his favorite sweater is buried.

8. **Set Up a Chore Wheel:** Make it fun and silly—don't take it too seriously. But make it clear what each person's weekly chores are by turning the wheel to line up daily chores with each of your names.

9. **Add It Up:** Together, write up lists of all the things each of you does around the house. Perhaps he *is* doing the laundry, just not exactly when you want him to. Seeing it on paper can help you (and him) see clearly who is pulling the bulk of the weight.

10. **Let It Go:** Just because the clutter bothers you doesn't mean it bothers him. It might be that you will do a little more of the housework, simply because you *notice* it. Don't turn it into anything. Just wash the dishes.

Keep Kids Confident

1 **Be More Confident Yourself:** Children are wonderful mimics. Practice what you hope to teach.

2 **Offer Tools:** If a child is disappointed she doesn't have a certain skill, do what you can within reason to help her acquire it.

3 **Encourage Natural Ability:** If you see some area in which a child naturally flourishes, point it out to him. See if he'd like to do more to make it even better.

4 **Show Compassion:** If she fails, let her know that it takes a brave person to do what she loves even if she has to work harder than others to achieve it.

5 **Be Realistic:** We all have our limits and limitations. Don't be afraid to help your child recognize his while also reminding him of where he excels.

6 **Show Up:** Kids notice when you aren't there, especially for the big stuff. No matter how busy you are, no matter what you have to do, make it a point to be there.

7 **Speak to Her with Respect:** Address children by name and be sure that your tone reflects what you believe her to be a capable of as a human being.

8 **Help Him:** Don't make life too easy for him. Life is not easy. He must learn to work hard and follow through with what he begins.

9 **Allow for Freedom:** Let a child test her boundaries. Do not put her in a bubble. Sometimes she will fall and fail. Help her regroup and move on.

10 **Hold Him Accountable:** Make him responsible to the household in which he lives. Reward him when he finishes chores. Have consequences when he doesn't.

Have Fun on a Long Flight

1. **Kiss Ass:** Bring an extra souvenir or bottle of wine onto the plane with you. Tell the flight attendant you have one too many and offer the extra to her. Be coy and then wait for that surplus first-class dinner, extra blanket, or even an upgrade!

2. **Get an Upgrade:** Outline any recent bad experiences you've had with the airline in a calm and friendly tone. Sometimes they will grant an upgrade to smooth things over. Also check for special promotions when you purchase your ticket.

3. **Stay Entertained:** Bring an iPod, a laptop, games, books, magazines, knitting, anything that will help you zone out for some period of your journey.

4. **Stretch:** While seated, make sure you remind yourself to stretch and flex your muscles. Get up a few times and walk the length of the plane.

5. **Hydrate:** Avoid alcohol and caffeine and do what you can to keep your body well hydrated. If you will end up in a new time zone, your tomorrow self will thank you.

6. **Make a Friend:** Chat with people. This is your chance to be anonymous. Interesting encounters often come with freedom like that.

7. **Close Your Eyes:** Whether or not you are a good plane sleeper, spend at least one hour of the flight with your eyes closed. It will refresh you.

8. **Schedule Yourself:** This is particularly important if you are traveling with kids. Know what you will do during each thirty- to sixty-minute block of time.

9. **Prepare for Comfort:** Bring a travel pillow and a sweater. Then, before you land, brush your teeth and wash your face.

10. **Bring Snacks:** No matter how long your flight is, it's *always* a good idea to have your own food in case you don't like what is served or it's too pricey.

What to Watch to Scare Yourself Silly

1. **The Ring (2002):** A week after watching the video, you die. That's the premise of the movie, and it's a pretty scary one.

2. **The Strangers (2008):** A couple + a dark, remote cabin + a band of crazy assailants trying to kill them.

3. **The Shining (1980):** Jack Nicholson at his creepy best makes your date's shoulder an imperative while "watching" this horror classic.

4. **Super 8 (2011):** J. J. Abrams creates a ton of suspense by keeping this alien out of frame until the very (scary) end.

5. **Psycho (1960):** Take a lovely, paranoid ingénue and put her in the hotel of a creepy man obsessed with his dead mother and cover your eyes.

6. **Poltergeist (1982):** Here you have a happy family and a ghostly kidnapper in the television.

7. **Paranormal Activity and Paranormal Activity 2 (2007 and 2010):** There is nothing like never revealing what's just around a corner or behind a door to scare the bejesus out of a girl. These movies have mastered this sadistic "art."

8. **Open Water (2003):** Two tourists left by their tour boat in shark-infested waters for days, or in the case of the movie, seventy-nine minutes. Enough said.

9. **The Mist (2007):** Stephen King invented this world where bloodthirsty monsters can't be seen through the fog.

10. **Aliens (1986):** A gritty Sigourney Weaver goes back to the terrifying planet where everything went awry in this suspense-filled sequel to 1979's *Alien*.

Pull Together a Last-Minute Party

1 **Assess What You Have:** Where did you stick the plastic cups from last summer's barbecue? How many tortilla chips are left? Where's the Halloween candy? Pour it all into bowls and set out the finger foods you have.

2 **Ask People to Pick Things Up:** Have guests bring booze or side dishes. In a pinch, run to a corner store and grab them yourself. If they only carry generic brands, decant the wine, prepare the cocktails, and serve the beer in pitchers.

3 **Tidy, Don't Clean:** You don't have time. Put anything you don't have time to put away in a room or closet with a door you can close. Then close it.

4 **Use the Old Stuff:** Prepare a pot of coffee. Make alcoholic punch with the opened bottles in your cabinet, and use up the rest of the sherbet in the freezer by throwing it on top.

5 **Excuse Yourself:** If necessary, start the guests with the basics and then run out for reinforcements.

6 **Utilize Delivery:** Order whatever you can, from dinner to drinks.

7 **Invite a Good Friend:** If, for example, your husband is bringing a client over at the last minute, ask a friend to run out and grab some wine and pick up an order. It might be nice, however, if you also ask your friend to stay.

8 **Prioritize:** Do you really need a shower? Will a washcloth and the sink do the trick? Only do things that you absolutely have to.

9 **Set the Mood:** A party only requires nice company, good music, something to eat, something to drink, and appropriate lighting. Get each of those checked off your list and the rest is gravy.

10 **Enjoy It:** Have a ball. You've earned it.

Get Yourself Noticed

1. **Host:** Host either your own event or someone else's. It will get *you* noticed as well as anything you are promoting.

2. **Start a Blog:** Writing a blog about something that interests you or something you know a lot about is a great way to put your voice out there and get feedback.

3. **Build an Audience:** Use social networking to begin. Let people know when you've done something newsworthy.

4. **Keep on Plugging:** Don't just post once. Keep posting. Try to do so in the same place each time. Eventually someone will take notice.

5. **Be a Guest on Someone's Website:** Write to people with websites, blogs, and other public information forums with a suggestion for a guest piece. See if someone will feature you.

6. **Review Something:** Write down what you think of a new movie, restaurant, or book. Then post it yourself on a site like Yelp, or ask someone to post it for you.

7. **Have Something Reviewed:** Ask a friend or acquaintance with a large following on Facebook or Twitter to review something you've written or created.

8. **Write a Press Release and Release It:** Write up a press release and send it out to marketing and press agents.

9. **Ask for Feedback:** Send a direct e-mail or call someone and ask him to give you feedback. One voice might be all you need to get the ball rolling.

10. **Advertise:** Take out an ad about yourself, your skill, or your product.

Take a Walk Through History

① **Owen Lovejoy House (Princeton, Illinois):** This depot on the Underground Railroad still stands and can be visited. Referencing this homestead, slaves referred to their journey north to freedom as "riding the Lovejoy line."

② **Washington Square Park (New York City):** The original potter's field, there were more than 100,000 people buried there. New York's last public gallows stood where the arch stands today.

③ **Winchester Mystery House (San Jose, California):** Built by the wife of the Winchester Rifle empire, she believed it full of the ghosts of people shot by her husband's rifles, who could only be satisfied by continual, disorganized construction.

④ **Titanic Docking Point (New York City):** Driving down the Westside Highway you can see the ghostly remnant of an iron dock, formerly of the White Star Line, where the *Titanic* would have arrived.

⑤ **Ah-Tah-Thi-Ki (Clewiston, Florida):** This museum, whose name translates to "A Place to Learn," teaches about the Seminole Indians, the only tribe that signed a peace treaty with the U.S.

⑥ **Taliesin (Spring Green, Wisconsin):** The summer home Frank Lloyd Wright built for his mistress. She and her children were murdered in a fire on premises upon its completion. It was later restored.

⑦ **League Park (Cleveland, Ohio):** You'd never know it, but part of one of the great neighborhood baseball parks still exists—the ticket area at the corner of E. 66th and Lexington.

⑧ **The Freedom Trail (Boston):** Follow the red line through downtown Boston and explore some of America's earliest days.

⑨ **Taos Pueblo (Taos, New Mexico):** Thought to be one of the oldest continually inhabited residences in the world, built between 1000 and 1450 A.D.

⑩ **C. A. Nothnagle Log House (Gibbson, New Jersey):** The oldest log house in America that you can still visit.

Plan a Day at an Art Museum

1 **Consider Your Footwear:** Art museums tend to require quite a bit of walking. Not only that, but when you stop to look, there will also be standing. No need to have sore feet.

2 **Have an Open Mind:** Art is subjective. You may not like everything you see, but you might appreciate technique and materials.

3 **Read the Descriptions:** There is a lot to learn—artist's name, date of the work, media used (paper, oils, acrylic, stone, etc.), and details of what is going on in the piece.

4 **Splurge on the Headphones:** Besides having the voice of a celebrity playing in your ears, you learn the real scoop about items on display.

5 **Check out the Gift Shop:** Stop in before or after seeing the exhibits. The gift shop is a great place to find a way to remember what you saw . . . and share it!

6 **Ask the Docent or Go on a Tour:** Museum staff love talking about art, and it's what they're there for.

7 **Check the Schedule:** Before you go, look online or call ahead. Exhibits change regularly, or close for cleaning or restoration. Many art museums close on Mondays, too. Better to check first than be disappointed.

8 **Bring a Friend:** You can discuss what you're seeing and learn what she knows. Or, you can simply marvel together over how *that* got into a museum.

9 **Enjoy the Peace:** Art museums are often havens of stillness and quiet in an otherwise hectic world. Embrace the silence.

10 **Go to the Café:** Most art museums have places where guests can eat surrounded by art. Enjoy coffee and refreshments among the statues and pretend it's your own private sculpture garden.

Love a Long-Distance Relationship

1 **Embrace Technology:** Upgrade your technology so that you are always up to date on the best and easiest ways to stay in touch. Gems like Skype and picture phones make long-distance dating practically easy!

2 **Be Open:** Obviously your relationship is challenged by the fact that you don't get to see each other all the time. Be sure to prioritize openness and honesty.

3 **Be Available:** Answer each other's calls when possible and respond in a timely manner to e-mails and texts to protect each other from insecurity and doubt.

4 **Always Have a Plan:** At the end of every visit, have the next visit lined up. Occasionally plan more than one ahead if possible.

5 **Enjoy the Perks:** Love that you have your life in one place and that his is elsewhere. Embrace that you get to live in two cities.

6 **Be a Good Traveler:** Keep a mini wardrobe and the basics at his place so that you need only take the bare minimum on flights, in the car, or on the train.

7 **Explain It:** Tell your friends it's like dating a modern-day cowboy. He leaves and then he comes home. It sounds much hotter that way.

8 **Be Fair:** Split your time evenly between your two homes so that neither feels more put out than the other.

9 **Have a "Fight" System:** Since your time together is so precious, don't waste it fighting. Agree to weekly phone check-ins, during which frustrations may be raised. Keep in-person fights short and concise.

10 **Rejoice:** It isn't like you have to hitch up a horse and ride for days. The modern world is made for this kind of lifestyle. Enjoy it.

Say Goodbye with Style

1 **Great Wishes:** This modified version of "Best wishes" or "Warmest wishes" cuts back on the schmaltz by wishing them something that's attainable.

2 **Warmest Regards:** You somehow seem like a good person with this signoff, someone the recipient would like to meet for a scone and coffee.

3 **Best:** A brief end to a quick note or off-handed response, this one works as a casual but professional way to end things.

4 **Thanks in Advance:** If you just asked for something that you're pretty sure you'll get, this is a good signoff. If there is some question, however, this might read as pushy.

5 **Thanks Again:** If you just wrote a thank-you, a totally appropriate way to end it is by restating your gratitude.

6 **Respectfully or with Respect:** This one is especially good after you have given someone a critique of some sort. It reminds everyone involved that it came from a place of professionalism and respect.

7 **You're the Best:** Careful with this one. It's a little shallow and might read as flip. But if you feel you can pull it off, it can be meaningful at the end of a thank-you.

8 **Cheers:** This is both polite and charming in that old world sort of way.

9 **My Thanks for Your Time:** This one is great for someone you've never met. It is polite, simple, and honest.

10 **Be Original:** End your note with a quick, "I'll see you at the meeting," or "Hope all remains well with your family," or some other indicator that you have an ongoing relationship with the recipient.

Plan a $20 Date Night

1 **Make Dinner:** You'd be surprised how many fresh ingredients you can get for under twenty bucks. Stick to vegetarian food and you'll save some money for candles.

2 **Go to a High School Football Game:** Remember how great it was when you were sixteen? The best part is that it is almost always free. Eat a hot dog for dinner and get ice cream before heading home.

3 **Have an '80s Night:** What's great about this is that you can go out dressed accordingly. Then hit a roller-skating rink or an arcade.

4 **Gallery Hop:** Some cities have special nights when stores in a gallery district stay open late. They are usually free, and some even offer free glasses of wine and snacks.

5 **Make It a Morning Date:** Meet in the morning and go to a flea market or to garage sales. Then have lunch, which is always less expensive than dinner.

6 **Attend Theater in the Park:** In the summertime, many theater groups use parks as their venues, and nearly all of them are free. Bring a blanket and a bottle of wine.

7 **Go to a Book Reading:** See what's going on at local bookstores. Readings are almost always free and if you like what you hear, maybe you and your date can split the cost of a book, have it signed to you both, and read it aloud together on your next date night.

8 **Go on a Night Hike:** Find a park that stays open after sundown. Then, using head lamps or flashlights, carefully pick your way down a trail into the spooky darkness.

9 **Test-Drive:** Go to a dealership that has your dream car and test-drive it. Then go to a dealership that has *his* favorite car and test-drive that.

10 **Go to a Fair:** County fairgrounds have events all year round. Found out what's going on at yours.

Don't Work so Hard: Organize Your Desk

1. **Take It Out:** Put everything in your desk out in the open so that you can see it.

2. **Clean:** Using a damp cloth and a wood polish, clean up the entire desk, inside and out. Also dust your computer and clean your keyboard.

3. **Fix the Spiders:** Are there cables all twisted up under the desk? Get them organized by binding with a plastic tie.

4. **Separate:** Put things in piles to be filed, to be moved to another location, or set aside. Leave yourself with only the items to be put away.

5. **Make Lists:** Put all the phone numbers you use regularly in a file on your desktop or on a note on the wall. Do the same with any info you find yourself regularly looking up.

6. **Sort Your Mail:** When mail comes in, sort it immediately. Keep pertinent information in a "USPS" folder on your computer desktop and recycle the actual item.

7. **Transcribe and Throw Away:** Any general notes jotted on small pieces of paper should be compiled into one file on your computer desktop. Then throw out their physical counterparts. Organize phone numbers or other contact information in a virtual or single actual contact list.

8. **Make Room:** Hang a shelf above your desk for notebooks and pertinent reading materials and reference books you'd like to keep on hand. Hang a second shelf for a tray for important papers.

9. **Reset the Stage:** Put supplies together in one drawer, files in another, and invoices or receipts in a third.

10. **Come Up with a System:** Now that everything is put away and cleaned up, decide how you will keep it this way. Perhaps at the end of any workday you will put everything where it belongs.

Easy Moves for a Hot Body

1. **Do Crunches:** Lie on your back with your hands supporting your neck. Pull your knees and shoulders toward each other while contracting your ab muscles.

2. **Lift Weights:** You can use bricks or unopened water bottles if you don't have weights. Stand with your feet together and arms at your sides holding the weights. Raise arms to shoulder height at your sides and then out in front of you. Repeat.

3. **Hold Your Body Weight:** If you can't do a pushup, simply lie on your stomach and push yourself up as high as you can and hold it. Do several times a day. Don't hyperextend your arms.

4. **Do Cardio:** Jump rope or do jumping jacks in your living room 50–100 times per day.

5. **Side Plank:** Lie on your side. Place your forearm so that you are positioned over your elbow at a 90-degree angle. Using your other hand as a guide on the floor in front of you, raise your hips and straighten your arm so that your body makes a straight line to your toes. Repeat.

6. **Get a Workout:** Buy a stationary bike or a rowing machine and work out in your living room.

7. **Do Standing Pushups:** Place your hands shoulder-width apart against a clean wall. Bend your elbows and tighten your core. Hold yourself against the wall for five breaths and then push yourself back to standing. Repeat.

8. **Squat:** Stand between two chairs if you require a little extra balance and then raise and lower your body at the knees and waist. Use your muscles to lift you back to standing. Start with 50–100 per day and add one additional every day.

9. **"Swim":** Lie on your belly. On an inhale, lift your legs, arms, and head. Do ten front strokes while kicking your feet, then relax. Repeat five times.

10. **Do Leg Lowering:** Lie on your back. Maintaining a relaxed upper body (especially back and neck), raise your legs together, then lower them as you count out ten seconds. Repeat ten times, adding a second each time you lower them.

Date a Much Younger Man (Without Feeling Like His Mom)

1. **Be Young:** No matter how old you are, this is one time it's okay to "act your shoe size." You might find it's a lot of fun.

2. **Don't Act Like His Mother:** Although the temptation might be there, if you don't want to feel like his mom, don't act like one.

3. **Don't Dress "Young," Dress Well:** Don't dress young if you think it means dressing ridiculously. Instead make sure you look good in your clothes and that they suit you.

4. **Play to His Strengths:** A younger guy might be intimidated by an older woman, so make sure you put him in situations where he feels confident, and focus on things he knows.

5. **Enjoy Him Exactly as He Is:** Don't take on your younger man as a "project," no matter how tempting it might be.

6. **Know His Cultural References:** While it's okay to share some of the music and movies you like, it isn't a bad idea for you to learn about some he likes as well.

7. **Let Him Wine and Dine You:** He is still the man and you are still the woman. It's okay to act like it.

8. **Allow Yourself to Have a Fling:** Some younger guys might be with you for the experience of it and not for the long term. If that's okay with you, enjoy it.

9. **Impart an Education:** Women everywhere will thank you if you leave your young man better than when you found him. Show him how to treat a *real* woman.

10. **Let the Insults Roll Off:** Some people might be critical of your relationship. So what? Don't let it get to you—your reaction could come off as desperate or overly defensive.

Ace an Interview

1 **Research:** Know a bit about the company and the plans for the department in which you'd be working. Ask for clarification and make insightful comments about the direction you see things going.

2 **Offer Practical Examples:** Have a few ideas prepared about your plans once you land the position. Would you restructure things? If so, how? Will you implement helpful tools? If so, what? Make it easy to really imagine your filling the role.

3 **Practice:** Ask a few friends to sit down with you for a practice interview and for a full critique afterward.

4 **Be Prompt:** Arrive fifteen minutes early and give yourself some time to calm down and mentally prepare before walking in.

5 **Be Prepared:** Know with whom you are meeting and for what position you will be interviewing.

6 **Know the Basics:** A lot of candidates make the mistake of knowing several big details about a company without knowing the basics, like store hours or the name of the CEO.

7 **Present Your Best Self:** Interviewers say it isn't uncommon for a candidate to lose a job before she opens her mouth. Dress the part and appear calm, warm, and in control.

8 **Be Enthusiastic:** It's okay if they think you want the job. You don't have to play the cool card. In fact, you will up your chances if you allow yourself some level of exuberant interest in the job.

9 **Prepare Stories:** Keep them concise but entertaining and make sure they illustrate the point that you are capable and well suited to the position.

10 **Use Notes and Take Notes:** Treat the interview like it's your first day. Look like you are preparing to get started. By the same token, you can use your notes to jog your own memory if you find your nerves getting the best of you.

Make It a Perfect First Date

1 **Go Someplace Memorable:** Research to find an unusual destination. Even if you've lived in a place your whole life, you might be surprised about a few places you never thought to go.

2 **Put Your Date First:** If you are planning the date, try to choose something your date will enjoy. If he's mentioned that he plays fantasy baseball, go to a game. But if he seems like the kind of guy who likes eating, for heaven's sake, don't go hiking!

3 **Keep It Public:** Go on your first date in a group or at least make sure you are out and about where you are both comfortable and the sexual pressure stays at a minimum.

4 **Don't Overspend:** Try not to choose an activity that costs too much. One or both of you might be distracted by the costs.

5 **Don't Overshare:** Also, keep your tales of woe to a minimum. This is a first date. Breezy is best.

6 **Give Yourself Time to Prepare:** If you had fun getting ready, even if the date is miserable, at least it wasn't a total wash.

7 **Lower Your Expectations:** Don't go in asking yourself if this is the future father of your children. Just ask yourself if he is your future second date.

8 **Pay . . . or Don't:** Just don't let it ruin your date. If it seems appropriate to pay, then pay. If he offers to pay, let him and be gracious.

9 **To Kiss or Not to Kiss:** Let him know early in the date if you don't kiss on a first date. This will remove any future awkwardness.

10 **Let It End:** At the end of the date, go home. It's that simple.

Plan an Extreme Adventure Weekend

1 **Zip-Line:** Find a nearby zip line or ropes course. Climbing and flying through the trees is not something you do every day. And as long as you are properly supervised, you don't need time to learn how.

2 **Skydive:** First-timers need to jump tandem with an experienced skydiver in charge of pulling the parachute. You still get the same breathtaking thrill.

3 **Spelunk:** Professionally led tours of aboveground caves and underground worlds can be exhilarating. Find some in your area.

4 **Ski:** Go to the closest ski area and take a lesson. Many places offer them free with a ski rental.

5 **Rock Climb:** With the proper equipment and know-how you can find your Zen on the slippery face of a cliff.

6 **Hot-Air Balloon Rides:** No practice required so long as a licensed pilot takes you.

7 **Scuba Dive:** From pools to lakes to the deep blue sea, a day of diving with the proper equipment (or free diving with a snorkel and mask) can open your eyes to a world you never imagined.

8 **Kayak/Canoe:** Follow a river's current down any of America's great waterways. If you're new to the sport, make sure you are pointed in the direction of an easy river—or go with a guide to kick it up a notch.

9 **Fly:** Take a lesson or sign on as a passenger in a small two-passenger plane or a helicopter.

10 **Storm Chase:** As long as you take someone experienced with you and don't do anything stupid, storm chasing is an exciting extreme adventure you can have almost anywhere.

Comfort a Friend Who Just Got Dumped

1. **Let Her Talk:** Listen with patience and compassion. Try not to preach or cast blame.

2. **Distract Her:** Take her out to places she likes to go. Try to see her more than usual and check in by phone and e-mail a few extra times a week.

3. **Make Her Smile:** Generally try to lighten the mood. Sometimes the world is funnier when we are experiencing deep pain. Help her get through it by pointing out something to laugh about.

4. **Perform a Cleansing Ritual:** Take her to a body of water to dip herself. If it's cold out, burn dried herbs in her home and help her clean out her space—if not physically, then spiritually.

5. **Work on Filling Her Schedule:** Encourage her other friends to step up and make plans with her. If she'll go, it will be better than sitting at home, dwelling.

6. **Fix Her Up . . . Later:** Mention guys you know that you are excited for her to meet. Begin to reawaken her positive energy about the future.

7. **Make an Online Profile with Her:** If she feels ready, ask her if she'd like help making on online profile. Take her picture and point out her best qualities.

8. **Be Her Wingman:** Go out with her and try to spark up conversations on her behalf. She doesn't have to date anyone, but getting attention can be helpful.

9. **Don't Judge:** All is fair in love and war. If they get back together, you don't want to find yourself in an awkward position. Offer only general opinions as they pertain to her healing.

10. **Remind Her That She Is Okay:** In the end she will find someone better suited and more right for her.

Make the Cut:
Reasons to Cut Your Hair Right Now

1 **To Keep It Looking Healthy:** Trim it regularly to remove split ends and faded color, leaving the bouncier, healthier hair.

2 **To Fix Damage:** If you have been skipping your regular trims, it might not be a bad time to start from scratch. Cut your hair short and begin anew.

3 **For Fashion:** From Emma Watson to Dakota Fanning, all the kids are doing it. Maybe it's time to join the wave.

4 **Because It's Cool:** Women with short hair are hot stuff. They are sexy and confident. They even move differently.

5 **Because You Have to Try It Once:** If you've never had short hair, you really ought to give it a try. If there is one thing that is guaranteed in this life, it's that it will grow back.

6 **To Quit Dyeing It:** The best way to give up the bottle—of dye—is to cut your hair to your roots and let it grow in au naturel.

7 **Because It's Hot Outside:** A big heavy head of hair is no fun in the middle of a humid summer. A short, light pixie cut, on the other hand, is easy, breezy, and fun!

8 **Because Styling Your Hair Is Driving You Nuts:** The frizzing, the flyaways, the flat, boring mop. Cutting it short will make all of that so much simpler.

9 **Because Your Neck Is Delicious:** Admit it, your neck is so kissable even your dog can't get enough. Short hair will frame it like the artwork that it is.

10 **Because You Need a Change:** Whether you are going through a breakup or falling in love, maybe it's time for a change. Cutting your hair isn't forever, but it will energize any new phase of life.

Vacation Off the Beaten Path . . .

1 **Toy Robot Museum (Adamstown, Pennsylvania):** This museum is built in a medieval-style shopping square, which alone is worth the trip. But this amazing museum is a wild place to visit while you're there.

2 **Carhenge (Alliance, Nebraska):** It's Stonehenge. Out of cars. In Nebraska.

3 **Madonna Inn (San Luis Obispo, California):** Every room is different in this kitschy dream hotel. The best part is that its website lets you pick one.

4 **World's Largest Basket (Dresden, Ohio):** Around the corner from the Longaberger Basket Company (which you can also tour) is this enormous woven landmark.

5 **Motorcyclepedia (Newburgh, New York):** All you should know is that the owner of this massive and impressive collection of motorcycles subtitled his exhibit "Wall of Death."

6 **Chandelier Drive-Thru Tree (Leggett, California):** This fallen sequoia tree just north of San Francisco is large enough to allow most cars to drive through it. Luckily it has been paved so that you can do just that.

7 **Corn Palace (Mitchell, South Dakota):** If you can go at the end of August, Mitchell also features a corn festival. However, this life-size castle is worth it whenever you can get to it between April and November.

8 **The Holy Land Experience (Orlando, Florida):** A living re-enactment of biblical Israel during the first century, featuring a replica of the caves where the Dead Sea Scrolls were discovered.

9 **The Coral Castle (Homestead, Florida):** Said to have been built by one man using supernatural powers, these monolithic stones, mostly coral and limestone, will make you ask yourself, how else could it have been done?

10 **UFDC Doll Museum (Kansas City, Missouri):** Considered one of the finest doll museums in the country, their shop is also the go-to place for doll collectors world wide.

Shop for Kids—with Kids— Without the Stress

1 **Think of Them and What They'd Like:** Remember when your mom thought you'd look really sweet in the bowtie smock? Don't do that.

2 **Make It One Stop:** Don't put yourself in a situation where you have to go to multiple places. Go to a store where you can find just about everything you need.

3 **Give Yourself Time:** Don't think you can do it all in an hour. If you're swamped, as long as no one is naked, wait until a workable block of time opens up.

4 **Look for Imperfections at the Store:** Scan for holes in the seams, stains, and general wear.

5 **Shop Where There Is a Good Return Policy:** Target, for example, only accepts returns for three months. Make sure you will have plenty of time to return the items your family doesn't like, need, or fit into.

6 **Keep Track:** Keep a journal or computer folder where you can write down a household clothing and general inventory.

7 **Keep an Overstock:** If you run into sales or there is a shirt your child really likes to wear, buy more than one in more than one size.

8 **Avoid Real-World Sales—Go Online:** The chaos of big sale days will cost you big time emotionally. So go online to shop them.

9 **Accept Labels:** This is another one you might remember from childhood. All you wanted was that Forenza sweater and your mom bought you the knockoff. Do what you want with socks and underpants, but otherwise get your kids what they'll actually wear.

10 **Take Them:** If possible, make it a family day and also a learning day. Give your kids a budget if they are old enough and have them choose the supplies they need and the clothing they want to wear. Of course, guide them as they go.

Look Great Without Setting Foot in the Gym

1   **Straighten Your Hair:** Heat is an amazing producer of silky, shiny hair, no matter what your before photo looks like. Tame flyaways and frizzies, and teach curls a lesson.

2   **Use Makeup:** If your face seems puffy, bloated, or plain old fat, use dark makeup, tanning sprays, or concealers to help you reshape your face.

3   **Invest in a New Bra:** Go to a store where they specialize in lingerie and get yourself fitted properly. The right size bra can pull you in, up, and hot.

4   **Put on Red Lipstick:** Just a coat of fire engine red will have men doing a double take. Make sure you pull your finger through your lips to keep the lipstick off your teeth.

5   **Wear Heels:** Even if you can't do stilettos, a nice platform or wedge will lengthen your legs and make you look leaner.

6   **Rethink Your Wardrobe:** What are you wearing that might make you look heavy? Embrace lines that are fitted at the smallest point on your waist. And make sure you are wearing the right size.

7   **Change Your Walk:** A hot little bounce in your walk can make all the difference in how sexy you seem. Practice and then own the runway.

8   **Change Your Attitude:** Sourpusses are not hot. Neither are anxious, flustered, or unhappy people. So embrace the positive and be the hottie you never knew you could.

9   **Gird Yourself:** Girdles are not just for grannies. Buy a pair of Spanx or invest in something a little more squeezy.

10   **Smile:** Smile and men will swoon.

Thank People You
Never Think of Thanking

1 **Your Mail Carrier:** It's hot out there, or it's cold and rainy. But still, he gets you your mail every day. If you see the carrier, say thank you.

2 **Your Neighbor:** Even if she hasn't watered your plants lately, she allows you to live in peace in your home. That deserves at least a modicum of gratitude.

3 **A Transportation Worker:** If you take a bus or train to work, offer a thank-you as you get off. Similarly, tell a pilot or flight attendant that you are grateful for the ride.

4 **A Police Officer:** If you see one, let him know you appreciate the work he does every day and the danger in which officers put themselves to keep us safe.

5 **Your Parents:** Thank them for the life they helped you to achieve. After all, you spend enough time blaming them for it.

6 **Someone Who Angers You:** It sounds counterintuitive, but thanking someone for causing you grief makes a negative a positive—you are saying that you learned a lesson, and that has value.

7 **Social Networkers:** People who retweet your ideas or share your projects with friends deserve a thank-you. It will make them feel good and encourage them to keep it up.

8 **A Clergyperson:** Thank someone at your place of prayer for a great sermon or an interesting lesson.

9 **A Friend:** Whether she helped you to feel less lonely or inspired you to do something with your life, thank a friend for being your friend.

10 **A Soldier:** Members of the military are fighting for you and to protect the country in which you live. A little gratitude can't hurt.

Survive Moving Day
Without Killing Each Other

1 **Bring in Reinforcements:** Ask everyone you know if they will help you in exchange for a lovely dinner, copious amounts of alcohol, and good moving karma.

2 **Have a Plan:** Before the day arrives, write up a complete schedule for what has to be done. Parcel out chores among those will be helping and prepare them for what they will have to do.

3 **Eliminate the Baggage:** And by "baggage" we are talking about leaving the small children with a babysitter and the dog at the kennel.

4 **Take Union Breaks:** Every two hours, call out for a break. People get fifteen to thirty minutes to drink water (or beer), have a small snack, and generally regroup.

5 **Gather Supplies:** You will need boxes, markers to label them, packing tape, a truck or several cars, snacks, drinks, and a sense of humor. Pull all of them together.

6 **Label Everything:** Make sure a room designation and thorough description are on every box and attached to every bag. Items that you will need sooner should be kept separate from things like "Grandmother's China."

7 **Give Yourself More Time:** Overlap your move-in and move-out dates and then start slowly, taking a few small trips with things like plants and books.

8 **Downsize:** Donate as much as you can and throw away the rest.

9 **Have a Plan for the Big Stuff:** Moving larger furniture can injure people, so try to get it out of the way earlier when people are still fresh. And make sure everyone is careful so that it is done right.

10 **Hire Movers:** Some of them will even pack the boxes while you give yourself a manicure and watch their rippling muscles do the heavy lifting.

Try a Style Icon on for Size

1 **The Audrey Hepburn:** Put on pearls and a little black dress a la *Breakfast at Tiffany's*, or a cigarette pant and a button-down shirt. But always do your black eyeliner in a swoop on your upper lid.

2 **The Jackie O:** Big black sunglasses and a shift dress made Jackie O the fashion icon of her generation.

3 **The Princess Diana:** Always glamorous and understated, Princess Di had one look she perfected—those feathered waves in her short blond hair.

4 **The Princess Kate:** Flawless and endlessly comfortable-seeming, Kate is the perfect fashion icon of today. Her outfits simply look like something she'd wear.

5 **The Helen Mirren:** Although a celebrity in Britain for years, Dame Helen was in her fifties when she first made a big splash in the United States. Now her impeccable fashion choices border on the iconic.

6 **The Josephine Baker:** Finger waves and long strand pearl necklaces form the base of this American expatriate's oft-copied style.

7 **The Marlene Dietrich:** High-waisted pants and feminine neckties are the staples of Dietrich's androgynous look.

8 **The Gwen Stefani:** This pop icon is known for her bright, brazen fashion choices. Break out the ruby red lipstick and rock it.

9 **The Oprah:** Oprah's full hair and simple style always flatter her. But she's not afraid to make bold choices, either—perhaps the reason her flashback reels are so entertaining.

10 **The Lady Gaga:** You don't have to dress in raw meat, but once, just once, see how it feels to be as theatrical as a drag queen and as beautiful as you imagine yourself to be.

Keep This "Junk" in Your Trunk

1 **A Blanket:** You'd be amazed how many different ways a blanket can come in handy. You can protect a seat from a muddy pet, use it to keep the car from getting dinged in moves, or cover yourself if you get stuck.

2 **First-Aid Kit:** A travel size is all you need in case you are in or come upon an accident and need to tend to some minor scrapes while you wait for help.

3 **Jumper Cables:** You never know when you might need a hand starting your car . . . or when you might come across someone else who needs your help.

4 **Tool Kit:** Keep the basics—a screwdriver to get to your battery, a tire iron for your spare tire, and a steel wire brush to clean cables, etc. Elastic cables are helpful too, when the trunk is overstuffed and you can't quite close it.

5 **Spare Tire:** Keep it full of air and easily removable in a pinch.

6 **A Jack:** In the event of a flat, you'll need a jack to elevate your car and directions for changing it.

7 **Flares and Marker Flags:** Especially at night, changing a flat can be dangerous. Placing flares and markers in the road can save your life.

8 **A Change of Clothes:** You never know when you'll spill your coffee while driving. Plus real life can be messy.

9 **Oil, Antifreeze, and Wiper Fluid:** These three fluids can be crucial to the proper functioning of your car. If any runs out at the wrong time, you'll be more than glad to have them.

10 **A Bottle of Water:** Not just for drinking if you get stranded, but also in case your car overheats—mix it with antifreeze.

Get Back into the Game

1. **Make Sure You're Ready:** Take some time alone to get over your ex and prepare to move on.

2. **Find a Single-Friends Group:** If all of your friends are coupled, the first thing you need to do is find a group of single people to spend some time with.

3. **Join a Support Group:** You can meet people in the same boat as you in support groups sponsored by churches and mental health centers, or even online.

4. **Up Your Own Stock:** Take classes or go on adventures either locally or around the world. Do things you never dreamed of doing and become a more well-rounded you.

5. **Be at the Center of Things:** If your life feels dull, host or organize events. Invite people you know and people they know.

6. **Be Pick-Up-Able Anywhere:** Consider that available men are everywhere, from the grocery store to the park. Look around and make eye contact regularly. Also practice your banter in checkout lines.

7. **Find Yourself Attractive:** Buy new clothes, join a gym, or get a manicure and begin to improve your look.

8. **Go on a Mission:** Seek out available guys. Tell your friends you are interested in dating and ask if they know anyone. Go online. Do what you can to put yourself in the path of love.

9. **Keep Your Kids Out of It at First:** At some point a new partner will have to meet your children, but in the beginning, it's okay and often necessary (especially if your kids are young) to keep the two worlds separate.

10. **Focus on the Future:** No matter how painful your past was, it is time to move on. Keep negative talk about your ex to a minimum and focus on the here and now.

Vacation on the Cheap

(1) Choose Your Destinations Wisely: If you travel abroad, choose a destination where the dollar is strong. If you travel nationwide, go someplace few people think to go.

(2) Prepare Your Own Meals: You can save a lot of money by buying groceries and preparing your own food while on vacation.

(3) Spend a Day in a Café: People-watch, read a great book, or write love letters to your partner, best friends, and children—even if your young ones haven't been born yet.

(4) Use Your Legs to Travel: Don't take cabs or rent a car. Use public transit or your own two feet.

(5) Dine with Locals: Eat where the locals eat to save some money. Tourists almost always pay more.

(6) Do Fun Cheaply: Find off-the-beaten-track adventures. Don't look in guidebooks. Those places have already "happened." Get recommendations from locals and friends who have already been where you are going.

(7) Own Your Own Equipment: Invest in snorkels, skis, a bike, and anything else you might want on vacation. You'll save a lot in the long run.

(8) Camp: Weather permitting, camping is a great way to stay anywhere for a lot less.

(9) Visit Friends: If you can stay someplace free, surviving cheaply in most places still allows you to live high on the hog, so choose destinations where you have friends with guest rooms.

(10) Apartment Swap: Nowadays there are all kinds of places where you can find people who want a break from their lives by stepping into yours. Trade apartments for a place to stay and save a lot of money.

Movies That Make You
Cry Your Heart Out

(1) *Marley and Me:* Yes, it's about the life of a dog and the family that loves him. And yes, by the end of the movie you love him, too. And yes . . . the unthinkable happens.

(2) *Bambi:* You know what happens to this fawn's mother. There is no reason to put yourself through this other than if you need a good cry.

(3) *P.S. I Love You:* It starts with the love of Hilary Swank's life already dead. And then you have to endure him teaching her, from beyond the grave, how to enjoy life.

(4) *E.T.:* When your best friend goes home, it's just sad, even if he is an alien.

(5) *Steel Magnolias:* This gut wrencher will turn on the waterworks but tempers it with a little kindhearted belly laughter.

(6) *Forrest Gump:* A lot of people die or lose limbs before Forrest even gets to Jenny's house. And you know it's not looking good for Jenny when he gets there.

(7) *Cinema Paradiso:* The projectionist Alfredo must break the heart of his young protégé in order to see him succeed.

(8) *Places in the Heart:* A mother tries to keep her family together and keep her farm after her husband dies. Sally Field knows how to bring home the tearjerkers.

(9) *Sophie's Choice:* It is impossible to type out what Sophie's choice actually is without weeping tragically. So if you'd like to cry, you'll have to rent it and let Meryl Streep tell you.

(10) *Terms of Endearment:* Shirley MacLaine and Jack Nicholson both won an Oscar for their roles, and Debra Winger was nominated. You will weep buckets.

Make Your Family Listen

1. **Speak:** Don't use passive aggression or pouting. Neither will get you anywhere.

2. **Choose Your Time and Place:** If you have something serious to say, say it when you think it will be heard. Don't bring it up during a fight or when people are tired, stressed, or otherwise not listening.

3. **Pinpoint:** Say what you mean. If you are looking for help around the house, don't yell at someone for forgetting to make a bed. If you want to be appreciated, say so.

4. **Be Clear:** When naming your request, don't get emotional. Just lay it out as simply as possible and with confidence.

5. **Don't Cry Wolf:** If you become untrustworthy you won't be taken as seriously. Try to maintain your integrity with your family from the outset.

6. **Prepare a Faultless Presentation:** If you have something important to convey, have your facts lined up in advance. A compelling argument is stronger when it's presented thoughtfully.

7. **Listen:** In any family there is more than one view, so listen to the others fairly and objectively.

8. **Remember That Rome Wasn't Built in a Day:** Not getting overnight change isn't the same thing as not being heard. Give it time, or enlist tools like family therapy or charts for feedback on progress.

9. **Communicate by Writing:** If you get flustered during conversation, try writing down your points and reading them out loud. It cuts out the emotion of the situation and maximizes clarity. Just don't write a novel.

10. **Establish Patterns:** If you and your family are stuck in a pattern where one voice is stronger and better heard than the others, you might need an outside party, like a therapist, to help you break it down and eliminate it.

Turn a Guy Down Gently

1 **You're Taken:** Tell him you would go out with him but your boyfriend probably wouldn't like it.

2 **Be Gay:** Admit that it is taking you some time to accept it but that you probably play for the wrong team.

3 **Qué?:** Look apologetic as you pretend you don't speak English.

4 **Is That a . . . ?:** Just as you are telling him how you'd love to go out with him, notice something over his shoulder as you exclaim, "Wait! That's my car!" and run out the door.

5 **Too Drunk to Date:** Tell him that as part of your ten-step program you are not dating for a year.

6 **Religion Calls:** Ask him if he'd mind if your parents and several cousins came along on your dates until you are engaged, per religious custom.

7 **Then Comes Baby:** While agreeing to the date, launch into a very long-winded explanation about how relieved you are to have found someone as ready to have kids as you are.

8 **Pass Him Along:** Tell him your friend sort of "called him" when you first saw him and that you'd feel bad encroaching on "her territory." Don't get into details unless this is a true story.

9 **Walk Away:** This only works if you see him coming—but if you do, turn and walk away quickly.

10 **Just Say No:** After he asks, simply reply, "Thank you so much for asking but I just have to say no," and leave it at that.

Green Your Life, Save the Planet

1 **Switch to Cloth:** Stop buying paper towels. Instead invest in some dishtowels—keep one out for wiping up messy spills and one for "clean" messes like water. Also, use the second towel to wipe counters and tables after meals. Switch them out weekly.

2 **Cut Two to Five Minutes Off Your Shower:** Shave out of the shower or with the water off and generally speed things up to save water.

3 **Fill Your Dishwasher:** Don't run it after every meal. Wait until it's full before you start it up.

4 **Drive One Less Time Per Day/Week:** Whatever you can do—take the bus, ride a bike, or walk, but give up your keys as often as possible.

5 **Recycle:** If you don't already, start recycling. If your city offers a program to pick up recyclables, start paying for it. Otherwise, get your neighbors together and agree to a schedule where someone takes everything to a recycling center once a week by rotation.

6 **Bring Your Own Bags to the Grocery Store:** Use totes and cloth shopping bags to bring your groceries home.

7 **Unplug Everything:** Before bed, unplug what you can.

8 **Dry Outside:** When it's warm out, hang your clothes outside to dry. Your dryer is harsh on the planet. Give it a break.

9 **Give Up Meat One Day a Week:** Be vegetarian-only one day a week and you'll make a huge difference to our planet.

10 **Read Books, Papers, and Magazines Electronically:** It's hard to give up the paper versions, but every now and then it's the right thing to do.

Open Up a Cramped Kitchen

1 **Hang a Pegboard:** It's inexpensive and a great place to hang your pots, pans, and kitchen tools. It will free up a lot of cabinet space, and if you paint it bright blue, it will wake up any standard white wall.

2 **Get a Freestanding Pantry:** Add a cabinet for food so that the built-in cabinets can be used for dishes.

3 **Mount a Magnetic Knife Strip:** Hang your knives instead of taking up precious counter space with a big wooden block.

4 **Add Cabinet Inserts:** Use an inexpensive wire-frame version from any organization or kitchen store. It will double the shelf space inside your cabinets.

5 **Hang Shelves:** Hang a shelf over the counter and get the toaster out of the way. You can hang dishtowels and a paper towel holder below.

6 **Use Every Inch of Storage . . . :** . . . no matter how inconvenient. Keep less-used equipment on top of cabinets or in tough-to-reach places.

7 **Keep Counters Clean:** Remove anything you can and wipe down the countertops. Small spaces get more cluttered more quickly.

8 **Swap Out Wooden Shelves for Clear Glass:** It's a great trick for making it seem like there is more room by removing visual bulk.

9 **Trade Big Appliances:** Use a French press coffeemaker in place of your electric one, or a handheld blender instead of an upright.

10 **Drape a Chain:** Suspended from the ceiling, a simple stainless-steel chain looks good, is inexpensive, and can hold baskets for fruit storage, a nice plant, or additional pots and pans.

Live Your Life Without Regret

1 **Don't Lock Yourself into Marriage Too Young:** Some people find the love of their life at eighteen. More don't. Make sure you have given yourself time to know yourself.

2 **Travel:** Before you are committed to a job or a family, make sure you have seen a place or two beyond the city in which you were born.

3 **Answer Your Parents' Calls:** They won't live forever. So enjoy them now, for better or worse.

4 **Vote:** If you don't like how your government is doing and you didn't vote, you can only blame yourself.

5 **Don't Switch Careers Too Many Times:** Staying in one field will one day make you an expert. Switching around will make you look flaky, indecisive, and untrustworthy. Which would you prefer?

6 **Don't Break the Law:** Not having a police record in the retirement home is a thing of beauty.

7 **Keep Your Clothes on in Front of Cameras:** The humiliation of having naked pictures leaked publicly outweighs the vanity of showing off your hot body.

8 **Don't Do More Than Experiment with Drugs:** If you try something once, make sure it's just once. They can be physically and spiritually damaging and are capable of ruining your life.

9 **Don't Get Too Many (or the Wrong) Tattoos:** Tattooing your neck might force you to continue to follow your dreams toward becoming a famous musician. But it is more likely that it will keep you from deciding that life is full of all kinds of paths and maybe at forty you will be ready to start on a new, neck-tattoo-free one.

10 **Don't Rack Up Too Much Credit:** Live within your means when you're young and enjoy the freedom of having done so when you're old.

Make Your Kitchen Garden Grow

1 **Herbs:** Everything from basil to cilantro, chives to parsley, and rosemary to mint, herbs are easy to grow inside or outside, in the ground or in a pot.

2 **Tomatoes:** As long as you plan for a way to keep the squirrels from thieving them, you can buy plants that are already started and keep them yielding fruit with regular watering and suckering.

3 **Squash:** Yellow zucchini is a great option, and the vegetables are easier to find among the leaves. This way they are less likely to grow as big as your thigh before you remember to pick them.

4 **Lettuce:** It's a cinch to grow, plus you can clip a head and another will grow back in its place. Swiss chard is another leafy green that grows easily and is full of important nutrients.

5 **Peppers:** This heat-loving vegetable comes in so many shapes, colors, and varieties. Get seedlings from a trusted nursery and they'll make an excellent addition to your garden.

6 **Watermelon:** This hydrating fruit practically grows itself! As long as you can provide around eighty frost-free days in a row, a steady water supply, and a lot of room for them to vine, you will have watermelon.

7 **Purple Carrots:** This heirloom vegetable is both beautiful and surprisingly easy to grow. Since traditional orange carrots come from relatively weak seedlings, these are a great, somewhat hardier alternative.

8 **Root Vegetables:** Provide deep, loose soil and you too can grow root vegetables, including beets, turnips, parsnips, and radishes.

9 **Sunflower Seeds:** All you need is sun (and maybe some support) to grow a sunflower. From there, harvesting the seeds only involves drying out the head of the flower.

10 **Pumpkin:** The old saying goes, "To be a successful gardener, grow pumpkin." This saying exists for a reason. There isn't much more to it than sowing the right variety—and giving it *lots* of room to grow.

Sharpen Your Wit

1 **Use the Art of the "Play on Words":** See if you can exercise a few puns and make them punny . . . er, funny.

2 **Joke about Sex:** As long as you keep it appropriate, a good joke about a failed or struggling sex life (yours or someone else's) can get a chuckle out of anyone.

3 **Have Some Stock Responses:** Plan ahead. Think of some great one-liners and see if you can build them into conversations.

4 **Keep It Universal:** You can avoid offending people by steering clear of jokes about religion or politics. Try to stick with the light stuff over which people *don't* start wars.

5 **Embrace Sarcasm:** A dry comment stating the opposite of what is true can lighten the mood and is generally thought hilarious.

6 **Practice:** If you aren't so witty, practice a little. When people are talking, relax your mind and think of funny comebacks. You can begin by trying them out around people with whom you are comfortable.

7 **Take a Comedy Class:** In a class setting you might find yourself free to open up and say whatever you like. A good teacher will give you tips for finding the funny in everyday situations.

8 **Look for Irony:** When people are saying one thing but doing something else, it's always fun to call them out on it.

9 **(Gently) Tease People:** Ribbing your friends and loved ones every now and then is both funny and a good way to lighten any mood.

10 **Keep Your Smile On:** Just remember, in your delivery it is important to relay with your face that you are kidding. Nothing's worse than a joke you have to explain.

Dial Back Your Calorie Count, Change Your Life

1 **Sweet Potatoes:** This starchy food is loaded with vitamins. Soften a few in boiling water and put them away in your fridge. Peel and use them as a great thickener in a delicious and healthy chocolate shake (add milk and chocolate sauce—no ice cream!), in cakes and pies, and even in soups.

2 **Wraps:** Lose the heavy bread in your lunch sandwiches and make them wraps instead.

3 **Cauliflower Mash:** Instead of potatoes, use a handheld blender to make this winning side dish. Mix in low-fat milk, fresh dill, and a teaspoon of butter. Add some Greek yogurt to taste.

4 **Breakfast Bird:** Give up the bacon and eggs. Only fruit, nuts, and grains for breakfast.

5 **Cannellini Beans:** Anytime a savory recipe calls for cream—particularly soups and sauces—substitute by adding these creamy beans blended smooth to both thicken the dish and make it richer.

6 **Natural Sweeteners:** Marmalade, honey, and maple syrups are great ways to lightly sweeten chili recipes, sauces, and even desserts. Toss the sugar and give them a try.

7 **Greek Yogurt:** A delicious and healthy sour cream or mayonnaise alternative. Put it on tacos or mix into potatoes when you mash them, or add to coleslaw.

8 **Coconut Milk:** This healthy savory/sweet liquid works well in both sweet and salty dishes. Use instead of milk on cereal or mixed into sauces for a creamy taste.

9 **Applesauce:** Replace butter and oil with applesauce in many baked goods for a low-calorie and tasty dessert.

10 **Olive or Canola Oils:** Stop cooking with butter, margarine, or oils high in saturated fats. This one little swap is a great way to improve your health.

Perfect Your at-Home Manicure

1 **Remove Old Polish:** Use a cotton ball to get off the remnants of your last manicure.

2 **Soak:** Mix up a warm bowl of Epsom salt, water, and rose petals. Soak your hands for ten minutes.

3 **Rinse Hands:** Using a clean water bath, rinse your hands, then wrap them in a towel.

4 **Push Back Cuticles:** Using a wooden stick, gently push back your cuticles. Cutting them can be damaging to your nails in the long run. Remove any dirt under your nails as well.

5 **Cut and File:** Cut and file your nails exactly how you like them. Don't file on top of the "face" of the nail or you will damage it.

6 **Moisturize:** Cover your hands in a creamy moisturizer, put them inside a clean pair of socks you no longer wear, and let them soak it up for twenty minutes. Then wipe them clean. Don't forget to clean under your nails one last time.

7 **Paint Your Dominant Hand First:** If you are right-handed, paint your right hand first. Left-handed, paint your left hand.

8 **Minimize Your Strokes:** Apply your nail polish in as few strokes as possible—three to five is best.

9 **Apply Base, Color, Color, and Top Coat:** Each nail should be painted four times, first with a base, then with color, followed by a second coat of color, and finally a top coat.

10 **Dry Them Well:** Let your nails dry for at least thirty minutes before you attempt to do anything with your hands.

Play Like a Kid

1. **Celebrity:** Write names of five celebrities on slips of paper and put them in a hat. In two teams, players pull names, describing the celebrities for one minute until all the slips are gone. Round 2, those names go back in the hat but now they must be described in one word.

2. **Pictionary:** Two people face off by pulling out phrases from a hat and drawing them on a board until one of their teams guesses it.

3. **Charades:** One person tries to get everyone to guess books, movies, celebrities, or actions without words in two minutes or less.

4. **Freeze or LA Tag:** Two people improvise a scene. Someone watching calls out "Freeze" and stops the action (freezing the actors in place). That person takes the place of one of the actors and starts up a new scene with an entirely new situation.

5. **Dance Contest:** Split everyone into groups of two or three. Play an agreed-upon song three times, while the groups write dances to perform. You cannot vote for yourselves as the winners.

6. **Spin the Bottle:** No matter your age, if you are having a singles bash, this classic will take you back to high school.

7. **Truth or Dare:** Write down questions and dares on slips of paper to be answered or performed.

8. **Light as a Feather, Stiff as a Board:** A person lies on her back. Everyone else puts their fingers underneath her. Sitting at the head, someone tells the story of how she died. At the end, the group chants the name of the game and lifts her floating body.

9. **Poker:** Have a group over for pizza, beer, and five-card stud.

10. **Personal Trivia:** Write and then ask trivia questions about each person in the room. Works best with a group of close friends.

Work Through the Pink-Slip Blues

1. **Go to the Movies:** You just need some time to process and grieve. Treat yourself to a movie and zone out.

2. **Scream:** Find an open field and let it out. Scream at the top of your lungs. Generally have a tantrum. It's a sad time. Do what you need to.

3. **Cry to Your Best Friend:** Call her up and vent it all out. Go on and on about the bitch who badmouthed you, the boss who hated you, and the client that screwed up everything. You'll feel better.

4. **Schedule Something Exciting:** Call up an old friend and see if she wants to grab dinner, or see if your sister is up for a girls' weekend. Just give yourself something to look forward to.

5. **Go Get a Hug:** Even if you have to swing by your honey's office or your kid's school, do it. You really, really need one.

6. **Take a Yoga Class:** Working out your grief physically is a great move in the throes of a work-related trauma. Somewhere a yoga class is starting. Go take it.

7. ***Don't* Freak Out:** At least, not until you've left the building. You might need a reference from this place. You have to keep it together.

8. ***Don't* Beg:** Not the day you got fired. The paperwork has already been filed. Take it as an absolute. Walk away with dignity and contest it later if you have just cause.

9. ***Don't* Plan Your Future:** Not today. Don't worry about it, don't think about it, and don't cry about it.

10. **Begin Thinking about Your Time Off:** What will you do? Where will you go? Maybe you should take up photography . . .

Teach Your Man to Turn You On

1. **Kiss Long:** Ask him to take his time with the kiss. A long, slow, and passionate smooch can usually get a girl going.

2. **Don't Forget Our Hot . . . Brains:** Tell him how much it helps you to feel hot and how hearing it from him is the best way to get there.

3. **Use Him:** Grab his hand and show him what to do.

4. **Necks, Nipples, and Knees:** Tell him how good it feels when he remembers to spend time kissing, licking, and tickling your erogenous zones before getting to the main event.

5. **Tease:** Suggest that he touch you and then pull away with his fingers, tongue, and/or penis repeatedly until you are begging him for it.

6. **It Is Not a Button:** Remind him that like his penis, a clitoris is full of nerve endings and should be treated as such.

7. **No Pulling, Pinching, or Biting—at Least, at First:** Before we are turned on, he should know that pulling, pinching, and biting feel pretty much like pulling, pinching, and biting. But once we are turned on they usually start to feel *really good*.

8. **Angles Are Important:** During sex it's good to show him that his pelvic bone is a wonderful place for you to rub against if it helps you to achieve orgasm. Show him how!

9. **Copy Cat:** Ask him to mimic you, then slowly show him on his body how you want to be touched.

10. **Dominate Him:** Order him around using your best dominatrix moves. You can even dress the part if you feel like it. Maybe you both will discover new ways to enjoy each other.

Surprise Him with the Perfect Dinner

1 **Be Creative:** Hand-make an invitation for your date. Get him excited before the big day and prepare him by letting him know the dress code.

2 **Personalize the Menu:** Choose food you know he loves. This is not the time to make dishes requiring skills you don't possess. Nothing will ruin your party faster than a flambé disaster.

3 **Do a Practice Round:** If you are keen to try something new, however, give yourself a test run and see how it goes.

4 **Decorate:** Indicate that it's a special night by decorating. Use twinkling white lights, flowers, and candles to create a romantic display.

5 **Turn Off:** No cell phones, no television, no computers allowed.

6 **Dress for It:** Look great when he gets home. Whether you decide to wear your cutest cocktail dress or just his favorite tie, look like you tried.

7 **Set the Mood:** Music and low lighting will help inspire the right tone. If your man had a long day, maybe start him with a bubble bath while you finish up in the kitchen. But make sure the house is clean and that you are using the good linen.

8 **Make It Special:** Add one or two touches to make it extra special. If you can't bring in a string quartet, even a little under-the-table "action" will make things memorable.

9 **Go on a Picnic:** Take him to a nearby park or into your backyard and lay a blanket out with a picnic basket full of food, wine, and romance.

10 **Make a Reservation:** If you don't have the time to put into it, don't. Choose a romantic restaurant and let them do it for you.

Turn Around an Offensive Coworker

1. **Gossips:** Don't engage, but in order not to become the next target, don't condemn. Simply nod and smile and go about your business.

2. **Liars:** If you notice a coworker is prone to lying, point out her inconsistencies in a compassionate way. Ask her if she is okay. Then drop it. If it continues and is problematic, send an anonymous memo to a superior.

3. **Foulmouths:** Use echo correction, like a mother to a child learning to talk. When he says, "Is this fucking piece of shit ready to go?" reply, "Is the memo ready? Let me check."

4. **Lazies:** If someone isn't pulling her weight, make a point of offering her additional work anytime you have some. Don't force it. Just ask.

5. **Nosey Nellies:** Are they in your business a little too closely? Put some distance between you. Offer nothing until they give up and move on.

6. **Cutters:** Does a coworker leave the minute the boss turns around? Out him by feigning a phone call and checking to see if anyone has seen him after he has left the premises.

7. **Star-Crossed Lovers:** If it has become a problem—there are disruptive sounds or distracting fights—you might have to report them to HR.

8. **Customer Service Failures:** Have a talk with them. Let them know that word will eventually make its way to the top if they're not careful.

9. **Fighters:** Give them a warning and suggest they find a better way to make their point. If it continues and they are your subordinates, let them go.

10. **Saboteurs:** Attempt to step in and fix it, and if you can't, get someone in who can—or send them packing.

Magically Transform Leftovers

1 **Tacos:** Any leftover meat can be heated in a hot pan with cilantro, lime juice, and some taco seasoning. Add cheese and veggies, warm up a can of beans, and put it all in a taco shell.

2 **Casserole:** Cook egg noodles until soft, then add your leftovers and a can of cream of mushroom soup. Top with bread crumbs and bake at 350°F for forty-five minutes.

3 **Fried Rice:** Mix cooked white rice (Chinese leftover is best) with any leftover meat and veggies. Fry in olive oil over a hot skillet or wok. Add low-sodium soy sauce. At the end stir in one egg and cook an additional two minutes.

4 **Salad:** Put your leftovers cold onto a bed of greens. Green beans, potatoes, beef, fish, chicken—it all tastes good the day after!

5 **Omelet:** Beat three or four eggs and pour into a warm skillet. After eggs set, add the leftovers and then close up the omelet. Serve with sour cream.

6 **Sandwiches:** Some people swear you can even do this with spaghetti on garlic bread!

7 **Soup:** Boil up any bones and make a delicious stock as a base for most soups and sauces. You can toss in the leftovers after the stock is finished and call it "garbage soup."

8 **Kebobs:** Skewer leftovers and heat them up, add colorful fresh veggies, and then re-serve as an entirely new (and fun) meal.

9 **Patties, Cakes, and Loaves:** You can make potato pancakes, salmon croquettes, crab cakes, and meat loaves of every flavor. Just mix with bread crumbs and eggs, then bake or fry as you desire.

10 **Lunch Wraps:** Mix your leftovers with mayo and mustard and wrap them up in a tortilla shell for a delicious treat.

Be Nice to Your Future Self

1 **Turn Down the Music:** Your future ears will thank you for keeping your ear buds at a reasonable level and the rock shows to a minimum.

2 **Get Out of the Sun:** You've heard it before. The sun is not your future self's skin's friend.

3 **Quit Smoking:** The longer you smoke, the more long-term damage you do your body. You've been meaning to quit anyway. Do it now.

4 **Refuse to Let Him Go Condom-Free:** Some STDs last a lifetime. The best way to protect a future you is to make sure you know your partners' sexual histories or at the very least, use condoms *every time you have sex.*

5 **Be Careful:** Accidents can leave you with permanent physical ailments. So think before engaging in dangerous behaviors.

6 **Foster Close Relationships:** Good friends and loved ones keep you healthy and happy. Make sure you create relationships you trust and value today. You'll be glad you did in the future, for a lot of reasons.

7 **Learn How to Eat Right:** Losing weight becomes harder with age. But even if you stay skinny and eat poorly, be aware, metabolisms slow. You need to practice good eating habits now.

8 **Work in the Right Field:** Choose a career path that makes you feel motivated and happy. Don't just settle. Studies have shown that loving your job keeps you healthier longer.

9 **Surround Yourself with People Who Value You:** Toxic relationships are bad for you, period. The more you surround yourself with supportive people, the better your overall health will stay.

10 **Forgive:** Unburdening yourself from anger and indignation is a step toward health and wellness you will be glad you took for the rest of your life.

Bite Back:
Keep Mosquitoes from Chomping You

1. **Wear Repellent:** Nowadays you can find repellents that are not also repellent to humans. Find one with a bearable smell or with no smell and slather it on. Opt for natural, as deet is nasty stuff.

2. **Hang a Mosquito Net:** Or buy several and hang them tentlike over a portion of your backyard for a more comfortable outdoor experience.

3. **Stay Cool:** Mosquitoes are attracted to warmer bodies, so make sure you have done your time next to the A/C before proceeding into the hot and sticky wilds.

4. **Drain Standing Water:** While it's true that mosquitoes can breed in a teaspoon of water, that doesn't mean you should give up the war. Empty baby pools after use, and after rain, drain puddles and any standing water in toys near your home immediately.

5. **Don't Exercise Outside:** Mosquitoes are attracted to lactic acid, which is given off during exercise. Plus, as mentioned, they like you hot and sweaty.

6. **Drink Wine:** Studies have shown that a mosquito will take a beer drinker over a wino any day. So skip the brewski and make it a spritzer.

7. **Get Bitten:** The more bites you get from a particular species of mosquito, the more immune you become to it.

8. **Hold Your Breath:** This is not the most practical way to avoid mosquitoes, but the fact is, carbon dioxide is what attracts them. If you are only going outside for a second, holding your breath can't hurt.

9. **Kill Them:** A flat swatter has more surface area and increases your chances of hitting the mosquito. If it's mid-bite, trap it by tensing your muscle and then kill it.

10. **Clean Up:** Gather your neighbors and clean up any standing water and also any garbage that's attracting bugs to your neighborhood.

Make Getting the Guy Look Easy

1 **Make Eye Contact:** Spot the guy you like and then lock in on his eyes as much as possible.

2 **Smile:** Nerves and shyness can sometimes get in the way of a good, heartfelt smile, but if you can manage to expose your pearly whites repeatedly in a conversation, you will increase your chances of scoring digits exponentially.

3 **Dance:** There are few better ways to show a guy you are confident and feeling good than by getting out on the dance floor. Showing him that you like to be watched will make him want to watch you.

4 **Buy *Him* a Drink:** Figure out what he's drinking and then order and deliver his next round. He'll be charmed and intrigued—or at least grateful for the drink.

5 **Stand Nearby:** Proximity is everything. So sidle right up to his side and stay there until he notices you.

6 **Engage Him in Conversation:** If you are with friends, ask him a question relevant to your conversation to get him talking.

7 **Use a Cheesy Pickup Line:** Starting things off with, "So, what's your sign?" will probably make him laugh and start things off on the right foot.

8 **Compliment Him:** What was it you liked about *this guy* when you first saw him? Why not tell him? "I like your T-shirt," or "I've been trying to get my friend to shave his head like that, it looks so good!" are friendly (not creepy) compliments that will make him feel good.

9 **Guide the Conversation Toward a Date:** Mention something going on in town you've been wanting to do, or a movie you're hoping to see. If he sounds interested, offhandedly suggest you go together.

10 **Close the Deal:** If the evening is ending and he hasn't asked for your digits, don't be afraid to get his. If he says no, be glad he isn't going to waste your time. If he says yes, make sure you call.

Return the Favor for Your Aging Parents

1 **Stay Respectful:** As parents age, sometimes it's difficult not to feel like you have become the parent. You haven't. Don't forget that. Maintain a semblance of respect.

2 **Don't Be Guilted into It:** You are allowed to have a life. Your parents want you to live it. They also just want a phone call every now and then.

3 **Share the Schedule:** If a parent has fallen ill, organize a schedule with siblings and friends to help ease the burden of care.

4 **Look into Retirement Communities:** Especially if a parent is alone and/or lacking mobility, a retirement community can be a great place to regain a social life and a life in general.

5 **Keep a Health Journal for Them:** In particular, health issues become perplexing, as they have trouble remembering things or generally don't want to be a burden. Keep track in a journal. You can do this whether or not you live nearby.

6 **Have a Relationship with Their Doctors:** If you can, go with them to doctor's appointments. If not, get signed permission to call and speak with them afterward.

7 **Know Their Neighbors:** Collect numbers you can call in case of an emergency, especially if you know you can't get to where they live immediately.

8 **Encourage a Roommate:** A roommate can help turn a single or widowed parent's life around. It will also give you some peace of mind. Just make sure they are trustworthy.

9 **Check In:** Call and visit as often as possible so that they know you care and so that those around them know you do, too.

10 **Move Closer:** If a long-term illness strikes and no one else can do it, you might have to consider moving closer to them. They'd do it for you.

When to Turn Off That Phone

1 **At the Gym:** Many gyms have no-phone policies due to overuse on the gym floor and in locker rooms, where people are trying to focus. Turn it off and get into your workout.

2 **On Elevators:** Since everyone can hear everything you and the person you're on the phone with are saying, you may as well hang up. After all, elevators are also notorious for bad reception and dropped calls.

3 **In the Doctor's or Dentist's Office:** It's important for you to take care of yourself, not someone who might need you on the other end of a call.

4 **On a Date:** Unless you want to end the date, leave your phone off.

5 **At Family Meals:** Your kids and your spouse want to have a relationship with you. It's best if you turn off your phone and refocus your attention.

6 **At the Checkout Counter:** Retail is hard enough without having to repeatedly ask a customer "Debit or credit?" after she swipes her card. Use common courtesy and talk to the cashier. You can call back later.

7 **In Houses of Prayer:** Even when the sermon runs long, it's frowned upon to let your phone ring during services.

8 **In the Bathroom:** Let's face it, it's bad etiquette to talk on the phone and use the bathroom, but if you're trying to get out of a bad date and need someone to call you to end it, this is where exceptions come into play.

9 **On the Beach:** Be at the beach when you're at the beach.

10 **In Yoga Class:** For many, yoga class is where they go to engage in a meaningful spiritual practice. Any action you may be getting on your phone will not help them accomplish their goal.

Have Sex Like You Just Met

1 **Start with Words:** Send him a text telling him you miss him. Call him just to say hello. Even if you aren't burning for him, find ways to reach out.

2 **Add Touching:** The next time you are sharing a space, remind yourself to touch him—rub his back, stroke his arm, or simply hold his hand.

3 **Then Stop Touching:** One night, try a sensate focus on each other. Sex therapists suggest this technique, whereby one person lies naked with eyes closed while the other runs his or her hands just above the skin. There is no contact, but quite a bit of sensuality.

4 **Take Orgasms Off the Table:** Agree to touch each other and kiss each other for a specified period of time without the pressure of an "end point."

5 **Use Fantasy:** Describe to each other detailed sexual encounters, either generally or between the two of you. See if it leads anywhere.

6 **Use Tools:** Porn, vibrators, and other tools can sometimes help a couple in a slump. Go shopping together, either online or at a sex shop where you both feel comfortable, and see what turns you on.

7 **Masturbate Together:** Kiss and caress him while he masturbates and ask him to reciprocate for you.

8 **Regress:** Remember necking? Dry humping? Try having sex like a teenager, keeping your pants on. It's hotter than you remember.

9 **Don't Roll Over:** No matter what, make sure you touch each other. Cuddle, hold hands, or massage each other, even if you both agree sex ain't happening.

10 **Make It a Game:** Throw ten sex acts into a hat and each of you draw one. If you don't do what it says, you have to do all the household chores for a week.

Don't Be a Chicken:
Whole-Bird Meals You Have to Try

(1) **Whole Herb-Roasted Chicken:** Place garlic cloves under the skin, stuff with fresh herbs and a half an orange, squeeze the other half of the orange over the outside of the bird, and sprinkle with salt and pepper. Then bake.

(2) **Fried Chicken:** Cut up the pieces. Bread them and fry them until they are golden brown.

(3) **Chicken Soup:** Boil the whole bird—bones, giblets, and all—for two hours (add water as needed). Add celery, carrots, parsnip, parsley, salt, pepper, and onion and let simmer for another forty-five minutes. Add rice or noodles.

(4) **Lemon Chicken:** Cut the chicken into pieces. Mix the juice of one lemon, mustard, white wine, and olive oil together. Pour over the pieces. Garnish with slices of lemon. Then bake.

(5) **Pulled Chicken:** Roast or grill the chicken. Boil the meat for an additional hour in chicken or beef stock until it falls off the bone. Drain, add barbeque sauce, and serve on a bun.

(6) **Beer Can Chicken:** Stand a salted and peppered chicken over a beer can and set it on the grill.

(7) **Rotisserie Chicken:** Sear the chicken on the grill; add butter and seasoning. Put on a spit, close the lid, and let the chicken cook for an hour and a half.

(8) **Tandoori Chicken:** Cut into pieces and cover with the sauce (yogurt and a mix of spices) overnight. Roast or grill.

(9) **Honey Mustard Chicken:** Cover a whole chicken with honey, mustard, salt, and pepper. Pour two cups of chicken stock and a cup of white wine into the bottom of the roasting pan to steam. Add potatoes, chunked carrots, celery, and onion.

(10) **Fried Whole Chicken:** Using an infrared or deep fryer, cook the whole chicken in about thirty minutes.

Get Energized During Your Lunch Hour

1 **Skip the Sugar:** Simple sugars wake you up and then knock you out. Better to skip things like bad carbs and other sugary treats at lunch.

2 **Keep It Cold:** Soups, stews, and fried foods are called "comfort food" for a reason. Sometimes, the psychological implication is enough: If it sounds cozy, save it for dinner.

3 **Go for a Walk:** After you are done eating, instead of sitting back down at your desk, go for a walk outside. A little fresh air will do you good.

4 **Hold the Chicken and Beef:** Choose proteins like salmon or quinoa for a hearty lunch that will keep your brain function high.

5 **Snickers? Not So Satisfying:** Make sure you actually eat during your lunch hour and don't just snack. If you are trying to cut calories by eating less, choose nuts and fruit.

6 **Work Out:** If you can slip in a twenty-minute workout at the beginning of your lunch hour, you will unlock the secret to feeling great in the afternoon caffeine-free.

7 **Turn Up the Music:** Listen to an energizing mix of songs while you eat or while walking to and from the cafeteria. *Eye of the Tiger* never put anyone to sleep.

8 **Close Your Eyes:** After you've eaten, go somewhere you can close your eyes for ten or twenty minutes. Just remember to set your phone alarm!

9 **Wash Your Face:** Bring extra makeup, some face soap, moisturizer, and a clean towel to the office. At the end of your lunch break, visit the bathroom and do a refreshing cleanse.

10 **Don't Skip Dessert:** Just make it fruity! Go ahead and indulge in strawberries, blueberries, and/or cantaloupe, all of which boost blood flow and wake you up.

Make It Work with an Older Man

1   **Get Smart:** Learn a thing or two about his generation's set of cultural references, whether he's five or twenty-five years older. Listen to music and watch movies so that you can better engage with him and his friends.

2   **Show Respect to Get Respect:** You are not his daughter, so don't act like you are.

3   **Be Self-Respecting:** Behave in a way that shows you are serious and on top of your game. Others' opinions will follow.

4   **Dress the Part:** Dress the way you want to be treated. If you are the only midriff-barer in a sea of shift dresses, you will be treated accordingly.

5   **Be Open to an Education:** Whether you intend this to be your forever relationship or just for now, let your older man teach you anything he has learned from those extra years of life.

6   **Sometimes Let It Be Your Turn to Be the Grownup:** Even if your dynamic is otherwise, once in a while, be the one taking care of him.

7   **Be Low-Maintenance:** Make sure everything isn't about you. No matter how hot you are, it gets old quick.

8   **Understand Your Relationship:** Why are you dating each other? Do you feel safe with him? Do you make him feel young? Understanding the reasons you got into your relationship in the first place will help you to keep it going strong.

9   **Treat His Past with Due Respect:** He has one, and some of it might creep into his present (ex-wives, children). Let it become as much a part of your life as it has to.

10   **Be Prepared:** It pays to retain a sense of realism over what it means in the long term to be the younger woman. Know in advance if you are prepared to be with him in sickness and in health.

Focus on the Big Picture

1. **Don't Anticipate:** Try to be present and avoid concerning yourself with "mights" or "coulds."

2. **Death and Taxes:** Remind yourself that your grandpa was right: you are beholden to two things, and neither of them is likely happening right now.

3. **Don't Be a Victim:** You can only control your piece of the situation. Don't look for vindication or place blame. Own your culpability and go from there.

4. **Be Wrong:** There is a reason a husband's defeated "Yes Dear" got laughs on all the old sitcoms. The fact is, sometimes it's easier to concede than to fight for a moot or insignificant point.

5. **Pick Your Battles:** Obey the speed limit and park legally so that you don't find yourself running into unnecessary confrontations. You know the speed limit is 65, so drive 65.

6. **Be Flexible:** When presented with a new idea or a new direction, go with it. Why be rigid?

7. **Focus:** Now is not the time to tackle every conceivable problem or challenge. Look at what is happening in front of you and get it under control before moving on to its ramifications.

8. **Ease the Tension:** When things go wrong, be the one who lightens the mood. Make a joke to soften the blow, then regroup and move on.

9. **Not Everything Is about You:** Becoming emotionally invested in every area of your life signifies some level of narcissism. Try to let it go and give someone else a chance to manage it.

10. **Accept It:** Life is messy. But it's a helluva ride.

Don't Be Afraid to Ask These Questions (Even on the Sly)

1 **To Reveal What He Is Looking for:** Do you envy the relationships of anyone you know? Why or why not?

2 **To Gauge His Depth:** What's the best book you've ever read?

3 **To Understand His Ambition:** If you could have any job in the world without going back to school or working your way up the ladder, what would it be?

4 **To See if He Can Bring the Funny:** What was your most embarrassing moment?

5 **To Unearth His Patience Level:** If you were trapped on a desert island with the music of only one musician or band, who would it be?

6 **To Analyze His Vanity:** What part of your body would you change if you could?

7 **To Unlock His Secrets:** Who from your whole life do you miss the most?

8 **To Scrutinize His Creativity:** What super power do you wish you had?

9 **To Flesh Out His "Type":** Which celebrity would you want to have a fistfight with, which one would you marry if you could, and which one would you just sleep with?

10 **To Deduce Your Compatibility:** Dogs or cats?

Sing Out These Great Lyrics Like No One's Listening

1. **"Heard 'Em Say" (Kanye West):** This song breaks down what it means to be honest with yourself in a dishonest world.

2. **"Chelsea Hotel" (Leonard Cohen):** A revealing snapshot into a brief romance between two very lonely hearts.

3. **"Fade Into You" (Mazzy Star):** Best. Make-out. Song. Ever. These lyrics are so sensual and heartfelt, they might make you moan.

4. **"Neighborhood #1 (Tunnels)" (Arcade Fire):** Desperate and a little bit funny, the singer wants to reach out to his love during a snowstorm by tunneling from his window to hers.

5. **"While My Guitar Gently Weeps" (The Beatles):** Written by George Harrison, this song came about as he was studying Eastern philosophy and wondering if perhaps there is "no such thing as coincidence . . . "

6. **"Strangers" (The Kinks):** This ballad speaks remarkably of the fact that everyone is bound irrefutably by being alone in this world together.

7. **"Dreams" (Fleetwood Mac):** This classic by Stevie Nicks is a song about breaking up that cuts to the quick and bleeds truth.

8. **"Empire State of Mind" (Jay-Z):** This hip-hop masterpiece pays homage to the Big Apple with powerful lyrics that inspire as well as any Frank Sinatra ode.

9. **"Tangled Up in Blue" (Bob Dylan):** Defying time and space, this epic song is a snapshot spanning an entire relationship from beginning to end. Dylan, arguably the greatest lyricist of our time, claims to have written it during his studies of the Cubist art movement.

10. **"America" (Simon and Garfunkel):** The lyrics take the listener on a Greyhound bus across the country and inspire us, no matter our age, to look for ourselves.

Take a Perfect Picture
and Make the Moment Last

1 **Use Film:** Back when every picture mattered, people were much more careful about their photographs. Break out an old camera and force every picture to matter.

2 **Practice:** Before you take a single shot, go for a walk with your camera. Look through the viewfinder and see how things look in frame.

3 **What to Look for:** Consider what colors look good together. Also, try to make the image clear and specific. Nothing muddled.

4 **Portraits:** Crop around the faces more closely so that there is less in the background. Or use a plain background. A good portrait features the person.

5 **Landscapes:** The idea in a landscape is to get as much detail in the picture as possible. Use a manual setting on your camera so you can control the depth, and make sure you widen the field.

6 **Framing:** Begin with things that are stationary. Try buildings, windows, or interesting doorframes and see if you can find an image that is intriguing and/or attractive.

7 **Shoot from the Hip:** Challenge yourself to take a few shots in the direction of some interesting action without looking through the viewfinder and see what you get.

8 **Try Shooting Outside:** It is easier to photograph in natural light than in artificial light. Set up a still life on an picnic table, limiting yourself to two colors—the color of the tablecloth you use as a background, and a single-colored item in the foreground. Think a red apple on a yellow cloth. Add additional items one at a time.

9 **Zoom:** Use your zoom to see if there is a better shot if you pull in tighter. Also, move around and see if there is a better shot at a different angle.

10 **Point and Shoot:** In the end, taking pictures should be fun. Practice and care will make you the master of your photographs.

Apply Makeup Like You're a Model

1 **Practice on a Melon:** Practice tracing predrawn lines in the shapes of eyes and lips as you reach around from behind the melon.

2 **Watch YouTube:** The Internet is a remarkable source of information about applying makeup. Find styles you like and learn what it takes to re-create them.

3 **Gather Your Tools:** You might only need a cotton swab and your finger, but plan ahead.

4 **Test Colors:** You can sample makeup at most stores (just make sure it's hygienic). Test lipsticks, foundations, and eye shadows on the underside of your arm, since the skin color there is usually less affected by the sun.

5 **Buy Seasonally:** Different foundations should be purchased for summer skin and winter skin. Similarly, colors will look better or worse on you depending on how much sun you've gotten.

6 **Hydrate Your Canvas:** Make sure you drink water, cleanse and moisturize your skin, and keep it well sun-screened.

7 **Use a Primer:** Makeup artists swear by it to help makeup go on more smoothly and stay on longer.

8 **Watch Your Wrinkles:** One basic problem a lot of women have is that they use foundations that settle into their wrinkles. Use light whipped makeups that don't accentuate the negatives.

9 **Focus on One Feature:** If you go for a bold eye, do a subtle lip, and vice versa. One day, give yourself bright, glowing cheeks with a little mascara and some lip gloss; another day, do a smoky eye and a pink lip. On a red lipstick evening, maybe just a dab of pink on the cheekbone is all you need.

10 **Set It:** Use a sheer powder as a final step to hold everything in place for as long as you need it.

Class Up Your Tat
(and Other Regret-Free Body-Art Rules)

1 **Put It Out of Sight:** Unless you are already Tommy Lee, you never know how a tattoo on your face will affect your career. Plus, this way you won't get sick of it.

2 **Avoid Pop Culture References:** You might not believe it but someday, far down the road, Stewie from the TV show *Family Guy* might not be cool anymore. You do not need him living on your shoulder blade.

3 **Don't Be Impulsive:** Take your time deciding on your design. Give yourself several months to choose wisely.

4 **Know What It Means—in English:** Let's just say there is a girl out there who tattooed a Mandarin symbol thinking it meant "The Power of the Feminine," only to discover it was on all the bathrooms in China.

5 **Steer Clear of Names:** Other than your parents and children, there might come a time when that name doesn't make you feel quite as good as it once did.

6 **Look Within:** Make a list of things in which you have found real meaning over time and consider the best way to convey one of them in body art.

7 **Make It Changeable:** Simple colors and lines can be added to or inked over if down the road you change your mind about your tattoo. You might be glad you considered this option.

8 **Try a Temporary Version:** Test it out first in washable pen.

9 **Choose an Artist Wisely:** Make sure you like her artwork and that she has good references. You wouldn't choose a surgeon with a bad rep.

10 **Imagine:** . . . what your eighty-year-old self will think.

Have a Blast Without Breaking the Bank

(1) Do a River Walk: Many cities have rivers running through them. Follow yours on paths or through nature until it ends or you get tired.

(2) Go Fishing: Borrow your grandpa's rod, dig up some tackle, and fish off a bridge or off a lakeside dock where you don't think anyone will mind.

(3) Look for Seashells, Rocks, or Glass: Go to a beach and walk along slowly, combing it for beautiful found objects.

(4) Go to the Library: Remember how great it was when you were a kid? Stroll through the stacks and read some magazines or peruse a few classic novels.

(5) Go Sledding: If you don't have a sled, use a garbage bag or borrow the neighbor's. Then follow the kids to the nearest hill.

(6) Walk Around a College Campus: The ivy-covered brick walls and old oak trees will make you feel smarter just looking at them. See if there are any free exhibits going on while you are there.

(7) Have a Cooking Contest: Using only what you have in the house, challenge a friend or partner to a cooking contest.

(8) Go Look at Real Estate: Tell the broker you are just looking to get a sense of what's out there, and then look at a property you could never afford.

(9) Try to Have a Lucid Dream: Lie down and see if you can focus your mind enough to guide yourself through a dream. When you wake up, write it down either way.

(10) Play a Game in the Park: Get your friends together to play a team sport. Use a huge yoga ball to play a really fun game of kickball. Or if it's cooler out, try touch football.

Penny-Pinch Your Way to a Perfect Party

1 **Make It BYOB&S:** Have your guest bring the drinks and snacks.

2 **Use Leftovers:** Don't know what to do with that huge pot of chili you made? Pretty sure you won't eat the rest of that pot roast? Have a "Help Me Eat My Leftovers" party.

3 **Make It Last-Minute Casual:** Send out an invite text the day of the party and tell guests to feel free to bring their half-empty drinks, mixers, and snacks. You do the same.

4 **Order Pizza:** When your guests arrive, collect money for pizza and use any leftover cash for a beer run.

5 **Have It Someplace Else:** Don't host the party at your house. Invite everyone to meet you at a bar or restaurant and let them split the bill.

6 **Take Donations:** Front money for drinks, food, and decorations, then ask a friend to ask people to chip in.

7 **Charge a Cover:** You could make that "donation" more formal by charging guests at the door. Most people will spend five or ten dollars to drink for free and socialize.

8 **Rely on a Theme:** Be the venue for the big game or the Oscars. Those who want drinks and food can bring it or order it.

9 **Host a Potluck:** Ask everyone to bring over one dish for a dinner party. As the host, you merely provide the venue and plates.

10 **Have a Jam Session:** Ask your guests to bring musical instruments and throw an awesome rock 'n' roll party.

Sitcom Wisdom to Date By

1 **From *Friends*:** Don't sleep with someone else, even if you're on a break.

2 **From *Seinfeld*:** Try to remember your date's name, especially if it rhymes with a part of the female anatomy.

3 **From *The Brady Bunch*:** At the beginning, look into how many kids a future mate has, or you could find yourself living in a three-bedroom house with six kids, a dog, a cat, and a maid.

4 **From *Three's Company*:** If your date tells you he's only pretending to be gay to fool his landlord, you might want to talk to his two female roommates about it.

5 **From *How I Met Your Mother*:** While any woman would enjoy it if her man told their kids a long rambling story about how they met, after five years and a lot of random sex with *other* women peppered in, it might be time to wrap it up.

6 **From *The Big Bang Theory*:** The least geeky guy in the room actually has a chance with the hot girl as long as he never leaves the room.

7 **From *Happy Days*:** Know a guy your whole life and one day it will turn out that you really do love Chachi.

8 **From *Mork and Mindy*:** It's cool to date an alien, but only if he's wearing rainbow suspenders.

9 **From *Gilligan's Island*:** If you're going to end up shipwrecked after a three-hour tour, make sure you bring along one smart single guy who is hot, even if the rest of the guys are old, annoying, or taken.

10 **From *30 Rock*:** Dating in your thirties is tough, especially if you are a workaholic commitmentphobe with a codependent relationship with your boss.

From Friends to Frenemies: Know When Things Are Getting Bad

1 **They Are Trash-Talking You:** If you are going on rumor, check in with the friend. It's possible your source misunderstood. But if you know for a fact that your friend is talking about you behind your back, it's time to let the friendship go.

2 **They Let You Down:** If you find you are always expecting one thing from them and getting another, relying on them has become your dumb move. Stop doing it.

3 **You Avoid Them:** If your relationship has gotten so that you are actively trying *not to see them*, you will be doing them a favor to ask them to stop seeking you out. Just be kind about it.

4 **You Feel Criticized or Judged:** Some people just have very strong opinions about everyone around them. If you are falling victim to their judgments, move away—unless they are right.

5 **They Try to Build Up Sides Against You:** If you've noticed that a friend will look to your partner, other friends, or even your family to point out your flaws, this is not a healthy relationship.

6 **Only One of You Makes an Effort:** If only one person cares about the friendship, step away.

7 **They Use Guilt and Passive Aggression:** Feeling guilty or embarrassed is not a good way to proceed in a relationship. Tell them to stop or end the friendship.

8 **It's All about Them:** And what's worse, they're not all that interesting. Find people that give you "you time" as much as "them time."

9 **They Leave You Hanging:** If you make plans and they forget or cancel at the last minute, then they don't respect you or your time.

10 **You No Longer Care:** If you're over it, chances are, so are they. Move on.

Safely Navigate a Dark Parking Lot

1 **Ask Someone to Watch You:** If you are leaving someplace where you know people, ask someone to stay within hearing distance until you get to your car.

2 **Stay Alert:** Don't listen to an iPod or distract yourself with your cell phone.

3 **Be 9-1-1 Ready:** Ready your phone to dial 9-1-1 and keep your finger on the "send" button. If anything happens, dial and continue to repeat your name and location, even if the phone gets knocked away.

4 **Learn Self-Defense:** Take a self-defense course to establish a game plan in the event of an emergency. Never rely on thinking on your feet.

5 **Walk with Confidence:** Keep your head up and eyes sharp, and walk with purpose.

6 **Avoid It:** If you can anticipate that when you return to your car the area will be dark and vacant, find somewhere else to park.

7 **If There Is an Occupied Vehicle Beside Yours . . . :** Enter from the door farthest from that vehicle. Be especially cautious around vans. If the windows are tinted, err on the side of caution.

8 **Use the Security People:** But remember, not everyone in a uniform is a good person. Make a note of his name and use it when speaking to him. Ask him to listen for you, not to walk you to your car. Call out when you are safely inside.

9 **Avoid Stairwells:** An empty elevator or one with multiple passengers traveling separately is your best bet. If it is occupied with one person or a group that is obviously together, wait for the next one.

10 **Park with Purpose:** Pick a parking spot closest to the entrance or exit of the garage. If you can, park near the garage office, cashier booths, or in the most well-lit space you can find.

Wear a Wardrobe That
Will Never Go Out of Style

1. **The Preppy Look:** Button-down shirts, cigarette pants, and a pair of white tennis shoes look good on everyone at any age.

2. **The Earth Mother:** Channeling your inner Earth Mother requires flowing dresses and tops, and of course, long hair. If it's gray hair, even better.

3. **Chic and Sophisticated:** This classic look—a pencil skirt, white shirt, and a low bun—is easy to pull off. You will be respected in any room, even if you just graduated from college.

4. **Femme Fatale:** This woman takes Chic and Sophisticated, unbuttons the top few buttons, takes down her hair—and then shakes it out.

5. **'70s Cool:** A pair of comfy bell-bottomed jeans to elongate the legs and a blouse in bright colors is a look most can pull off and feel beautiful wearing.

6. **Sexy Librarian:** A pair of glasses and a messy bun make this look unforgettable and ageless.

7. **Sporty:** Sweats and a T-shirt or yoga pants and a sports bra are all pieces of clothing that indicate you care about how you look and feel.

8. **Beach Beauty:** A wide-brimmed hat and a coverup (or *his* button-down shirt) over a flattering bathing suit looks great on anyone beachside.

9. **Ski Bunny:** A fabulous ski jacket in the color of your choice with a tight pair of ski pants looks intriguing whether you are a Bond Girl or a Bond Girl's mother.

10. **Original:** Bringing your own style never goes out of style.

Be More Confident in Any Crowd: Soothe Social Anxiety

1. **Embrace Your Inner Wallflower:** Generally speaking, no one minds a quiet person. Listen to the conversation and react with nods, smiles, and appropriate laughter and think of yourself as a very good audience.

2. **Stop Looking in the Mirror:** Metaphorically speaking. Don't think about how you look, what you sound like, or whether or not it came out right. Once it's out, it's out. Move on.

3. **Get Good at Feeling Anxious:** In other words, step out of your comfort zone at least once a day if not more. Scaring yourself is no different from challenging yourself.

4. **Know the Cause:** Is it you? Or are you surrounding yourself with uncomfortable or negative people?

5. **Get Out of Your Head:** Analyzing everything people say (including you) can blow your mind. Listen and respond at face value. It's just easier.

6. **Choose the Right Friends:** Find a group of friends who share your interests and like having you around. If you haven't found them yet, keep looking.

7. **Experiment:** Do you feel more comfortable one-on-one or does it take some pressure off when you are in a group? Knowing yourself can curb anxiety before it begins.

8. **When in Doubt, Relax and Smile:** If you aren't sure how to behave, your best bet is to breathe and default to "friendly."

9. **Dial Down the Emotional:** Obviously when you have formed an intimate bond with someone, he should be able to handle your deepest thoughts and feelings. But in a light social gathering, it's okay to avoid topics and situations that you find upsetting.

10. **Know You're Not Alone:** Everyone feels awkward sometimes. Go easy on yourself, and remember that in the end the only opinion of you that matters is your own.

Tell Your Kids These Little White Lies

1. **"Never Touched the Stuff":** When your past experiences with drugs or alcohol comes up, and it will, your children are likely to be facing fairly complicated choices. Don't make it easier for them to choose wrong.

2. **"Rover Went to Live on a Farm":** When children are first exposed to death, they might be too young to get hit with the whole "We are all going to die" revelation. You know your children. Give them information they can handle.

3. **"I Always Like You":** You *don't* always like them. They don't have to know that.

4. **"Santa and the Tooth Fairy Are Real":** These are stories that provide children with a healthy sense of wonder. Plus they're fun. And as most of us know, they're ultimately harmless.

5. **"The Factory Shut Down":** It might be the only way to get them to move past getting that thing they won't stop asking for.

6. **"Babies Come from Storks":** When the question comes up, feel free to tailor the answer to a child's age and level of precociousness. If that means fibbing, so be it.

7. **"Your Face Will Freeze That Way":** If it gets them to stop making the face, everyone wins.

8. **"Alcohol Makes Adults Smarter and Children Dumber":** It might be the only way to keep them from wanting to taste your White Russian.

9. **"Thunder Is Just God Bowling":** This answer is much simpler than going into an explanation about the sound of a magnified electric shock. More importantly, it's calming at a time children are looking to be soothed.

10. **"It's Already Nine O'Clock!":** Bedtime is a state of mind when you are under five. Feel free to choose the time based on that and little else.

Make Working from Home Work for You

1 **Set Up a Home Office:** Get your house ready to take on the requirements of working from home.

2 **Research:** Look into ways that working from home benefits businesses. Find examples of increased productivity and figure out how you will take on some of the costs that an office would have.

3 **Talk to Your Boss:** Be prepared with statistics and concrete examples to explain why this will be a successful venture *for the office*. That should be your focus.

4 **Work During Work Hours:** Once you get the green light, consider that the benefit of working from home is solely to save on commute time. When you are supposed to be at work, work.

5 **Make Frequent Visits to Your Office:** Make sure, especially at first, that you come into the office even more often than you've been told to—not so much that your boss will think you'd be better off there, but enough to show that you are still available.

6 **Remain Visible:** Even though you are not sitting at a desk down the hall, make sure that your boss and coworkers hear from you throughout the day and know you are working.

7 **Become Your Own IT Powerhouse:** Prepare yourself to deal with any glitches that come up. You will be your primary source of technical support, so learn the basics in advance.

8 **Start Off in the Right Field:** Working solo and/or remotely is often a major perk in computer-based jobs.

9 **Be Your Own Boss:** That way, you only have to convince yourself. Start your own business and you get to decide where you work.

10 **The Future Is Now:** The number of employees working from home continues to increase. There are close to thirteen million Americans working one or more days a week from home. You might be next.

Cook Healthy Meals That Even the Pickiest Palate Will Love

1 **Meatloaf:** Substitute turkey meatloaf for beef or pork and stuff it with low-fat mozzarella. Mix it up with mustard, Worcestershire sauce, and fresh garlic for flavor.

2 **Mac-and-Cheese:** It doesn't have to come out of a box to be delicious. Mix noodles with low-fat cheese, top with bread crumbs, and bake. (Mix in diced tomatoes and tofu dogs for an extra delicious kick.)

3 **Buffalo Burger:** Buffalo, or bison, is a sweet, flavorful, and tender meat that is also low in cholesterol and fat. Add a slice of low-sodium bacon and skim mozzarella.

4 **Chicken with Mole Sauce:** Give your favorite chocoholic this treat by substituting almond butter for peanut butter and honey for the sugar in a traditional mole recipe, and then pour it over white-meat chicken.

5 **Fish Tacos:** Bake up your family's favorite fish and add lemon and cilantro. Then put it on your favorite whole wheat taco shell with low-fat cheese.

6 **Cincinnati-Style Chili:** Prepare your favorite chili recipe swapping marmalade for sugar, and ground chicken, turkey, or bison for beef. Then pour over a bowl of whole wheat spaghetti and top with cilantro and low-fat Cheddar.

7 **Egg-White Omelet Pizza:** Put all your favorite pizza toppings over an egg-white omelet. Swap out red sauce for pesto for an even healthier version!

8 **Almond Butter, Banana, and Honey Sandwich with Baked Sweet Potato Fries:** This PB&J alternative with a plate full of baked crispy sweet potato fries is healthy *and* delicious.

9 **Turkey Sliders:** Make silver-dollar-size turkey burgers and put them on top of mini whole wheat buns with lettuce and tomato and one low-sodium pickle.

10 **Crispy Chicken Tenders:** Coat your chicken with rice or corn cereal and then lightly pan-fry in olive oil until cooked through. Dip in a honey mustard you love.

Take Time for Yourself

1 **Conduct a Ritual:** Do something cleansing—swim in natural water, go for a hike, burn incense—to purge negative energy.

2 **Work Out:** A good workout will ensure that you feel better, stronger, and ready to move forward.

3 **Get Your Blood Flowing:** Do something extreme, like BASE jumping or snow boarding—anything to remind you that you are vital and alive.

4 **Catch Up on Sleep:** The body heals through sleep, so use your day off to reinvigorate your body.

5 **Organize Your Life:** Burnout can signal problems anywhere in your life. If there's time, start cleaning up some areas in your home or hire someone to come and do it for you. Order might help you realign and feel better.

6 **Get a Haircut and a New Outfit:** It sounds shallow, but a new look can make you feel like a new you, which might be exactly what the doctor ordered.

7 **Have a Spa Day:** Lounge in mineral baths and get a deep tissue massage.

8 **Look at Job Postings:** Just to remember that you aren't trapped, see what else is out there, take notes, and do some light research.

9 **Vent to a Friend:** Take a friend out for drinks and unload. See if an outside perspective can't help you find a little inside perspective.

10 **Go See a Shrink:** Make an appointment and see if therapy can't help you navigate your way back to mental well-being. If the answer is yes, make a second appointment. If not, go out for ice cream on your way home and forget it.

Pick Perfect Sunglasses for Your Face

1 **Heart-Shaped Face:** Try colored glasses that match your skin tone in order to keep the wider part of your face from looking even wider. Or try a wire frame.

2 **Oval-Shaped Face:** Most sunglasses work well with oval faces. Try aviators for that rock goddess look, or a pair of classic black Ray-Ban shades.

3 **Round-Shaped Face:** You ladies need to look for glasses that will help narrow and slim your face. Try an Olsen Twin "Bubby" frame that is wider than the broadest part of your face.

4 **Square-Shaped Face:** Go for the John Lennon wire frame or something a little jazzier, like the cat-eye frame.

5 **Diamond-Shaped Face:** Like the oval, you can get away with a lot of styles. Try a pair of BluBlockers and keep your eyes protected as well as looking good.

6 **Dark Complexion:** Darker skin tones can pull off brightly colored frames like reds and oranges. They also look great in basic black.

7 **Fair Complexion:** Brown and gray frames are best, but some fair-skinned people can get away with blues and greens as well.

8 **If Your Eyes Are Your Best Feature:** Find sunglasses with complete UVB protection that are also lightly tinted so that your eyes are still visible beneath the glass.

9 **Use a Camera, Not a Mirror:** When trying on sunglasses, trust your photograph since that is how people actually see you, rather than your reflection.

10 **They Should Make You Feel Good:** Sunglasses should make you feel mysterious, cool, and sexy. Wear a pair that makes you feel like a million bucks.

Life Lessons from Your Favorite Cartoon Characters

1. **The Flintstones:** At the end of the day, if you can't run your car under the power of your own feet, you won't get anywhere.

2. **The Powerpuff Girls:** Fight the good fight no matter how small you are or how babyish your voice (right, Bubbles?). With your sisters beside you, you can do anything!

3. **The Simpsons:** Never try—or at least find a way to give up gracefully. Eventually everyone will have to.

4. **Dragon Ball Z:** For there to be good, there must be evil. And strength can only be measured against something weaker or of even greater strength.

5. **The Smurfs:** Women are rare and beautiful creatures that should be allowed to have their way no matter how whiny they get. (Tell everyone!)

6. **Tom and Jerry:** Battle your enemies with humor. If it gets too violent, you won't die, you'll just come back in the next scene with a mallet.

7. **Josie and the Pussycats:** Girls who play instruments in a band are cool. Girls who solve crimes and mysteries while on tour with their cool band are even cooler.

8. **The Jetsons:** In the future we will all carry cars in briefcases and have robots that clean the house. Where are you, future?

9. **Scooby Doo:** Don't talk to strangers, or if you do, expect them to be creative criminal masterminds, especially if they own a creepy mansion or dark mine.

10. **Bugs Bunny:** Enjoy the moment. If it's not your problem, don't make it your problem. And when the fit is hitting the shan, taunt them by munching on a carrot and then use your speed to get away.

Be On-Call in Any Emergency

1 **Take a Class:** Community centers and local universities very often offer community CPR courses, where you can amass lifesaving first-aid skills.

2 **Call 911:** Make sure help is on the way. If you are the only one around, do it yourself. If not, ask someone nearby to make the call.

3 **Keep Your Wits:** Assess the emergency and calmly and deliberately take charge if there is no one else qualified to do so.

4 **Remember Your ABCs:** Airway, breathing, and circulation. Check to see that the victim has a clear airway, that she is breathing, and that she has a pulse.

5 **Don't Move:** Never move an injured person until you know what happened. If there is a back or neck injury, one wrong move could be devastating.

6 **Stop the Bleeding:** If there is blood, begin by applying compression on the wound to stop the blood flow.

7 **Unclog and Open Airways:** For an unresponsive victim, tilt the head back to open the airway. Check to see if his tongue, food, or anything else is blocking it. If so, clear it out.

8 **Keep Her Awake:** A person who is awake can take part in her own treatment. If possible, keep her talking and lucid.

9 **Breathe for Him:** If a victim is not breathing and no one is trained in CPR, and you've checked for cleared airways, pinch his nose, place your mouth over his, and gently fill the lungs with two breaths. If he has no pulse you will need to add chest compressions—which is why you should learn to do CPR.

10 **Stay with the Victim Until Help Arrives:** Talk to him and comfort him if that's the most you can do.

Get Dirty:
Things You Should Know How to Do

1 **Look Like You Like It:** A little closed-eye ecstasy never hurt anyone and looks fantastic. Remember, men are visual creatures!

2 **Talk:** Even if it doesn't seem very "you" to go all breathlessly Demi Moore during sex, every once in a while a little running dialogue about how good he feels can improve everyone's time.

3 **Enjoy Porn:** You don't have to love all porn, nor do you have to love every minute of every porn flick, but you should enjoy something about some porn.

4 **Perform Fellatio:** The Charlottes of the world might take offense, but the truth is, if you expect him to reciprocate, you are going to have to be prepared for oral sex. Give it a soapy wash before you begin if it helps you get through it.

5 **Put a Condom on Him:** You don't have to master doing it with your teeth, but a delicate, sexy, and *safe* application of a condom is a dirty skill no woman should be without.

6 **Moan:** A few strategically timed sighs and moans can kick the whole sexual experience up several notches pretty quickly.

7 **Masturbate:** Learn your body. If you don't know what you like, you can't expect anyone else to.

8 **Orgasm from Intercourse:** Getting to the big O through intercourse is not always easy. Learning how to do it is not only fun but will make you feel even sexier!

9 **69:** This is not a move you have to add to every sexual encounter, but giving and receiving oral sex at the same time as your man can be bonding and is pretty much always fun.

10 **Do a Strip Tease:** Learn to take it all off in such a way that you leave him begging for your body.

Keep It Clean:
Things You Never *Have* to Do

1 **Swallow:** You've done enough, so go ahead and spit it out in the sink if you want to.

2 **Have Sex Without Love:** There is nothing wrong with a good romp for its own sake. But if it's not your bag, don't do it.

3 **A Threesome:** Rarely have you heard, "I sure do regret *not* having a threesome." There are good reasons for this.

4 **A Foursome, Fivesome, or Sixsome (and so forth):** See number three.

5 **Have Sex in Public:** Public sex is not a forum for the vaguely or entirely disinterested. Your neighbors agree—it's okay to keep it in the private confines of your home.

6 **Have Sex on Top of Anything Breakable:** From roofs of cars to cases of wine, don't get on if you're not sure you'll come off without injury.

7 **Have Sex with Your Legs on His Shoulder:** It's not fun for everyone, and that's okay.

8 **Have Sex with an Inanimate Object:** If a penis is enough for you, then congratulations! Enjoy it and save the cucumber for the salad.

9 **Allow Anything in Your Anus:** It can be a no-entry zone. It's entirely up to you. If your man wants to slowly, carefully, and gently prove that it shouldn't be, it's up to you if you want to let him try, but you do not have to let him try again.

10 **Have a Lesbian Phase:** The lesbian phase is not for everyone. Sometimes it's strictly for lesbians and coeds. And that's okay. There are other ways to prove you are cool and open-minded, like eating escargot and watching French film.

Travel Alone Without Feeling Lonely — or Unsafe

1. **Share Your Itinerary:** Have someone at home know where you'll be at all times and establish check-in points. If they don't hear from you, make sure they know whom to contact (hotels, police, etc.).

2. **Take a Cruise:** Choose a cruise for singles, where people go expecting to meet new people.

3. **Bring Plenty to Do:** Occupy yourself with reading, journaling, and personal games. That way it won't matter if you meet anyone or not.

4. **Smile:** Be open and friendly and you will attract people to you. Before long you won't feel like you are on vacation alone.

5. **Take a Class:** It's easy to meet people in classes. Try surfing or ski lessons, take a yoga class, or learn about local cuisine.

6. **Go on a Tour:** Obviously, if you want an easy way to meet people on vacation, share a bus and a tour guide with them.

7. **Join a Retreat:** There are all kinds of artist retreats, from sculpture to writing to cooking to yoga. Choose the one that most interests you.

8. **Make a Plan:** Have a plan for when you arrive at a destination. Rely heavily on reviews and suggestions when it comes to places to stay. And always be alert, move with confidence, and stay safe.

9. **Make Eating a Casual Activity:** Dining for many is the hardest thing about traveling alone. So keep it simple and stick to the fun stuff.

10. **Buy a Guidebook:** Guidebooks are often written with the solo traveler in mind. They will help you streamline your plans.

Throw a Party for Your Guy

1. **Dress the Part:** If it's a party for a sporting event, put on a team logo T-shirt. Even if you don't care about the game, at least look like you fit into the scene.

2. **Make the Snacks in Advance:** It's okay to have the food prepared but not as cool to be the one running around and serving it. Tell the guys where it is and ask them to bring it in.

3. **Order Pizza:** This is not the time for crudités and salmon puffs. Get some pizza, beer, and chips.

4. **Go with the Flow:** You are not the mother in the room, even if you are the only female. Let everyone have fun. Deal with the mess later.

5. **Don't Turn Up Your Nose:** You don't have to do shots of tequila if that's not your thing, but when you turn them down, keep it light and breezy, not judgmental and bitchy.

6. **Be One of the Guys:** You can still be cute and feminine, but you can also get in on the guy fun. Talk the talk and join in on the action.

7. **Offer Up Ideas That They'll Like:** They will fully appreciate it when you offer a suggestion like "Every air ball, we drink!"

8. **Don't Get Too Fancy:** If you try to organize too many things, it might begin to feel awkward or forced. Keep the events to one activity and try not to complicate it.

9. **Don't Sexualize Yourself:** If there are several guys and one girl, no matter your relationship to them, it can get awkward if you take the flirting and the sex talk too far.

10. **Leave:** Once the party is under way, if it doesn't feel like your scene, excuse yourself.

Secrets You Should Never Reveal to Him

1. **Your Number:** Not your *phone* number—the number of sex partners you've had. Unless there is a good reason he should know (there isn't), it helps no one to share it.

2. **About a One-Time Shoe Purchase:** As long as it isn't a regular thing. Sometimes a girl just needs great shoes.

3. **That You Had a Sex Dream and He Wasn't in It:** We can't control our subconscious, and if it will make him feel bad, why tell him about it?

4. **That You Find His Best Friend Annoying:** There's no reason to put a rift in a relationship that has nothing to do with you. Let him enjoy his friends.

5. **That You Find His Best Friend Hot:** Similarly, there is no reason to make him insecure when his best friend is around, which is exactly what revealing this bit of info will accomplish.

6. **That You Won $100 in the Lottery:** Some things are just better spent on something impractical. If you don't think he'll understand that, don't mention it.

7. **That You Slept with Someone He Knows:** As long as it was in the past, it might be more comfortable for everyone *not* to tell if you have remained friends with a former lover.

8. **That You Don't Like His Mother:** Make an exception only if she is doing something damaging to you or your relationship. There isn't much he can do about his mother.

9. **How Much Your Shampoo Costs:** Guys will not understand why we spend $40 on shampoo. Same goes for makeup and moisturizer. Do not even try to explain it.

10. **That You Had *and Cured* an STD:** You don't want to remember, and trust me, he doesn't want to know.

Have Fun at Family Game Night

1. **Games Make You Smart:** Studies have shown that many games, even online games, can provide excellent learning and social tools for kids and parents.

2. **Kids Like It:** You don't have to be involved in everything they do, but it's nice to know what they're up to.

3. **It's Bonding:** Whether you organize a family game night or an online raid in a virtual world with everyone playing as his or her avatar, it is something fun you can do together!

4. **Play Is Serious:** Although play is what we associate with frivolity and fun, there are actually studies suggesting that game play lowers stress, gives us an important sense of purpose, and improves our lives for the better.

5. **Games Invoke Wonder:** As a family you might reawaken your sense of wonder through fantasy card games, drama exercises, and online worlds that remind us to keep dreaming.

6. **They Embolden Creativity:** Sports require creative thought for beating an opponent. Some board games make us think creatively about expressing ourselves without words.

7. **They Obliterate Loneliness and Isolation:** Social games bring people together and give them a sense of community, something every family should feel.

8. **They Improve Your Mood:** Why not feel better as a path to loving your family and your life more? Healthy competition is energizing and mood enhancing.

9. **They Help You Learn to Lose:** They help us learn how to survive in a world where we will sometimes win but also sometimes lose.

10. **They Are Healthy:** Overall, games improve your health and life. So get playing!

Take Time with a Toddler

1   **Blow Bubbles:** Do something magical for them. Fill the room with bubbles and watch their eyes pop with delight.

2   **Chase Them:** Enjoy the peals of laughter as you chase them around and around. Or at least enjoy the exercise you are getting.

3   **Bake Cookies:** Give them sprinkles to apply and help them use a cookie cutter to make shapes.

4   **Color:** Draw enormous pictures on a large roll of paper you tape to the driveway or kitchen floor. (Hint: You can tape down more than one piece so that it gets even bigger!) Or just give each child one piece and have them draw over newspaper.

5   **Make Sock Puppets:** Help them glue googly eyes and little mouths on an old sock. Then do a show together.

6   **Go to a Children's Museum:** Play with them in a museum where they can touch anything, do anything, and be anything.

7   **Read a Book:** Go over what they see in the pictures as you read. Once you finish, go back and read it again.

8   **Go on an Adventure Walk:** You don't have to go far. For a little one, everywhere is an adventure.

9   **Finger Paint:** Put on smocks or old shirts and finger paint together.

10   **Play Instruments:** Dry out gourds so that they shake like maracas. Bang on tambourines, triangles, or bongos. In a pinch use an oatmeal box for a drum, or a spoon and a pot. Then rock out.

Learn the Jargon of Your Job

1. **404:** A person with no idea, totally clueless. Its origin is in a web error message alerting that a document could not be found. "Mary's 404. Call Sally."

2. **Betamaxed:** When one technology renders another obsolete. "Blu-Ray has totally Betamaxed DVD."

3. **Alpha Geek:** The smartest tech guy in the room. "I don't know what's happening with the network. I'm calling our alpha geek."

4. **Doritos Syndrome:** The feeling you have after not eating anything but processed food and empty calories.

5. **Gray Matter:** Older employees hired by young companies to provide a look of respectability.

6. **Agreeance:** A way to say "agreement" but schmantzier. "So then, we're in agreeance."

7. **Wallpapering Fog:** Doing nothing. "Sarah is just wallpapering fog at this point with the Swanson accounts."

8. **Glazing:** The art of sleeping with your eyes open. "I was glazing; sorry about that."

9. **Percussive Maintenance:** The precise work of thwacking your electronic device until it comes back to life.

10. **Wow Factor:** That little detail that is going to bring the project to life and take it to the next level. "All we need now is the wow factor."

Breathe Through the Worst of It

1 **Visualize:** Imagine yourself anywhere but where you are. Find a calm and peaceful place where the sun is shining and birds are singing.

2 **Analyze the Pain:** Really consider the pain. How does it feel? What color is it? What does it want? What is it trying to teach you?

3 **Know It Will End:** Focus on the fact that discomfort is not a permanent state. It will end and a new feeling will take its place.

4 **Transcend the Physical:** Focus solely on your breathing and ignore everything else. When your mind wanders to the discomfort, help guide it back.

5 **Sleep:** If you can, allow your body to sleep more often than normal if the pain will last for days or weeks. It is healing and will help to restore you.

6 **Elicit Discomfort Elsewhere:** Bite on your lip or dig the nails of one hand into the other. Psychological control over the discomfort can help you through it.

7 **Sing Your Favorite Song Lyrics:** Choose songs you like, running them through your head and hitting all the words to the best of your memory's ability. Depending on how long you must endure the discomfort, decide how many songs you will have to sing.

8 **Stay Positive:** Look at the many ways discomfort alerts us to problems that can teach us and finally save us.

9 **Pray:** No matter how you feel about God, now just might be the time to find Him or Her.

10 **Plan Revenge:** While once you are in a better place you hopefully won't carry it out, but for now, go ahead and plan your revenge on any person or thing that led you to this moment.

When to Believe Your Mother

1 **Bring a Sweater:** It's 100 degrees outside. So what? Someone somewhere does not know how to properly set a thermostat. You will almost always be glad you have that sweater.

2 **Treat People the Way You Want to Be Treated:** Being kind is excellent advice.

3 **Sit Up Tall and Stand Up Straight:** All kinds of back problems come from slouching, but that isn't even the only reason she was right about this—it turns out that tall people get better jobs and more respect.

4 **Just Be Yourself:** Too bad it sometimes can be tricky figuring out exactly who that is. But once you do, learn to like her and others will too.

5 **You Need Your Beauty Rest:** It happens to be true. A good night's sleep helps your skin, helps your digestive system break down fats, and generally keeps you looking better.

6 **Write Thank-You Notes Right Away:** Putting it off causes you stress and then you forget. If you write them immediately, you feel good *and* you make someone smile. Win-win.

7 **Do Your Best:** Luckily, with mom, your best could always come in just over adequate. But it's true. If you do something to the best of your abilities, you can be proud no matter the outcome.

8 **You'd Lose Your Head If It Wasn't Attached:** This one is probably correct. Lucky for everyone, it's hard to test.

9 **Don't Hang Around with *Those* Kids:** In your heart you knew she was right back then, but they were so much fun! Still, aren't you glad you had her voice in your head?

10 **Be Home by Twelve:** Few good things happen afterward. It's true.

When Not to Believe Your Mother

1. **Sometimes They *Do* Respect You in the Morning:** The fact is, not every guy is a scumbag.

2. **Cracking Your Knuckles Won't Give You Arthritis:** Turns out, this is a myth. It's a little gross, however, so try to limit it to private time.

3. **Shaving Does *Not* Cause Increased Follicle Activity:** In other words, the hair won't grow back thicker. However, sometimes breakage or the appearance of stubble makes it seem like it does.

4. **It Doesn't Give You Warts:** This is both for playing with toads *and* playing with yourself. Toads can be dirty in other ways, though, so washing your hands afterward is a good idea. Actually, in both cases.

5. **Starve a Fever, Feed a Cold Changes Neither the Fever nor the Cold:** Being sick is being sick. You still have to eat and maintain good, balanced nutrition.

6. **Your Face Won't Stay Like That:** It turns out, a pissy puss is a temporary, if impolite, condition.

7. **Cleaning Your Plate Is a Bad Idea:** Actually, most Americans put way too much food on their plates to begin with. Decide to only eat half and put the rest away for lunch. Or start with half and *then* your mom will have been right!

8. **Cold Air Does Not Cause Colds:** A deficient immune system combined with germy practices does. Cold air, however, causes discomfort. So still wear a jacket. She was right about that.

9. **Swallowing Seeds Does *Not* Yield Fruit Crops in One's Stomach:** Otherwise, wouldn't we just always be full?

10. **It's Okay to Go Near Boys:** Even if every time you asked her about a boy she told you to take up soccer, it turns out she was wrong. Aren't you glad you didn't listen?

Write That Book Already!

1   **Choose Your Genre:** Do you have a fascinating personal story? Choose memoir. Some wonderful expertise? Go for nonfiction. How about a great story idea? Try fiction.

2   **Get It on Paper:** Prepare a brief outline so that you know the arc of your story in advance. Or if nothing else, decide where your story starts and ends.

3   **Research:** Collect any research you will need to round out your story. Even fiction sometimes requires some extra information to inform the narrative.

4   **Write:** The best way to write a book is to write it. The moment it occurs to you to do so, don't turn on the TV. Get out some paper and start your manuscript.

5   **Exercise Discipline:** Choose a practical workload. Some people write a page a day. Just one year later, they have a complete book.

6   **Build Your Audience:** In the meantime, take to social networking sites and build up friend and follower numbers. These quantifiable data points will help you sell your book later.

7   **Start a Blog:** Using your book's general themes or topic, begin a blog so that you establish yourself as an expert.

8   **Choose a Title:** Your title should sum up your book's themes and ideas while also being catchy and memorable. If you have a hard time titling, get input from friends.

9   **Allow for Critique:** Share your manuscript with friends and family. Basically any and all resources can be helpful. And you never know who someone knows.

10   **Decide How to Publish:** If you want to self-publish, there are many inexpensive ways to do it. If you want to sell it, go to editors and agents. And if you want to keep it for yourself, enjoy your hard work!

Bucket-List Your Life Before Kids Come Along

1. **Fall in Love:** The kind that when he looks at you, you blush. The kind that when you look at him, you cry.

2. **Don't Get Out of Bed:** Stay in bed for twenty-four hours with someone you love or like a lot and do some not-sleeping.

3. **Write a Book:** When you have kids, it will be a lot harder to do it. So do it before.

4. **Be Foreign:** Visit a place where you don't speak the language or know the culture. Then get drunk with a local.

5. **Start a Savings Account:** Create a nest egg. Once you have kids, you will want a little something to fall back on during hard times.

6. **Know How to Cook Five Things Well:** Spaghetti, chicken, carrot-ginger soup, stir-fry, and an omelet will work.

7. **Finish School . . . for Now:** Have most of your formal education completed.

8. **Gain Depth:** Go someplace and see true poverty with your own eyes. Understand starvation, illness, and lack of water.

9. **Live in a Major City:** At least once, move out of the sticks and see how the animals live.

10. **Do at Least One Extreme Sport at Least Once:** Jumping out of an airplane doesn't fall under the purview of responsible parenting.

Apologize to Your Parents . . . and Make It Sincere!

1. **You Snuck Out . . . Once:** No need to break out the whole sordid history, but for the sake of a good story, now that you are clearly living the life of a responsible grownup, you can admit it.

2. **You Dated the Guy They Hated for a Lot Longer Than They Thought:** It doesn't matter anymore, so it no longer has to be a secret.

3. **That Dent? It Wasn't the Neighbor:** But be warned, if you admit this one, you might find yourself having to apologize to the neighbor.

4. **You Once Hosted a Forbidden Party:** They were out of town and you got most of the stains out of the carpet.

5. **You Forged Their Signatures for Most of Senior Year:** You either made it to college or you didn't. That little indiscretion is water under the bridge.

6. **They Were Right:** You never thought you'd believe it, but it turns out, a septum pierce would have been a very bad idea.

7. **You Liked Camp More Than You Didn't:** You made a big deal about leaving every summer, but overall, it was a good experience and you made a lot of good friends.

8. **You're Glad They Took Care of the Dog:** You said you'd walk it and feed it, but you never did. Admit it, be gracious, and move on.

9. **The Safe Car Was the Better Choice:** A part of you knew it then, but you *really* wanted the cool one.

10. **You're Grateful:** Just . . . for everything.

Fill Your Plate with Superfoods

1 **Broccoli:** It single-handedly keeps your immune system boosted all winter long. Boil the whole bunch, especially the antioxidant-packed stems, and use a hand-held blender and plenty of Cheddar to make a delicious soup you can eat every day.

2 **Blueberries:** This low-fat sweet treat is loaded with fiber and vitamin C. Add to cereal or a smoothie.

3 **Sweet Potatoes:** A vitamin A powerhouse, sweet potatoes are lower in calories than white potatoes—so you don't have to feel as bad when you eat them with butter and chives. Plus they taste amazing.

4 **Yogurt:** Great for any gastrointestinal tract, yogurt is also high in protein and potassium. Low-fat yogurt is a great substitute for people who have sensitivities to milk.

5 **Green Tea:** Known to help regulate everything from headaches to obesity to depression, green tea in place of your morning coffee is a brilliant way to get healthy.

6 **Pumpkin:** High in fiber and low in fat, it isn't just the meat of this gourd that is a source of remarkable, disease-fighting nutrients but the seeds.

7 **Eggs:** A great, inexpensive source of protein that keeps you feeling full. And when boiled or shirred without butter or oils, eggs are low in fat.

8 **Kiwi:** Antioxidant and nutrient rich, this sweet little fruit will supply you with a full day's worth of vitamin C.

9 **Nuts and Seeds:** High in proteins and heart-healthy fats, nuts and seeds are great foods to add to your list of excellent snack foods, especially when they are low in sodium.

10 **Kale:** This superfood is off-the-charts high in vitamin K, which helps the body transport calcium and build bones.

Dye Your Hair at Home

1 **Do a Test:** Every dye has different chemicals in its makeup. If you are particularly prone to allergies, it is imperative you follow the testing instructions before you proceed.

2 **Choose a Reasonable Color:** Dyeing at home is not the time for drastic change. Pick a color that closely resembles your hair color—or at least the nongray parts.

3 **Match Your Eyebrows:** For the most natural look, your best bet is to go with a color that matches your eyebrows.

4 **Deep Condition:** Make sure your hair is healthy and hydrated before you dye. However, do not condition on the day you plan to dye your hair or it will keep some of the color from properly absorbing.

5 **Clean It:** Your hair should be clean when you dye it. Wash it that morning or the night before.

6 **Dry It:** Most store-bought hair dyes require that your hair be dry before applying the chemicals.

7 **Dress for It:** Wear an old button-down or a sweatshirt with a zip up front that you can take off and on without pulling it over your head.

8 **Keep It Clean:** Keep a warm damp towel nearby so that if you splatter any of the dye you can wipe it up quickly. Similarly, make sure you wipe it from your face, neck, and any other part of your body it drips onto.

9 **Skip the Eyes:** Never dye your lashes or brows. That's what mascara is for.

10 **Rinse It Out:** Make sure you rinse your hair thoroughly. Leaving even trace amounts of dye in your hair will actually cause the color to fade more quickly.

From Goat to Gruyère:
Serving Cheese to Your Guests

1   **Don't Mix Flavors:** If you are sampling from a well-filled cheese plate, cleanse your palate between each cheese so that you can enjoy the full experience of each.

2   **Eat Cheese at Room Temperature:** Actually, just under. Experts say that is when cheese is at the peak of its flavor.

3   **Smell It:** No matter how stinky it is, getting a good noseful will actually inform the flavor and make it richer and deeper.

4   **Describe It:** Once you have the taste in your mouth, use as many adjectives as you can to describe it, out loud or to yourself. This way the complexity of the flavor will be broken down and manageable.

5   **Move the Flavor:** Let the flavor begin at the tip of your tongue and move it slowly to the back of your mouth.

6   **Go from Mild to Strong:** Begin with mild cheeses and work your way to stronger cheeses.

7   **Think about the Details:** Cheeses come in soft, semi-soft, and hard. Their consistency is an important part of their overall taste. Experts suggest alternating your sampling between harder and softer cheeses.

8   **Combine It:** The taste of cheese is enhanced by other flavors, so make sure you pair it with wine, beer, fruit bars, nuts, and simple breads and crackers.

9   **Cover Sliced Cheese:** Cheese has a tendency to dry out, so make sure you keep it covered before serving. Leave it in a whole chunk and have a knife available so guests may slice their own pieces.

10   **Your Palate Is Right:** Don't let anyone tell you what makes a cheese delicious. At the end of the day, you like what you like.

Enjoy the Sun — Safely

1 **Embrace the Shade:** Being outside during pleasant summer months is important. But staying out of direct sunlight is important, too.

2 **Stay Inside from 10 A.M. to 3 P.M.:** Peak sun hours are the worst for your skin. So if you can, stay under cover unless it's early morning or early evening.

3 **Don't Trust Clouds:** Clouds are not sunscreen. In fact, some studies indicate that they magnify the negative effects of the sun. Be extra careful.

4 **Cover Your Eyes:** Your skin is not the only victim of the sun. Don't settle for cheap eyewear on bright days. Protect your eyes from UVB rays.

5 **Reapply Sunscreen:** Don't just put it on once, but continue to apply it every hour or two during the time you are in the sun. And always put some on before you leave the house.

6 **Remember to Get Your Head, Backs of Ears, and Lips:** The sun can burn your head through your hair, especially if your hair is thin or very dark, so wear a hat. Also, sunscreen the tops and backs of your ears and use SPF balm on your lips.

7 **Water Is Double Trouble:** Bodies of water actually reflect the sun and throw it back up at you just as it is beating down. Be warned.

8 **Bring a Tent or Umbrella:** If you are headed to a sunny field or the beach, bring your own shady structure.

9 **Dress Like a Bedouin:** Loose, light clothes will add a layer of protection from the sun and keep you cool, as desert dwellers have known for years.

10 **Eat Raw:** Some schools of thought suggest that the sun affects people differently based on their diet. Some people on raw-food-only diets claim they hardly ever burn anymore despite not wearing sunscreen.

Make Like an IT Pro

1 **Speed Up Your Copy and Paste:** Highlight a stretch of text and hit Ctrl + c to copy it, Ctrl + v to paste it.

2 **Cut and Paste:** You can also delete text from one place with Ctrl + x and then paste it elsewhere with Ctrl + v.

3 **Reboot:** If your computer is woefully frozen, press and hold down the Ctrl-Alt-Delete keys (for a Mac, Control-Apple-Escape) all together until your computer screen goes black and starts to reboot.

4 **Google the Problem:** There are hundreds of thousands of technical posts out there where people have asked a question, and others have responded with solutions.

5 **Take a Class:** If you feel like most seven-year-olds can work a computer better than you, take a class. Some companies offer beginner classes for free, and even if you think you are beyond them, you might still learn some surprising new tricks.

6 **Choose Your Computer Wisely:** Marketers "accessorize" to make bad machines look appealing. If you aren't knowledgeable, shop with a friend who is.

7 **Mouse Lessons:** There are two buttons on every mouse. The left is used for most clicks. The right, however, allows you to highlight text or shows you shortcuts and other options.

8 **Back Up Often:** Every computer experiences an epic failure at some point. There are many ways to back things up. Find one that works for you and put it into daily practice.

9 **Delete What You Don't Need:** Over time, a computer is like a huge ball of Velcro rolling around. Everything you view is in essence downloaded and saved. Load or use existing software that will help you clean up some of it.

10 **Keep It Clean:** Keep your keyboard clean and dusted and your screen free of dirt. Buy the appropriate supplies. Also, keep your computer desktop tidy and your files organized.

Survive a Holiday Dinner with Family

1 **Change Your Tactics:** Try not to engage in any unsuccessful past dynamics. Do things differently this year and change any patterns of unhealthy behavior.

2 **Be Dian Fossey:** Imagine your family as a band of gorillas in the wild. Nothing they do will disturb you as long as you do nothing to disturb them.

3 **Remain a Grownup:** No matter how easy it is to feel like the sixteen-year-old you once were, try to remain your grown-up self, or some version thereof.

4 **Bring a Partner:** Even if you are single, bring *someone* to the family event. If you have to offer to pay them, do it. The emotional expense of going alone might mean you end up breaking even.

5 **Put Your Best Self Forward:** Try to dress the way you want them to see you, not the way they expect you to be.

6 **Use Humor:** As often as possible, tackle the tension by easing in a joke or two. Have a few funny stories ready for when it's really time to change the subject.

7 **Take Breaks:** Give yourself some time away from them.

8 **Be Helpful:** Someone had to make this meal. Be a good guest and help serve and clean up. It will buy you points and keep people happy.

9 **Look for Complimentary Things to Say:** Families have a way with joking put-downs. See if you can't turn it around and slip in a cascade of compliments.

10 **Plan an Activity:** Get everyone together for an after-dinner game or a family movie to watch together, or even better, a DVD of home movies put together for everyone's enjoyment.

End Your Relationship the Right Way

1. **Make the Decision:** Weigh it out and be sure. If you are in the middle of an emotional time, wait until it passes.

2. **Don't Waver:** There are always going to be reasons to stay with someone. It's easy to get mired in fear. Don't.

3. **Go Someplace Public, but Neutral:** Take him someplace where past memories won't be ruined and where you are both basically anonymous in case there is a scene.

4. **Don't Offer False Hope:** There is nothing he can do to fix it. Even presenting threats makes it seem like he can still do something to get you back.

5. **Don't Give In:** He will bargain with you and make promises. Stand your ground. You will be vulnerable and insecure. Don't get pressured. Tell him you will consider what he's saying later, but for now your directive stands.

6. **Be Clear:** Do not mince your words. Tell him that you are breaking up and give a short explanation as to why. Then conclude the conversation as quickly as possible.

7. **Prepare for His Hurt Feelings:** It's just inevitable; there is very little way around it. It'll be uncomfortable and there might be strongly expressed emotions. Just be prepared for it and it might not sting quite as badly.

8. **Don't Be Cruel:** Cruelty is offering false hope, it's taking pity, it's pulling the Band-Aid off slowly.

9. **Cut Him Off for Now:** Say you won't see him for two weeks and make it clear you will not take his calls or open his e-mails.

10. **Plan a Final Meeting for Two Weeks Later:** Put this plan in place to keep things from escalating right after the breakup and to give him perspective and time to reflect. Field his questions honestly but with compassion. Then move on.

Learn to Love Opera

1. **Know the Basics:** Before you go, find out what show you will be seeing and who wrote it.

2. **Read the Book:** If you can get your hands on it, read the whole libretto (Italian for "small book"). It is generally short (less than an hour's read) and will tell you the whole story and what to look for.

3. **Know the Plot:** Generally speaking, opera is a play in a language you probably don't speak set to music you are unfamiliar with. It will be helpful to understand why that guy stabbed that other guy.

4. **Know the Music:** Try listening to a highlights CD or even the entire opera so that you will be familiar with some of the music before you go.

5. **Get Dressed Up:** Half the fun of an opera is dressing to the nines to see it. Granted, opening nights tend to be the fancier ones; still, go with it.

6. **Prepare for the Calm:** Nothing will explode. There will be no car chases or alien invasions. If you know that in advance, you might take it as an opportunity to sit quietly and calmly.

7. **Enjoy the Experience:** Opera is a complete experience. There is generally a live orchestra, live performers, and intricate sets. Take them in.

8. **Watch:** Pay attention to the exquisite, often old-fashioned costumes and the beautiful staging.

9. **Listen:** Enjoy the purity of the voices. Listen to how high the soprano sings, how low the bass sings, and the complexity of the notes for every character.

10. **Drink in the Drama:** It's supposed to be big, brash, and over the top. If you can't take it seriously, don't. Just have fun and wait for the fat lady to sing.

Craft a Gift in No Time

1. **Decorate a White T-Shirt:** Buy some fabric paint at the crafts store and make a cool shirt that is even more special because you made it.

2. **Frame Something:** Find a cool piece of fabric, paper, or better yet a great photo, and frame it. If he has a favorite book, find a copy with a cool cover at a used-book store and frame that!

3. **Make a Memory Box:** Drop in items that have some significance for your relationship. Examples include ticket stubs, photographs, and journal pages where you wrote about the person or event.

4. **Paint a Picture:** It might sound juvenile, but the fact is, you might have some talent hidden in there. Why not take it out for a test ride? You can always call it "modern art."

5. **Friendship Bracelets:** Knotting, braiding, or weaving colored string can lead to cool bracelets for men or women.

6. **Hit the Bead Store:** Choose a series of stones to put on a necklace or a leather cord. When you say, "I made it!" it will be that much cooler.

7. **A Cardboard Cutout:** Have a life-size photo printed of a pet, a loved one, or a celebrity crush, glue it to foam core, and cut it out. Your gift will be funny and memorable.

8. **A Memory CD:** Burn songs that remind you of your relationship through the years.

9. **Write Your Story:** Type up a complete version of how you met, fold it up, and hand it over.

10. **Make Up an Interpretive Dance:** Go ahead and give someone the gift of laughter. Make up a dance, bring in a friend to do it with you, and perform it as a gift the recipient will never forget.

Act Young, Feel Young, Live Young

1 **Play in a Sprinkler:** It doesn't have to be your own. Use a local park's or even a neighbor's and run back and forth. It's still as much fun as you remember.

2 **Listen to Music:** Find music that was popular when you were a kid and crank it up. Let yourself dance as wildly as if you were at a junior high or middle school party.

3 **Go Bike Riding:** Remember how riding up and down your block was fun every summer? Try it again today, but let yourself cross a few of the busy streets your mother wouldn't let you.

4 **Go on a Nostalgia Tour:** Drive yourself to your elementary and high schools. Swing by parks you used to play in and visit other old haunts.

5 **Go Sledding:** Dust off the sled in your parents' basement and find a hill. If this doesn't take you back, nothing will.

6 **Do Someone's Homework:** Do a little long division or write an essay about your summer.

7 **Watch a Kids' Movie:** If there is one you really loved as a child, watch that. If not, try a new classic like *Toy Story* or *Shrek*.

8 **Go on an Adventure:** Find a small opening to a wooded area and start your exploration there. Wander in and see where you end up.

9 **Roll Down a Hill:** The sensation—slightly nauseating but also fun—is one that will remind you of a summer day from long ago.

10 **Organize a Field Day:** Get some friends together for a day of field games. From relay races to water fights, split into teams and do your worst!

Make Those Knitting Needles Fly

① **Choose Your Needles:** Handle a few to see which feel best to you. Those made of bamboo are lightweight and are good for beginners.

② **Choose Your Color:** Think about who you are making the knitted item for and what would look best on her. If you don't know, choose a universally wearable color like blue. Darker colors can be more difficult, as can multicolored yarns. Choose a solid color that is light to medium-dark.

③ **Gather Additional Tools:** You will want scissors on hand to cut yarn. Also, a crochet hook is helpful for dropped stitches.

④ **Use Hand Lotion:** Odd though it sounds, you will find quickly that dry, cracking hands can hurt. Use an absorbent lotion so that it doesn't get on the yarn.

⑤ **Pay Attention in the Beginning:** Also known as "casting on," this is generally thought the hardest part of knitting. If you don't have someone to show you, read a thorough explanation before trying it yourself.

⑥ **Know Your Stitches:** Knitting is made up of two basic stitches, the knit stitch and the purl stitch. The knit stitch is the most basic, so for our purposes this list will deal with that one.

⑦ **After You Cast On:** Hold the stitches in your left hand. Insert your right-hand needle front to back into the first stitch under the left needle.

⑧ **Move the Yarn:** Transfer the yarn over the tip of the right needle. There will be a loop around your left needle.

⑨ **Finish the Stitch:** Pull the needle out from the loop to see your first stitch and repeat in the second stitch.

⑩ **Start a New Row:** Double-stitch over the last stitch and work your way back to the beginning. Keep going and eventually you will have a complete scarf!

Pick a Pet for All the Right Reasons

1. **They Provide Unconditional Love:** Pets know better than anyone how to treat the one who feeds them.

2. **They Offer a Sense of Purpose:** Owning a pet is a major responsibility. You are keeping another being safe and healthy. As such, your life's purpose will be more richly defined.

3. **They Help Stave Off Loneliness:** Having a pet provides companionship when you didn't even know you were starved for it. Even better, they don't talk back.

4. **They Provide Structure:** Pets need food, water, and exercise. Weaving them into your day creates structure that can help anyone who works from home or those who get bored easily.

5. **They Keep You Healthy:** According to many studies, pet owners stay healthier and live longer than others. Petting a companion animal is also proven to lower your blood pressure.

6. **They Are Very Good Listeners:** Need a shrink? Get a pet or two. They will listen intently to even your least interesting yarns and will give you a kiss to make it all better when you're done.

7. **They Get You Up and Out:** Some pets make very motivational exercise partners, especially when they come to you, leash in mouth.

8. **They Provide Pre-Parenting Training:** Cheaper than taking a class and less stressful than babysitting, having a pet will give you the confidence that you have the parenting chops.

9. **There's No Better Way to Meet People:** A pet gives you free entry into the "People with Pets" club. Dog walkers meet their neighbors and cute guys at the dog park. Other pet owners have things to talk about at the pet store.

10. **They Make You Feel Good:** Nothing beats coming home to a wagging tail or a purr and excitement that is palpable . . . and all for you!

Eat Gourmet Meals
on a Barely-There Budget

1 **Plan Meals:** Before you go to the store, make a general plan for the meals you will be making. You will have some sense of how much it will cost ahead of time and you will be more efficient.

2 **Make Extra:** Leftovers make great material for a new meal. Recycle leftover chicken on quesadillas. No one has to know!

3 **Use Everything:** Boil chicken bones and veggie ends for stocks you can use as base for sauces and soups. Keep them in the freezer. Think of other ways to stop yourself from throwing away food.

4 **Cook from Scratch:** You will make more (and healthier) chicken nuggets for less if you do it from scratch than if you use a frozen version. The same can be said for baby food, soup, and many other ready-made items.

5 **Cut Coupons:** Figure out the deals in advance and shop according to what you find. It will save you money and keep your family happy.

6 **Utilize Your Freezer:** Unfinished food can be kept for weeks in your freezer. When the roasted potatoes from Sunday's lunch are forgotten, they can appear a few weeks later with dinner.

7 **Keep Your Ingredients Seasonal:** Fruits and vegetables are cheaper in season. And better.

8 **Follow the Sales:** When you get to the store, feel free to throw your planned meal ideas out the window if you see a good sale. Or try to swap them in and save more.

9 **Eat Less:** Cut back on your portion sizes and general intake. Save money by paring back what you eat.

10 **Cut Your Own Vegetables and Meat:** Buying whole veggies and meat products really does save you dollars at the store.

Follow Your Bliss

1 **Find It:** Jot down the most exciting and engaging moments of your life. What did they have in common? Were you coaching or leading a person or team? Painting? Engaging in a physical rush like riding a roller coaster or cliff diving?

2 **Read Biographies:** Read books about passionate individuals who lived rich and profound lives and see if anything resonates with you.

3 **Set Up Opportunities:** Experiment by trying out new things that sound intriguing. See if any of them wakes up your bones.

4 **Weave It Into Your Life:** Once you know what your bliss is, add it to your daily life where possible. Buy a skateboard and ride it to work, or wake up an hour earlier to write.

5 **Imagine:** Think of ways you might make your bliss a central part of your everyday life. Even if you are miles from finishing a sculpture, imagine it completed and in a gallery.

6 **Stop Waiting:** Know that there will never be a "good" time to revamp your life. Start now instead. Life is too short to live it in boredom or misery.

7 **Ask for Support:** Tell people about your bliss and ask for feedback. Maybe someone knows about a community theater you could work with, or a ballroom-dancing opportunity.

8 **Do It Yourself:** Decide that no one is going to do it for you. Save some money by making your coffee at home or cutting out dessert and use the extra dough to buy supplies.

9 **Share It:** Ask friends and family to model clothes you've designed or come to your musical performance once you are ready to share what you are creating, doing, and enjoying.

10 **Let Yourself Be Happy:** Once you are doing it, enjoy it. Don't let guilt or greed creep in. Make the most of what you are doing and love your more meaningful life.

About the Author

Dee Dee Clermont prides herself on asking the questions that lead to the best advice. She has garnered her own series of life's lessons through the many articles she has written about the lives of modern women. She lives in Brooklyn, New York.